Business Taxation 2007/08

NVQ Accounting Unit 18
Diploma Pathway Unit 18

for June and December 2008 examinations

Aubrey Penning

Bob Thomas

osborne BOOKS

Published by Osborne Books Limited
Unit 1B Everoak Estate
Bromyard Road
Worcester WR2 5HP
Tel 01905 748071
Email books@osbornebooks.co.uk
Website www.osbornebooks.co.uk

Design by Richard Holt
Cover image from Getty Images

Printed by CPI Antony Rowe Limited, Chippenham

British Library Cataloguing in Publication Data
A catalogue record for this book is available from the British Library

ISBN 978 1905777 136

Contents

Please note that the eight chapters and subsequent sections of the book each have a self-contained numbering system, rather than the traditional form of pagination which runs through the book.

Acknowledgments

The author wishes to thank the following for their help with the editing and production of the book: Mike Fardon, Mike Gilbert, Rosemarie Griffiths and Claire McCarthy.

The publisher is indebted to the Association of Accounting Technicians for its generous help and advice to its authors and editors during the preparation of this text, and for permission to reproduce extracts from the Standards of Competence for Accounting.

The publisher would also like to thank HM Revenue & Customs for its help, advice and kind permission to reproduce tax forms obtained from www.hmrc.gov.uk

Author and Technical Editor

Aubrey Penning, the author, co-ordinates the AAT courses at Worcester College of Technology, and teaches a range of units including Units 8 and 9 and the two taxation Units. He has over twenty years experience of teaching accountancy on a variety of courses in Worcester and Gwent. He is a Certified Accountant, and before his move into full-time teaching he worked for the health service, a housing association and a chemical supplier. Aubrey is author of *Personal Taxation* and co-author of *Managing Performance & Resources Tutorial* and *Cash Management & Credit Control* from Osborne Books.

Bob Thomas, the Technical Editor of this book and the Osborne Books' *Personal Taxation*, has been involved with the Education and Training activities of the AAT since 1986, including the development and piloting of the current scheme. He is an external verifier, a simulation writer, a moderator and a contributor at workshops, training days, conferences and master classes. He is a member of the Learning and Development Board and Chairman of the Assessment Panel.

Introduction

Business Taxation has been written to provide a study resource for students taking courses based on Unit 18 'Preparing Business Taxation Computations' (2003 Standards). This Unit is common to both the NVQ and Diploma Pathway.

Finance Acts

The examinations for this Unit assessed by the AAT will be based on the following Finance Act and tax year:

Examinations in June and December 2008:	Finance Act 2007	Tax Year 2007/08

using the book

The text includes chapters that are designed to be progressive, so that issues covered in earlier chapters are referred to and applied in later chapters. The author believes that this approach will lead to readers building up a solid understanding as they progress through the book. Note that the pagination of each chapter is self-contained, eg Chapter 1 contains pages 1.2 to 1.23.

At the end of each chapter there are student activities to reinforce the work studied. The solutions to some of these activities are contained in this book, while some are contained in the *Business Taxation 2007/08 Tutor Pack* that is available to colleges and independent studiers (see below).

examination practice papers

In addition to the eight chapters (one introductory, four relating to limited companies and three relating to sole traders and partnerships), there are four 'half-papers' in examination style for practice use. Two of these reflect the possible content of Section 1 of an AAT examination, and two are based on Section 2 content. The Section 2 half-papers can be tackled after Chapters 1 to 5 have been studied, while the Section 1 'half' papers require familiarity with the content of Chapters 6 to 8.

There are also two full practice papers, together with the updated specimen paper that is published with kind permission of the AAT. The half-papers can also be linked together to provide additional practice of sitting a full paper. Recent examination papers, answers and examiners' comments can be downloaded from the AAT website at www.aat.org.uk

Osborne Tutor Packs

The answers to selected Chapter Activities and all the Examination tasks in this text are set out in a separate *Business Taxation 2007/08 Tutor Pack*, available to tutors and to students who have the permission of their tutors to have access to the answers. Please contact the Osborne Books Sales Office on 01905 748071 or visit the website for details of how to obtain the Tutor Pack.

Tax data

NATIONAL INSURANCE

Tax Year 2007/2008

Employer Contributions

Class 1 contributions are calculated as 12.8% of (gross pay less £100 per week).

Class 1A contributions are calculated as 12.8% of the assessable value of benefits in kind.

Self-employed National Insurance contributions (sole traders and partners)

Class 2 contributions are payable at a flat rate of £2.20 per week (unless the 'small earnings exemption' is claimed), and in addition,

Class 4 contributions are payable on the profits as follows:

8% of profits for the year between £5,225 and £34,840, plus

1% of profits above £34,840

CORPORATION TAX

'Profits'	Corporation Tax rate Financial Year 2006 (i.e. 1/4/2006 – 31/3/2007)	Corporation Tax rate Financial Year 2007 (i.e. 1/4/2007 – 31/3/2008)
£0 – £300,000	Small Companies Rate (19%)	Small Companies Rate (20%)
£300,001 – £1,500,000	Full Rate (30%) less marginal relief	Full Rate (30%) less marginal relief
£1,500,001 and over	Full Rate (30%)	Full Rate (30%)

Marginal relief

Marginal relief formula:

Marginal Relief Fraction x (Maximum of Band – 'Profits') x PCTCT / 'Profits'

or: *Fraction x (M – P) x (I / P)*

where	M	=	Maximum of Band
	P	=	'Profits'
	I	=	PCTCT (or Income)

The fraction is:

- 11/400 for the financial year 2006
- 1/40 for the financial year 2007

INCOME TAX

Personal Allowance for tax year 2007/08: £5,225

Tax bands	**2007/08**
	£
Starting rate 10%	0 – 2,230
Basic rate 22%	2,231 – 34,600
Higher rate 40%	over 34,600

CAPITAL GAINS TAX – FOR INDIVIDUALS

	2007/08
Annual Exempt Amount	£9,200
Rates	
Gains	10% / 20% / 40%

Taper Relief for Business Assets

Number of complete years	**% chargeable**
0	100
1	50
2 or more	25

RETAIL PRICE INDEX (FOR THE INDEXATION ALLOWANCE)

	Jan	Feb	Mar	Apr	May	Jun	Jul	Aug	Sept	Oct	Nov	Dec
2007	201.6	203.1	204.4	205.4	not available at time of going to press							
2006	193.4	194.2	195.0	196.5	197.7	198.5	198.5	199.2	200.1	200.4	201.8	202.7
2005	188.9	189.6	190.5	191.6	192.0	192.0	192.2	192.6	193.1	193.3	193.6	194.1
2004	183.1	183.8	184.6	185.7	186.5	186.8	186.8	187.4	188.1	188.6	189.0	189.9
2003	178.4	179.3	179.9	181.2	181.5	181.3	181.3	181.6	182.5	182.6	182.7	183.5
2002	173.3	173.8	174.5	175.7	176.2	176.2	175.9	176.4	177.6	177.9	178.2	178.5
2001	171.1	172.0	172.2	173.1	174.2	174.4	173.3	174.0	174.6	174.3	173.6	173.4
2000	166.6	167.5	168.4	170.1	170.7	171.1	170.5	170.5	171.7	171.6	172.1	172.2
1999	163.4	163.7	164.1	165.2	165.6	165.6	165.1	165.5	166.2	166.5	166.7	167.3
1998	159.5	160.3	160.8	162.6	163.5	163.4	163.0	163.7	164.4	164.5	164.4	164.4
1997	154.4	155.0	155.4	156.3	156.9	157.5	157.5	158.5	159.3	159.5	159.6	160.0
1996	150.2	150.9	151.5	152.6	152.9	153.0	152.4	153.1	153.8	153.8	153.9	154.4
1995	146.0	146.9	147.5	149.0	149.6	149.8	149.1	149.9	150.6	149.8	149.8	150.7
1994	141.3	142.1	142.5	144.2	144.7	144.7	144.0	144.7	145.0	145.2	145.3	146.0
1993	137.9	138.8	139.3	140.6	141.1	141.0	140.7	141.3	141.9	141.8	141.6	141.9
1992	135.6	136.3	136.7	138.8	139.3	139.3	138.8	138.9	139.4	139.9	139.7	139.2
1991	130.2	130.9	131.4	133.1	133.5	134.1	133.8	134.1	134.6	135.1	135.6	135.7
1990	119.50	120.20	121.40	125.10	126.20	126.70	126.80	128.10	129.30	130.30	130.00	129.90
1989	111.00	111.80	112.30	114.30	115.00	115.40	115.50	115.80	116.60	117.50	118.50	118.80
1988	103.30	103.70	104.10	105.80	106.20	106.60	106.70	107.90	108.40	109.50	110.00	110.30
1987	100.00	100.40	100.60	101.80	101.90	101.90	101.80	102.10	102.40	102.90	103.40	103.30
1986	96.25	96.60	96.73	97.67	97.85	97.79	97.52	97.82	98.30	98.45	99.29	99.62
1985	91.20	91.94	92.80	94.78	95.21	95.41	95.23	95.49	95.44	95.59	95.92	96.05
1984	86.84	87.20	87.48	88.64	88.97	89.20	89.10	89.94	90.11	90.67	90.95	90.87
1983	82.61	82.97	83.12	84.28	84.64	84.84	85.30	85.68	86.06	86.36	86.67	86.89
1982	-	-	79.44	81.04	81.62	81.85	81.88	81.90	81.85	82.26	82.66	82.51

Coverage of Standards

UNIT 18: PREPARING BUSINESS TAXATION COMPUTATIONS

This unit is about preparing tax computations for businesses and completing the relevant tax returns. There are four elements.

The first element requires you to prepare capital allowances computations, including adjustments for private use by the owners of a business.

In the **second element** you must prepare assessable business income computations for partnerships and self-employed individuals. This includes identifying the National Insurance Contributions payable.

The **third element** is concerned with preparing capital gains computations for companies and unincorporated businesses.

The **fourth element** requires you to prepare Corporation Tax computations for UK resident companies.

Throughout the unit you must show that you take account of current tax law and HM Revenue & Customs practice and make submissions within statutory timescales. You also need to show that you consult with HM Revenue & Customs in an open and constructive manner, give timely and constructive advice to business clients and maintain client confidentiality.

Please note that the Performance Criteria quoted throughout the book still refer to the Inland Revenue which is now HM Revenue & Customs.

Element 18.1

Prepare capital allowances computations

Performance Criteria

		chapter
A	Classify expenditure on capital assets in accordance with the statutory distinction between capital and revenue expenditure	3,6
B	Ensure that entries and calculations relating to the computation of capital allowances for a company are correct	3
C	Make adjustments for private use by business owners	6
D	Ensure that computations and submissions are made in accordance with current tax law and take account of current Inland Revenue practice	3,6
E	Consult with Inland Revenue staff in an open and constructive manner	1
F	Give timely and constructive advice to clients on the maintenance of accounts and the recording of information relevant to tax returns	1,7
G	Maintain client confidentiality at all times	1

Element 18.2

Compute assessable business income

Performance Criteria

		chapter
A	Adjust trading profits and losses for tax purposes	2,6
B	Make adjustments for private use by business owners	6
C	Divide profits and losses of partnerships amongst partners	7
D	Apply the basis of assessment for unincorporated businesses in the opening and closing years	7
E	Identify the due dates of payment of Income Tax by unincorporated businesses, including payments on account	7
F	Identify the National Insurance Contributions payable by self-employed individuals	1,7
G	Complete correctly the self-employed and partnership supplementary pages to the Tax Return for individuals, together with relevant claims and elections, and submit them within statutory time limits	7
H	Consult with Inland Revenue staff in an open and constructive manner	1
I	Give timely and constructive advice to clients on the maintenance of accounts and the recording of information relevant to tax returns	1,7
J	Maintain client confidentiality at all times	1

Element 18.3

Prepare capital gains computations

Performance Criteria

		chapter
A	Identify and value correctly any chargeable assets that have been disposed of	4,8
B	Identify shares disposed of by companies	4
C	Calculate chargeable gains and allowable losses	4,8
D	Apply reliefs, deferrals and exemptions correctly	4,8
E	Ensure that computations and submissions are made in accordance with current tax law and take account of current Inland Revenue practice	4,8
F	Consult with Inland Revenue staff in an open and constructive manner	1
G	Give timely and constructive advice to clients on the maintenance of accounts and the recording of information relevant to tax returns	1,8
H	Maintain client confidentiality at all times	1

Element 18.4

Prepare Corporation Tax computations

Performance Criteria

		chapter
A	Enter adjusted trading profits and losses, capital allowances, investment income and capital gains in the Corporation Tax computation	2,5
B	Set-off and deduct loss reliefs and charges correctly	2,5
C	Calculate Corporation Tax due, taking account of marginal relief	5
D	Identify and set-off Income Tax deductions and credits	5
E	Identify the National Insurance Contributions payable by employers	1,5
F	Identify the amount of Corporation Tax payable and the due dates of payment, including payments on account	5
G	Complete Corporation Tax returns correctly and submit them, together with relevant claims and elections, within statutory time limits	5
H	Consult with Inland Revenue staff in an open and constructive manner	1
I	Give timely and constructive advice to clients on the maintenance of accounts and the recording of information relevant to tax returns	1,5
J	Maintain client confidentiality at all times	1

1 Introduction to business taxation

this chapter covers . . .

In this chapter we examine:

- *the various types of taxes that businesses pay*
- *the role of HM Revenue & Customs*
- *the way in which Corporation Tax and Income Tax are calculated*
- *how tax returns work for individuals and companies*
- *when to pay the relevant taxes*
- *the way in which National Insurance affects businesses*
- *the duties and responsibilities of a tax practitioner*

PERFORMANCE CRITERIA COVERED

unit 18: PREPARING BUSINESS TAXATION COMPUTATIONS

This chapter introduces the background to business taxation, and covers some of the underpinning knowledge that is common to all four elements of Unit 18. In addition, it covers the following performance criteria that are common to each of these elements:

- *consult with Inland Revenue staff in an open and constructive manner*
- *give timely and constructive advice to clients on the maintenance of accounts and the recording of information relevant to tax returns*
- *maintain client confidentiality at all times*

There is also coverage of the following performance criteria:

element 18.2

compute assessable business income

F identify the National Insurance Contributions payable by self-employed individuals

element 18.4

prepare Corporation Tax computations

E identify the National Insurance Contributions payable by employers

WHAT IS 'BUSINESS TAX'?

The 'business tax' that we are going to study in this book is not a single tax, but instead is a number of UK taxes that have an impact on businesses.

The specific taxes that affect any business in the UK will depend primarily on the legal structure of the business. You will probably be aware from your accounting studies of the three main ways (listed below) that businesses can be formed. We are going to examine the tax situation for

- limited companies
- sole traders, and
- partnerships

Limited companies (whether public or private) are incorporated bodies and therefore have their own legal existence that is quite separate from that of the owners. The profits that limited companies generate are subject to **Corporation Tax**.

Sole traders and **partnerships** are both unincorporated businesses, which means that there is no legal separation between the owner(s) of the business and the business itself. For this reason the profits from these businesses are dealt with under **Income Tax**, where they are assessed directly in relation to the business owners – the sole trader or partners. This is the same Income Tax that most of us pay on our income from employment or savings. If you have studied personal taxation (Unit 19), you will have seen how Income Tax works in some detail. To succeed in the business taxation Unit you only have to understand the impact of Income Tax on business profits.

In the first part of this book we will be examining how Corporation Tax works, and how we can calculate how much Corporation Tax limited companies should pay. To do this we will need to work out the amount of trading profits that are subject to Corporation Tax. We will also need to work out the chargeable gains that result from the disposal of certain assets, and incorporate this along with other company profits in the Corporation Tax computation. The tax return for a limited company will also be studied so that we can complete it.

In the second part of the book we will be looking at how the profits of sole traders and partnerships are assessed under Income Tax. We will also see how Capital Gains Tax can affect these business owners if they dispose of certain business assets. We will also learn how to complete the part of the Income Tax return that deals with self-employment.

We will also look at the impact of National Insurance on all of the above businesses, and learn how to calculate the amounts that need to be paid.

The table on the opposite page shows the areas we will study this Unit. The content of Unit 19 'Preparing Personal Taxation Computations' is also shown for comparison. There are other taxes, such as Value Added Tax and Inheritance Tax, which affect businesses, but they are beyond the requirements of your studies and so are not covered in this book.

THE TAX SYSTEM

We will first look at the background to the way that the tax system works. We will then outline the way in which numerical tax calculations are carried out.

HM Revenue & Customs

HM Revenue & Customs was formed in 2005 by an amalgamation of the Inland Revenue and HM Customs & Excise. Income tax, Corporation Tax and Capital Gains Tax are all administered by HM Revenue & Customs, which also collects National Insurance Contributions and VAT. This is a government organisation that has an administrative structure containing the following three parts:

- Taxpayer service offices are the main offices that individual taxpayers deal with, and handle much of the basic Income Tax assessment and collection functions.
- Taxpayer district offices deal with Corporation Tax and more complex Income Tax issues.
- Tax enquiry centres deal with enquiries and provide forms and leaflets to taxpayers.

These three functions are located in offices throughout the UK. In smaller centres some functions may be combined into one office, while in larger towns and cities they may be located separately.

the law governing tax - statute law

The authority to levy taxes comes from two sources. The first is legislation passed by Parliament, known as **statute law**. You may have heard of the Finance Acts. These are generally published each year and give details of any changes to taxes. These changes will have been proposed by the Chancellor of the Exchequer (usually in the budget) and passed by Parliament. In this book we will be using information from the Finance Act 2007, which relates to the financial year 2007 for companies and the tax year 2007/8 for individuals.

We will see exactly what is meant by financial years and tax years later in this chapter. There are also other relevant statute laws that were designed to create frameworks for the way that certain taxes work.

Unit 18
PREPARING BUSINESS TAXATION COMPUTATIONS

Unit 19
PREPARING PERSONAL TAXATION COMPUTATIONS

limited companies	sole traders partnerships	individuals with personal income
CORPORATION TAX	***INCOME TAX***	
trading profits	trading profits taxable as personal income →	trading profits
+		+
other profits		income from employment
+		+
chargeable gains		savings and investment income
		+
		property income
=		=
profits chargeable to Corporation Tax		income taxable under Income Tax
	CAPITAL GAINS TAX	
Note that chargeable gains are included in the Corporation Tax computation	gains on disposal of business assets are taxable under Capital Gains Tax	gains on disposal of personal assets are taxable under Capital Gains Tax

NATIONAL INSURANCE

Companies, sole traders and partnerships pay employer's National Insurance Contributions related to the earnings of employees of the business

National Insurance Contributions are payable by sole traders and partners as individuals

the law governing tax - case law

The second source of tax law is called **'case law'**, and draws its authority from decisions taken in court cases. Taxation can be very complicated, and sometimes disagreements between HM Revenue & Customs and taxpayers result in court cases. The final outcome of such cases can then become 'case law' and influences future interpretation of statute law.

Although there is a substantial amount of statute law and case law that is relevant to the taxation of businesses in the UK, this book will try to keep references to specific law to a minimum. While it will be important to know the rules that apply to certain situations, you will not be required to quote from the legislation or cases in your examination.

information available from HM Revenue & Customs

In addition to the tax law outlined above, there are interpretations and explanations of various issues that are published by HM Revenue & Customs. The main ones are as follows:

- Extra-statutory concessions issued when HM Revenue & Customs agree to impose a less strict interpretation of the law than would otherwise apply in particular circumstances.
- HM Revenue & Customs statements of practice are public announcements of how HM Revenue & Customs interpret specific rules.
- Guides and Help Sheets are issued to help taxpayers complete the necessary return forms and calculate their tax.

A large array of publications and forms can be downloaded from the HM Revenue & Customs website at www.hmrc.gov.uk This website also provides data on Corporation Tax and Income Tax rates for a range of tax years. You will find it useful to have a look at what is available on this site when you have an opportunity. It will also mean that you can obtain copies of tax returns to practice on when you reach that part of your business tax studies.

CALCULATION OF CORPORATION TAX AND INCOME TAX

Corporation Tax

In Chapters 2 to 5 in this book we will be looking in some detail about the way in which Corporation Tax is calculated. At this point we will just show how the system works in outline, by using a simple format for a **Corporation Tax computation**.

We will then use a numerical example that reflects a straightforward situation for a company.

an outline Corporation Tax computation

		£
	Trading Profits	X
+	Profits from Investments	X
+	Chargeable Gains	X
=	Profits Chargeable to Corporation Tax (PCTCT)	X
	Corporation Tax on PCTCT	X

A simple Corporation Tax computation would look like this if we assume the following figures:

Corporation Tax Computation for AB Company Limited
for year ended 31/3/2008

	£
Trading Profits	1,300,000
Profits from Investments	400,000
Chargeable Gains	300,000
Profits Chargeable to Corporation Tax (PCTCT)	2,000,000
Corporation Tax on PCTCT (£2,000,000 x 30%*)	600,000

*We will see later the other Corporation Tax rates that can apply.

Income Tax

In the later chapters in this book we will be looking at how trading profits are assessed under Income Tax. Although we will not need to use a full Income Tax computation in this unit, we will now just briefly see how it will appear. This is so that you can envisage how the trading profit figures would be used to work out Income Tax.

an outline Income Tax computation

		£
	Income – earnings and other income	X
	Less personal allowance	(X)
=	Taxable income	X
	Tax payable on taxable income	X

A simple Income Tax computation for a sole trader might appear as follows:

Income Tax Computation

	£
Trading Profits	5,000
Other Income	1,000
	6,000
Less Personal Allowance	5,225
Taxable income	775
Tax payable at 10%*	77

*Other rates of Income Tax can also apply.

HOW INCOME IS CATEGORISED FOR TAX PURPOSES

The income that a company or an individual receives is divided into categories, depending on what sort of income it is and where it comes from. These categories apply to both Corporation Tax and Income Tax, and are based on descriptions of income. They were previously called 'schedules' and 'cases'. This is done so that:

- the correct rules on how to work out the income are used (since these vary with the categories), and
- the correct rates of tax are used (since they can also depend on the type of income when applying income tax)

When studying this unit we will only need to know the outline detail of most of these categories, because we will be mainly concentrating on trading income. The list and descriptions shown below have been simplified to include only the categories that you need to know about in this unit. It does not include, for example, the categories that relate to overseas income.

'Property Income' – Rental income from land and property

'Trading Income' – Profits of trades and professions

'Savings & Investment Income' – UK Interest

FINANCIAL YEARS AND TAX YEARS

Corporation Tax – financial years

The rates of Corporation Tax are changed from time-to-time (normally in the Chancellor's budget) and relate to specific **financial years.** These years run from 1 April in one calendar year to 31 March in the following year. The year that runs from 1 April 2007 to 31 March 2008 is known as the financial year 2007 – in other words, the financial year is named after the calendar year that most of it falls into. We will see in the next chapters exactly how companies use the tax rates that apply to each financial year to calculate the correct amount of Corporation Tax.

Income Tax – tax years

For Income Tax purposes time is divided into **tax years** (sometimes called **fiscal years**). Individuals' income and Income Tax is worked out separately for each tax year. The tax year runs from 6 April in one calendar year to 5 April in the next calendar year. The tax year running from 6 April 2007 to 5 April 2008 would be described as the 2007/08 tax year.

HOW TAX RETURNS WORK

A **Tax Return** is a document issued by HM Revenue & Customs and used to collect information about a company's or an individual's income and gains. The Company Tax Return (the CT600 form) is used to collect information for Corporation Tax purposes, whereas the tax return for individuals provides data relating to Income Tax and Capital Gains Tax. Both companies and individuals are subject to the **self-assessment** system of tax. This means that they declare their profits and other taxable income on the tax return, and can then work out their own tax and pay it without HM Revenue & Customs sending them a bill. Individuals who submit their returns within a certain deadline can ask HM Revenue & Customs to work the tax out for them, but otherwise the taxpayer (company or individual) or their agent must calculate the tax.

The tax forms relevant to your studies for this unit are reproduced in the Appendix to this book. The forms are also available for download from the HM Revenue & Customs website: www.hmrc.gov.uk or the Resources Sections of www.osbornebooks.co.uk As we progress through this book we will examine how the various relevant parts of the returns should be completed.

tax returns for limited companies

A company must submit a CT600 form (see opposite for page 1 of the short version) for every **chargeable accounting period** (CAP). Provided the accounts are produced for a period of twelve months or less, the company's normal accounting period will be the same as the CAP. Longer accounting periods are divided into two CAPs, one based on the first twelve months of the accounting period, and the other based on the remainder of the period. We will look at the practicalities of dividing up the figures for a long accounting period later in the book.

Note that the company tax return relates to the company's chargeable accounting period, not a particular financial year. The form sets out the information that is needed by HM Revenue & Customs, and provides a standard format for calculations. It must be submitted within twelve months after the end of the company's accounting period from which the CAP was derived. The short CT600 version shown in the Appendix to this book is the one that you will need to be able to complete. You will not be asked to complete any supplementary pages for the company tax return that you may see referred to within the form, or the 'full' version of the form.

tax returns for individuals

Individuals with complex tax affairs (including all those in business as sole traders or partners) need to complete a separate tax return for each tax year. Note that individuals' tax returns relate to tax years, not accounting periods. The normal way that accounting periods are linked to tax years under Income Tax is that the assessable profits for a particular tax year are derived from the accounting period that ends in that tax year. This is known as a basis period for the tax year. For example a sole trader who makes accounts up to the 31 December each year would use the accounts for the year ended 31/12/2007 as the basis period for the tax year 2007/08.

Later on in this book we will look at the rules that link accounting periods to tax years in various special situations.

Page 1

HM Revenue & Customs

Company - Short Tax Return form

CT600 (Short) (2006) Version 2

for accounting periods ending on or after 1 July 1999

Your company tax return

If we send the company a *Notice* to deliver a company tax return (form *CT603*) it has to comply by the filing date, or we charge a penalty, even if there is no tax to pay. A return includes a company tax return form, any Supplementary Pages, accounts, computations and any relevant information.

Is this the right form for the company? Read the advice on pages 3 to 6 of the Company tax return guide (the *Guide*) before you start.

The forms in the CT600 series set out the information we need and provide a standard format for calculations. Use the *Guide* which contains general information you may need and box by box advice to help you complete the return form.

Company information

Company name

Company registration number

Tax Reference as shown on the CT603

Type of company

Registered office address

Postcode

About this return

This is the above company's return for the period

from (dd/mm/yyyy) to (dd/mm/yyyy)

Put an 'X' in the appropriate box(es) below

A repayment is due for this return period

A repayment is due for an earlier period

Making more than one return for this company now

This return contains estimated figures

Disclosure of tax avoidance schemes

Notice of disclosable avoidance schemes

Transfer pricing

Compensating adjustment claimed

Company qualifies for SME exemption

Accounts

I attach accounts and computations

for the period to which this return relates

for a different period

If you are not attaching accounts and computations, say why not

Supplementary Pages

If you are enclosing any Supplementary Pages put an 'X' in the appropriate box(es)

Loans to participators by close companies, form *CT600A*

Charities and Community Amateur Sports Clubs (CASCs), form *CT600E*

Disclosure of tax avoidance schemes, form *CT600J*

structure of the income tax return

Because different individuals have different circumstances, the tax return is divided into two parts.

The first part is sent to every recipient of the tax return, and is therefore common to all returns. It requests general information, as well as details of certain personal income.

The second part of the tax return consists of a series of supplementary pages that are only sent to relevant taxpayers. In this text we will only be looking at these business-related supplementary pages, since the main part of the return is dealt with in Osborne Books' *Personal Taxation* text, which covers the personal taxation unit.

There are supplementary pages for income from **self-employment** (ie for sole traders) and income from **partnerships**. For those in partnership, the supplementary page is completed for the individual's share of partnership profits. The partnership as a whole will also need to submit a form that summarises the total profits of the partnership.

scheduling of the income tax return

Individuals and partnerships can submit their tax returns either in the traditional paper format, or online. HMRC are encouraging the use of online submissions, and have introduced the following different deadlines for each method of tax return submission:

- Submission of paper-based tax returns must be made by the 31 October following the end of the tax year. This rule applies from the tax year 2007/08 onwards, and means that the 2007/08 return would need to be submitted by 31 October 2008. If required, HMRC will calculate the tax relating to a properly completed return if it meets this deadline.
- Submission of an online return can be made at any time up to 31 January following the end of the tax year. The amount of tax is automatically calculated by the computer program once the online form has been completed, and the taxpayer can print out a copy for their records. An online return for the tax year 2007/08 would therefore need to be submitted by 31 January 2009.

WHEN TO PAY TAX

The payment dates for companies and individuals differ, so we will examine them separately.

companies – Corporation Tax

We saw in the last section that company tax returns are completed for each chargeable accounting period (CAP). Unless instalment payments are necessary, the Corporation Tax that has been calculated is normally payable nine months and one day after the end of the chargeable accounting period that it relates to. For example, the Corporation Tax relating to the chargeable accounting period 1/1/2007 to 31/12/2007 will normally be payable on 1/10/2008. If the period falls into more than one financial year this will be taken account of in the tax calculation, but it does not affect the payment date. The payment date relates only to the period, not to the financial year.

If a company is 'large', then it will pay most of its Corporation Tax in instalments, with only the final amount falling due on the date referred to above. We will look at this situation in more detail after we have seen how Corporation Tax is calculated.

Notice that for companies the payment of tax is due before the final filing date for the tax return. This means that the tax calculation will have to have been carried out by the payment date (so that the payment amount is known), even though the actual form need not be submitted until nearly three months later! The return can always be submitted early if desired.

individuals – Income Tax

For income from trading profits there is no system set up to automatically deduct Income Tax as there is for employees. The outstanding balance of Income Tax that relates to business profits and other income from which tax has not been deducted will need to be paid to HM Revenue & Customs according to the following rules.

The *final* date for payment of the Income Tax that relates to a tax year is the 31 January *following the end of that tax year.*

For some taxpayers there may also be payments on account that must be made before the final date. These are due as follows:

- first payment on account is due on the 31st January within the tax year
- second payment on account is due on the 31st July following the end of the tax year

For the tax year 2007/08 the payment dates would be:

31st January 2008 for the first payment on account,

31st July 2008 for the second payment on account, and

31st January 2009 for the final payment

Notice that when payments on account are required, two payments will be due on each 31 January. For example, on 31 January 2008 there would be due both:

the final payment for the tax year 2006/07, and

the first payment on account for the tax year 2007/08

Later in the book we will see how the payments on account are calculated, and which taxpayers need to make these early payments.

We saw earlier that 31 January following the tax year was also the final date for submitting an online tax return, so for Income Tax these two dates coincide.

The table below illustrates the main points relating to tax returns and payment dates.

Companies	Individuals (Sole Traders and Partnerships)
Corporation Tax	**Income Tax**
Company Tax Return (CT600) includes calculation of Corporation Tax for chargeable accounting period (CAP).	Tax return includes supplementary pages for sole traders and partners, and relates to tax year.
Return submitted by 12 months after end of period that accounts are based on.	Paper return submitted by 31 Oct following tax year, or online return submitted by 31 Jan following tax year.
Final payment by 9 months and 1 day after end of CAP.	Final payment by 31 Jan following tax year.
Large companies also make instalment payments.	Most taxpayers also make two payments on account.

Case Study

DIVERSE ACCOUNTING PRACTICE: TAX RETURNS

It is August 2007. You are a trainee employed by the Diverse Accounting Practice, working in their tax department. The practice uses online submission for Income Tax returns. You are currently scheduling work related to two clients as follows:

The Mammoth Company Limited produces annual accounts to the 31st January. The accounts for the year ended 31/1/2007 have been completed and are awaiting the necessary tax work.

Jo Small is a sole trader who has been trading for many years. The practice has produced accounts for her for the year ended 30/6/2007.

required

State the type of tax return that will need to be completed for each of the clients. Explain how each return is related to the client's accounting period, and the latest submission dates for the returns. State the final date for the payment of outstanding tax after any instalments or payments on account have been made.

solution

The Mammoth Company Limited will require a company tax return (form CT600). This will relate to the chargeable accounting period (CAP) 1/2/2006 to 31/1/2007. The form must be submitted by 12 months after the end of the accounting period - 31/1/2008. The final Corporation Tax payment must be made by 1/11/2007 (nine months and one day after the end of the CAP).

Jo Small will need a tax return for the tax year 2007/2008. The accounting period of 1/7/2006 to 30/6/2007 will form the basis period for this tax year. The main part of the form will need to be completed, along with the supplementary pages relating to self-employment. The online tax return must be submitted by 31/1/2009. The final Income Tax payment relating to 2007/2008 will also have to be made by 31/1/2009.

NATIONAL INSURANCE

If you are an employee, you are probably familiar with employee National Insurance Contributions (NIC), which are deducted through Pay-As-You-Earn, along with Income Tax. In our study of business taxation we will be looking at two types of National Insurance Contributions, payable by

- employers (companies or individuals) when they employ staff, and
- self-employed individuals (sole traders and partners) in respect of their own profits

employer's National Insurance Contributions

When a sole trader, partnership, or company employs staff, then the employer must operate PAYE and deduct tax and employee National Insurance contributions from gross pay.

The National Insurance (NI) contributed by the employees is known as **Primary Class 1 Contributions**. It is payable, along with the Income Tax deducted under the PAYE system, to HM Revenue & Customs by the 19th of the month after the month in which the payroll was run.

The employer must in addition pay **Secondary Class 1 Contributions**. These are a cost to the employer that is a direct result of employing people. In the accounting records of the organisation this cost is often allocated to the salaries and wages account, along with the gross pay of the staff.

The employer's contributions for each employee are separated into Class 1 contributions and Class 1A contributions, as follows:

- **Class 1 contributions** are calculated as 12.8% of each employee's gross pay (less the earnings threshold of £100 per week), and
- **Class 1A contributions** are calculated as 12.8% of the assessable value of the employee's benefits in kind

There is no upper limit for employer's NIC. The Class 1 employer's contribution (based on gross pay less the earnings threshold) is payable to HM Revenue & Customs monthly, along with the employee's NIC and Income Tax.

Benefits in kind relate to non-cash value received, for example use of a company car or an interest free loan. If you have studied personal taxation you will remember the complex rules for assessing benefits. For the purposes of this unit we only need to be aware that the Class 1A employer's NI contributions are based on the value of any benefits.

The Class 1A contributions (on benefits in kind) are payable by the employer to HM Revenue & Customs annually by 19 July following the end of each tax year.

example – employer's NI

Kevin is employed by KevCom Limited. He has gross pay of £479 per week, and also has use of a company car throughout 2007/08. The assessable benefit of the car is £3,120 for the tax year.

The secondary Class 1 contributions payable by KevCom Limited would be calculated as:

Employer's NIC Class 1: based on gross pay

(£479 – £100) x 12.8%

= £48.51 per week (£2,522.52 for the year)

This would be payable to HM Revenue & Customs on a monthly basis by the employer along with PAYE payments.

Employer's NIC Class 1A: based on the car benefit

£3,120 x 12.8%

= £399.36 for the tax year 2007/08

This would be payable to HM Revenue & Customs by 19 July 2008.

Where the employer is a limited company then primary and secondary Class 1 and Class 1A NI contributions are payable in respect of the earnings of all employees, including the directors (who may also be the owners of the business).

If the organisation is a sole trader or partnership then the owners are not treated as employees, but are instead subject to self-employed NIC, as we will now see.

self-employed National Insurance contributions

There are two classes of NIC that apply to both sole traders and partners.

- **Class 2 contributions** are payable at a flat rate of £2.20 per week (unless a 'small earnings exception' [see below] is claimed), and, in addition,
- **Class 4 contributions** are payable on profits above £5,225 per year

The profits for self-employed NIC purposes are the same ones that are used for Income Tax purposes – the assessable trading profits. Where profits are less than £4,635 (2007/08) then the small earnings exception may be claimed and Class 2 contributions need not be paid.

The rates for Class 4 contributions for 2007/08 are:

- 8% of profits for the year between £5,225 and £34,840, plus
- 1% of profits above £34,840

If profits are below £5,225 then there are no Class 4 contributions. You may recognise this lower limit figure as the same as the Income Tax personal allowance.

example – NI for the self-employed

Sonita is a sole trader with trading profits of £40,000 in 2007/08.

Sonita has no employees.

Her NIC liability for the year would be:

		£	£
Class 2 contributions:	£2.20 x 52 =		114.40
Class 4 contributions:	(£34,840 - £5,225) x 8%	= 2,369.20	
	plus		
	(£40,000 - £34,840) x 1%	= 51.60	
			2,420.80
			2,535.20

Payment of Class 2 contributions is made by the self-employed person by monthly direct debit or is invoiced on a quarterly basis. Class 4 contributions are calculated at the same time as Income Tax under the self-assessment system, and entered on the tax return and paid along with the Income Tax for the year.

THE DUTIES AND RESPONSIBILITIES OF A TAX PRACTITIONER

A person who acts as a professional by helping clients (either companies or individuals) with their tax affairs has responsibilities:

- to the client, and
- to HM Revenue & Customs

The AAT has published **Guidelines on Professional Ethics** that deal with these and other issues. These apply to both AAT students and members and the document can be downloaded from the website www.aat.co.uk
If you are studying the AAT Diploma Pathway, you will study this subject in more detail in the 'Professional Ethics' unit.

confidentiality

You will know from your studies that keeping a client's or customer's dealings confidential is an essential element of professional ethics. As far as confidentiality for a tax practitioner is concerned, the guidelines referred to above state that confidentiality should always be observed, unless either

- authority has been given to disclose the information (by the client), or
- there is a legal, regulatory or professional duty to disclose

taxation services

The guidelines state the following regarding taxation services:

> *'A member providing professional tax services has a duty to put forward the best position in favour of a client or an employee. However the service must be carried out with professional competence, must not in any way impair integrity or objectivity, and must be consistent with the law.'*

The guidelines also state that:

> *'A member should not be associated with any return or communication in which there is reason to believe that it:*
>
> - *contains a false or misleading statement,*

- *contains statements or information furnished recklessly or without any real knowledge of whether they are true or false; or*
- *omits or obscures information required to be submitted and such omission or obscurity would mislead the tax authorities'*

dealing with professional ethics problems

Dealing with professional ethics can be a difficult and complex area, and we have only outlined some main points. If you find yourself in a position where you are uncertain how you should proceed because of an ethical problem then you should first approach your supervisor or manager. If you are still unable to resolve the problem then further professional or legal advice may need to be obtained.

tax records

It is also important to know what records will need to be kept regarding the client's income and tax affairs, and to ensure that such records are kept secure. The records must be sufficient to substantiate the information provided to HM Revenue & Customs. This would include documentation such as invoices, receipts, and working papers.

These records must be kept as follows:

- **Companies** must keep records relating to the information in their tax returns until at least 6 years after the end of the accounting period. For example, records relating to the chargeable accounting period (CAP) from 1/4/2007 until 31/3/2008 must be kept until 31/3/2014.
- **Individuals** in business (sole traders and partners) must keep records for approximately 5 years plus 10 months from the end of the tax year to which they relate. For example documents relating to 2007/08 must be retained until 31st January 2014.

For both types of organisation this date for record keeping is 5 years after the latest filing date for the return (assuming the income tax return is submitted online). If there is a formal HM Revenue & Customs enquiry into a taxpayer's affairs then the records need to be kept at least until the end of the enquiry.

Chapter Summary

- The taxes that UK businesses are subject to will depend on the type of organisation.
- The profits and gains of limited companies are subject to Corporation Tax, while sole traders and partners' trading profits are subject to Income Tax, along with any other personal income. The self-employed are also subject to Capital Gains Tax on the disposal of certain business assets. National Insurance contributions are made by the self-employed on their profits, and all employers pay NIC in relation to their employees.
- Income Tax and Corporation Tax are administered by HM Revenue & Customs, which collects tax and National Insurance Contributions. It is also responsible for publishing documents and forms to gather information about how much tax is owed and is governed by statute law and case law.
- Under both Corporation Tax and Income Tax, the assessable amount is divided into categories so that appropriate rules can be applied to calculate the amount of each different form of income.
- Corporation Tax rates relate to financial years that run from 1 April. The tax is calculated separately for each Chargeable Accounting Period (CAP) that is linked to the period for which the accounts are produced.
- The Company Tax Return (CT600) is based on the CAP. Corporation tax is payable within nine months and one day after the end of the CAP. Large companies must also make instalment payments.
- Income tax, which applies to individuals (sole traders and partners), is calculated separately for each tax year (6 April to the following 5 April). An Income Tax computation is used to calculate the tax by totalling the income from various sources, and subtracting the personal allowance. Each tax year has a separate tax return, which is used to collect information about the income and tax of individuals. It consists of a common section plus supplementary pages relating to self-employment. Income tax must be paid to HM Revenue & Customs by the 31 January following the end of the tax year. For some taxpayers there is also a requirement to make payments on account before this date.
- Employers also have to pay National Insurance Contributions in respect of their employees. The amount payable for employee earnings is calculated as a percentage of all earnings above a certain level. The earnings figure includes the value of benefits in kind. National Insurance is also payable by the self-employed in respect of their profits. They must pay a flat rate (Class 2), plus an amount calculated as a percentage of their profits (Class 4).
- Tax practitioners have responsibilities to their clients (including confidentiality) and to HM Revenue & Customs. They must also ensure that all necessary records are kept for the required period of time.

Key Terms

Limited Company	A limited company is a separate legal entity from its owners (the shareholders). Its profits are subject to Corporation Tax.
Sole Trader	An individual who is self-employed on his or her own. There is no legal distinction between the business entity and the individual, and the sole trader is subject to Income Tax on the profits of the business.
Partnership	An organisation made up of several individuals who share the responsibilities and profits of the partnership. Since there is no legal separation between the partnership and the individuals who are partners, they are individually subject to Income Tax on their share of the profits. Effectively, a partnership is a collection of sole traders.
Corporation Tax	A tax that applies to the trading and other profits of limited companies, including any chargeable gains.
Income Tax	The tax that individuals (including sole traders and partners) pay on their income, including business profits.
Capital Gains Tax	The tax that applies to certain disposals that individuals make on business and private assets.
National Insurance	Effectively a tax that is applied to employed individuals, employers, and the self-employed.
Statute Law	Legislation that is passed by Parliament, for example the annual Finance Act.
Case Law	The result of decisions taken in court cases that have an impact on the interpretation of law.
Financial Year (Corporation Tax)	Each financial year runs from 1 April to 31 March. Corporation Tax rates are based on financial years.
Tax Year (Income Tax)	Each tax year runs from 6 April to the following 5 April. Tax years are also known as fiscal years.

Company Tax Return This document (the CT600) is filed for each Chargeable Accounting Period, normally the period for which the company prepares accounts.

Tax Return (individuals) The self-assessment tax return is issued for each tax year to certain taxpayers and relates to Income Tax and Capital Gains Tax. It is divided into a common section, plus supplementary pages including pages relating to sole traders and partners. It can be submitted in paper form, or online.

Student Activities

Answers to all these asterisked questions are to be found at the back of this book.

1.1* The following statements are made by a trainee in the tax department of Jenner & Co.

Indicate whether each statement is true or false.

(a) One of the reasons that income is divided into categories is so that the correct rules can be applied to each type of income.

(b) The only law that is relevant to tax matters is the current Finance Act.

(c) Companies must complete a separate CT600 tax return for every financial year in which they operate.

(d) A Corporation Tax Computation is the name given to the calculation of Corporation Tax, based on the profits chargeable to Corporation Tax for the chargeable accounting period.

(e) National Insurance contributions are only payable by the employed and the self-employed.

(f) A sole trader with profits assessable in 2007/08 of £6,225, and no other taxable income, would pay Income Tax of £100.

(g) It is the job of a tax practitioner to ensure that his client pays the least amount of tax. This may involve bending the rules, or omitting certain items from a tax computation.

(h) Most self-employed people pay tax under PAYE and so don't have to worry about completing tax returns.

1.2* DonCom plc has the following assessable income agreed for the chargeable accounting period from 1/1/2007 to 31/12/2007:

Trading Profits	£1,300,000
Chargeable Gains	£500,000
Profits from renting property	£100,000

Required:

Assuming a Corporation Tax rate of 30%, use a Corporation Tax computation to calculate the tax liability for DonCom plc.

State the filing date of the CT600 form, and the date by which the final Corporation Tax payment must be made.

1.3* Parmajit is trading in partnership. Her share of the partnership profits for the accounting period 1/6/2006 to 31/5/2007 was £4,300. In addition she had other taxable income in the tax year 2007/08 of £2,000. She uses paper-based tax returns.

Required:

Assuming that Parmajit is entitled to a personal allowance of £5,225 for 2007/08, and pays

Income Tax at 10% for that year, calculate her Income Tax liability.

State the date that her tax return must be submitted if HM Revenue & Customs were to calculate her tax, and the date by which the balance of Income Tax must be paid for the tax year.

1.4* John and Julian are brothers. John is self-employed, and has assessable trading profits for the tax year 2007/08 of £25,000. Julian is an employee of Walvern Financial Systems Limited, earning £25,428 per year.

Required:

Calculate the National Insurance Contribution liability under each class for

(a) John

(b) Walvern Financial Systems Limited

In each case state how each payment would typically be made.

1.5* You are a trainee employed by Osborne Accounting Practice, working in their tax department. The practice uses online return submission for Income Tax. You are currently scheduling work related to two clients as follows:

The Walvern Water Company Limited produces annual accounts to 31 July. The accounts for the year ended 31/7/2007 have been completed and are awaiting the necessary tax work.

Wally Weaver is a sole trader who has been trading for many years. The practice has produced accounts for him for the year ended 31/7/2007.

Required:

(a) State the type of tax return that will need to be completed for each of the clients.

(b) Explain how each tax return is related to the client's accounting period, and state the latest submission dates for the returns.

(c) State in each case the final date for the payment of outstanding tax after any instalments or payments on account have been made.

2 Corporation tax – trading profits

this chapter covers . . .

In this chapter we examine:

- *the Corporation Tax computation in outline*
- *the adjustment of trading profits for tax purposes*
- *dealing with accounts for long periods*
- *relief for trading losses*

PERFORMANCE CRITERIA COVERED

unit 18: PREPARING BUSINESS TAXATION COMPUTATIONS

element 18.4

prepare Corporation Tax computations

A *enter adjusted trading profits and losses, capital allowances, investment income and capital gains in the Corporation Tax computation.*

B *set-off and deduct loss reliefs and charges correctly*

THE CORPORATION TAX COMPUTATION

We saw in the last chapter that the Corporation Tax computation comprises a summary of profits from various sources that are chargeable to Corporation Tax. The computation then goes on to calculate the amount of Corporation Tax that is payable. A simple version of this computation is repeated here:

	Trading Income	X
+	Profits from Investments	X
+	Chargeable Gains	X
=	Profits Chargeable to Corporation Tax (PCTCT)	X
	Corporation Tax on PCTCT	X

You will notice that 'Trading Income' is listed as the first item in the computation, and is often the most important one. We will be looking in detail in this chapter at why and how the trading profits from the financial accounts are adjusted for tax purposes.

Before we do that, we will examine briefly the main steps that need to be undertaken to complete the full Corporation Tax computation. We can then refer to this procedure as we look at the components in detail over the next chapters. The following diagram shows in summary how it all fits together.

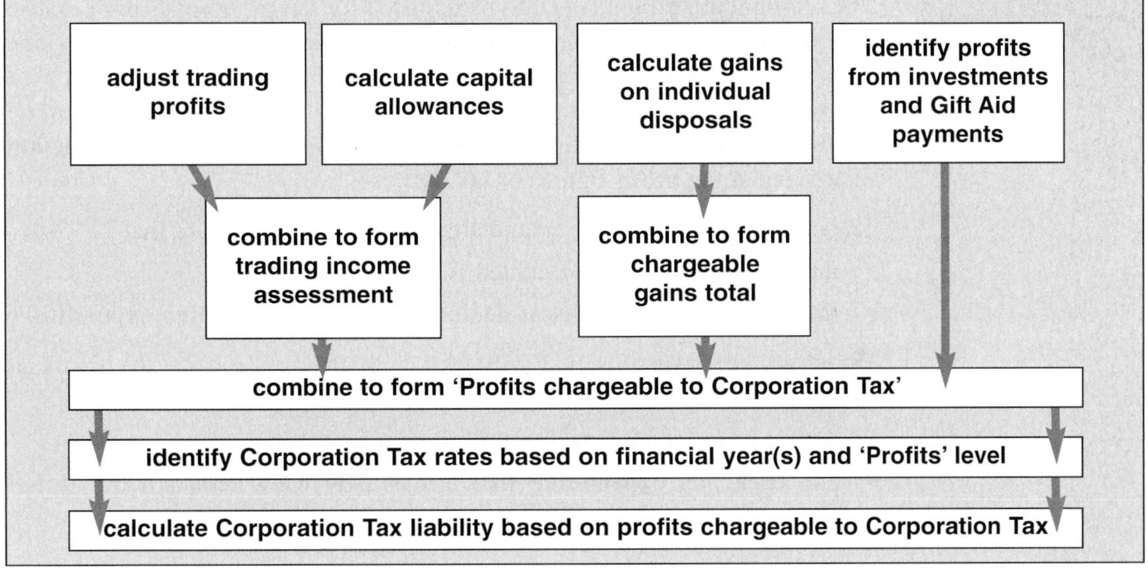

Corporation Tax computation – step-by-step procedures

In this chapter we are going to learn how to adjust the trading profit (the top left-hand box in the diagram). We will also see how trade losses can be set against profits to reduce Profits Chargeable to Corporation Tax.

In Chapter Three we will see how to calculate capital allowances so that we can incorporate the result into the trading income assessment.

In Chapter Four we will examine chargeable gains and then we will see how it all fits together.

In Chapter Five we will explain how to calculate the Corporation Tax liability.

ADJUSTMENT OF PROFITS

The starting point for the calculation of trading profits is the profit and loss account that has been prepared by the company. You may be asked to work from a set of accounts prepared for internal use, or in published format, but the process is the same.

The 'basis of assessment' for trading profits is the **tax-adjusted trading profits** of the **chargeable accounting period**, prepared on an accruals basis. In this section of the book we will start by using accounts that have been prepared for the chargeable accounting period (ie no more than 12 months). We will see later how we deal with accounts that have been prepared for a longer period. Since the financial accounts that will be our starting point will always have been prepared on an accruals basis, that aspect should not cause us any problems.

The reason that accounts need to be adjusted for tax purposes is not because they are wrong, but because Corporation Tax does not use exactly the same rules as financial accounting. We need to arrive at a profit figure that is based on the tax rules! For example, there are some costs that although quite legitimate from an accounting point of view are not allowable as a deduction in arriving at the profit figure for tax purposes.

The object of adjusting the financial accounts is to make sure that

- the only **income** that is credited is **trading income**
- the only **expenditure** that is deducted is **allowable trading expenditure**

When we adjust profits, we will start with the profit from the financial accounts, and

- deduct any income that is not trading income, and
- add back any expenditure that has already been deducted but is not allowable

This approach is much more convenient than re-writing the whole profit and loss account based on tax rules. It is quite logical, because it effectively cancels out income and expenditure that is not relevant for tax purposes.

example – adjusting the profits

Suppose that we wish to adjust a set of financial accounts (shown here in summary form):

	£'000
Sales	500
less cost of sales	200
Gross trading profit	300
Non-trading income	150
	450
less expenditure	120
Net profit	330

Analysis of the accounts has shown that the cost of sales is entirely allowable, but £40,000 of the £120,000 expenditure is not allowable for tax purposes.

To adjust the profits we would carry out the following computation:

	£'000
Net profit per accounts	330
Less non-trading income	(150)
Add expenditure that is not allowable	40
Adjusted trading profit	220

This provides us with the same answer that we could get by writing out the accounts in full, using only the trading income and allowable expenditure. If we did that it would look as follows. This is shown just for comparison – we won't actually need to rewrite the accounts in this way.

	£'000
Sales	500
Less allowable cost of sales	200
Gross trading profit	300
Less allowable expenditure	80
Net profit	220

We will now look in more detail at adjustments for income, followed by expenditure.

adjusting income

Provided the 'sales', 'turnover' or 'revenue' figure relates entirely to trading, this figure will not need adjusting. Other income may or may not be taxable, but if it is not trading income, then it will need to be adjusted for in the trading profit calculation.

The following are examples of income that are not assessable as trading income, and should therefore be adjusted for by deducting from the net profit shown in the financial accounts.

- non-trading interest receivable
- rent receivable
- gains on the disposal of fixed assets
- dividends received

All these examples should be adjusted by simply deducting the amount that was credited to the financial accounts. There is no need to worry about exactly how the figure was originally calculated. We will then have arrived at what the profit would have been if these items had not been included originally. Items that originate from the trade (eg discounts received) are taxable as part of trading income, and therefore need no adjustment.

Non-trading interest and **rent received** will reappear in the PCTCT computation as investment income and property income respectively. Throughout the examples in this book (and examination tasks) you can assume that any interest received is non-trading and is therefore dealt with as outlined here unless stated otherwise.

Gains on the disposal of fixed assets could result in chargeable gains. These gains need to be calculated according to special rules before being incorporated into the PCTCT as we will see in Chapter 4. **Dividends received** from UK companies are not assessable under Corporation Tax at all (since they have been paid out of another company's taxed income), although, as we will see later, they can have an impact on the rate of tax applied.

adjusting expenditure

We will only need to adjust for any expenditure accounted for in the financial accounts profit if it is **not allowable**. We do this by **adding it back** to the financial accounts profit. Expenditure that is allowable can be left unadjusted in the accounts. Although this may seem obvious, it is easy to get confused, especially during an examination!

The general rule for expenditure to be allowable in a trading income computation is that it must be

- revenue rather than capital in nature, and
- 'wholly and exclusively' for the purpose of the trade

Although we will look at how to deal with various specific types of expenditure shortly, the above rules are fundamental, and should always be used to guide you in the absence of more precise information. This part of the unit will require a good deal of study, since it is quite complex, and the rules and examples that follow will need to be remembered. The best way to approach this is to continually revise the topic and practice lots of examples.

expenditure that is not allowable

The following are examples of expenditure that is not allowable, and therefore require adjustment. Some clearly follow the rules outlined above, while others may have arisen from specific regulations, or court cases forming precedents (case law).

- **any capital expenditure**
  This follows the normal financial accounting use of the term, to mean expenditure on assets that will have a value to the business over several accounting periods. Capital expenditure includes expenditure to improve fixed assets, and installation costs and legal expenses in connection with acquiring fixed assets.
- **depreciation of fixed assets**
  This is because capital allowances are allowable instead, as HM Revenue & Customs alternative to depreciation, as we will see in the next chapter. Even where there are no capital allowances available, depreciation is still not allowed. Other items which are similar to depreciation (eg amortisation of certain assets, and losses on disposal of fixed assets) are also not allowable.
- **entertaining expenditure**
  This relates to business entertaining of customers or suppliers. Entertaining of the businesses' own staff is however allowable (see page 2.9).
- **gifts to customers**
  Virtually all gifts made to customers are not allowable. There is an exception for some low-value items, as we will see shortly.
- **increases in general bad debt provisions**
  Any such increase (that is debited to the profit and loss account) must be added back in the computation, and decreases in general provisions adjusted for by deducting from profits. A general provision could be based on a lump sum, or a percentage of total debtors. Increases in specific provisions and the actual write-off of bad debts are however

allowable. Where accounts have been prepared using 'impairment' as a means of calculating the bad debt provision, the provision will be treated in the same way as a specific bad debt provision. This applies as long as objective evidence was used to calculate the amount of impairment. This situation could arise if, for example, the accounts are prepared under International Accounting Standards. See also the additional note below.

- **charitable payments**
  These items can be deducted from the total profits of the company in the PCTCT calculation as Gift Aid payments. Where this occurs the expenditure cannot also be deducted in the calculation of trading profits. We will look a little more closely at gift aid payments in Chapter 5.
- **fines for law breaking**
  Although there are exceptions for employees' parking fines (if incurred while on business), all other fines (and associated legal costs) are not allowable for tax purposes when paid by a company.
- **donations to political parties**
  These are not for the purpose of 'the trade' and so are not allowable.
- **writing off non-trade loans**
  For example, loans to employees or directors (unless they were incurred in the normal course of trade).
- **dividends payable**
  The payment of dividends is not an allowable expense. However if these occur in the accounts after the net profit that we have used as the starting point for our calculation, there will be no need for an adjustment.
- **Corporation Tax**
  Logically, the tax payment itself is not tax deductible!

expenditure that is allowable

As already stated, revenue expenditure that is 'wholly and exclusively' for the purpose of the trade is allowable. We will now list some illustrative examples, a few of which were referred to above.

- normal **cost of sales**
- normal **business expenditure**, for example:
  – distribution costs
  – administration
  – salaries and wages, and employers' NIC
  – rent, rates and insurance
  – repairs
  – advertising

– business travel and subsistence

– accountancy services

– research & development expenditure

- **specifically allowable expenditure**:

– interest payable on trade loans

– staff entertaining (eg staff Christmas parties)

– trade bad debts written off (note, however, that writing off of a loan to an employee is not allowable, since it is not a trade item)

– increases in specific provisions for trade bad debts and impairment provisions based on objective evidence (see note below). Specific provisions are those based on named debtors

– gifts to customers that contain a conspicuous advertisement, costing up to £50 per recipient per year – this however does not apply to food, drink, tobacco or gift vouchers, gifts of which can never be allowable – allowable examples would include calendars and diaries

– employees' parking fines incurred while on business, but not those of directors

- **capital allowances**

  We will see how to calculate capital allowances in the next chapter. In the exercises in this chapter we will use capital allowance figures that have already been calculated. Because capital allowances will not be recorded in the financial accounts, they will be deducted as a separate item in the adjustment to the accounts.

note regarding trade bad debts and provisions

Whereas a sum written off a trade debt or an increase in a specific provision is allowable, any recovery of amounts previously written off and any decrease in specific provisions is taxable, and no adjustment is needed. This can be a confusing area, yet forms a popular examination topic. The following table summarises the position:

Expenditure	*Treatment*	*Action*
Trade Bad Debts Written Off	Allowable	No adjustment
Increases in Specific Bad Debt Provisions	Allowable	No adjustment
Increases in General Bad Debt Provisions	Not allowable	Add back
Income	*Treatment*	*Action*
Trade Bad Debts Recovered	Taxable	No adjustment
Decreases in Specific Bad Debt Provisions	Taxable	No adjustment
Decreases in General Bad Debt Provisions	Not taxable	Deduct

Case Study

TRADING ALOUD LIMITED: ADJUSTING THE PROFIT

Trading Aloud Limited is a company that specialises in selling acoustic equipment. The unadjusted profit and loss account for the year ended 31/3/2008 is as follows:

	Notes	£	£
Sales			900,000
less cost of sales			530,000
Gross profit			370,000
Rental income			120,000
Dividends received			140,000
			630,000
less expenses:			
Salaries and wages	(1)	95,400	
Depreciation		51,000	
Directors' fees		45,000	
Administration expenses		17,600	
Advertising	(2)	12,600	
Travel and entertaining	(3)	19,500	
Bad debts and provisions	(4)	21,650	
			262,750
Net Profit			367,250

Notes:

(1) Salaries and wages includes £4,350 employers' NIC.

(2) Advertising includes:
- (a) gifts of food hampers to 70 customers £3,250
- (b) gifts of 100 mouse-mats with company logos £500

(3) Travel and entertaining is made up as follows:

	£
Employees' travel expenses	7,400
Employees' subsistence allowances	5,450
Entertaining customers	6,650
	19,500

(4) Bad debts and provisions is made up of:

	£
Trade bad debts written off	13,400
Increase in general bad debt provision	5,000
Increase in specific bad debt provision	3,250
	21,650

Capital allowances for the period have been calculated at £15,000.

Required

Adjust the net profit shown to arrive at the trading income assessment for Corporation Tax purposes.

Solution

The computation is shown here with notes that explain the rationale behind each adjustment and allowed item. Items that are to be deducted are shown in the left-hand column, and those to be added kept in the main (right-hand) column for clarity.

		£
Net Profit per accounts		367,250
Add Back:		
Expenditure that is shown in the accounts but is not allowable		
Depreciation		51,000
Food Hampers		3,250
Entertaining Customers		6,650
Increase in General Bad Debt Provision		5,000
		433,150
Deduct:		
Income not taxable as trading income	£	
Rental Income	120,000	
Dividends Received	140,000	
Capital Allowances	15,000	
		(275,000)
Trading Income Assessment		158,150

Notes:

- The sales and cost of sales appear to be normal trading items.
- The rental income will be brought into the main Corporation Tax computation as property income.
- The dividends received are not subject to Corporation Tax.
- Salaries and Wages (including employers' NIC) are allowable.
- Depreciation is never allowable.
- Director's fees are treated in the same way as other staff salaries.
- Administration expenses appear to be wholly and exclusively for the trade.
- The advertising costs are allowable, including the mouse-mats that fall under the provision regarding items under £50 per person. The hampers cannot be covered by this rule as they contain food.
- Employees' travel and subsistence costs are allowable, but entertaining customers is never allowable.
- Changes in general provisions for bad debts must always be adjusted for, but specific provision increases and bad debts written off are allowable.
- The capital allowance figure is shown here as a final deduction in arriving at the assessable trading income.

working from published accounts

The principle of adjusting profits for tax purposes is the same when using a published version of financial accounts. The only issue that requires extra care is the choice of profit figure as a starting point from the range of figures available. It makes sense to use the profit figure that will require the least number of adjustments. The best profit figure to use will therefore be profit before tax and before dividends so that these items will not need further adjustment. We will now use a Case Study to illustrate this procedure. Since you will probably be familiar with the International Accounting Standards (IAS) format, we will use it here.

Case Study

FORMAT COMPANY LIMITED: ADJUSTING PUBLISHED ACCOUNTS

The published accounts of Format Company Limited under IAS for the year ended 31 March 2008 are shown below, together with notes that provide some analysis of the summarised data.

Capital allowances have already been calculated, and amount to £86,400.

	£'000
Revenue	963
Cost of Sales	(541)
Gross Profit	422
Other Income	390
Distribution Costs	(56)
Administrative Expenses	(123)
Finance Costs	(24)
Profit before Tax	609
Tax	(150)
Profit for the Year	459

Notes

- Cost of Sales includes depreciation of £140,000
- Administrative Expenses include the following:

–	Increase in Bad Debt Provision due to impairment calculation based on objective evidence	£7,700
–	Entertaining Customers	£9,600

- Other Income consists of:

–	Rental Income	£220,000
–	Interest Received from Investments	£60,000
–	Profit on Sale of Fixed Assets	£95,000
–	Dividends Received	£15,000

- Finance Costs relates to bank overdraft interest.

Required

Calculate the trading income as adjusted for tax purposes.

Solution

We will start our computation with the 'Profit before Tax' since the item that follows that figure is not allowable, whereas the items that precede it could be a mixture of allowable and non-allowable.

	£	£
Profit before Tax		609,000
Add Back:		
Expenditure that is shown in the accounts but is not allowable		
Depreciation		140,000
Entertaining Customers		9,600
		758,600
Deduct:		
Income that is not taxable as trading income		
Rental Income	220,000	
Interest Received from Investments	60,000	
Profit on Sale of Fixed Assets	95,000	
Dividends Received	15,000	
Capital Allowances	86,400	(476,400)
Trading Income Assessment		282,200

DEALING WITH ACCOUNTS FOR LONG PERIODS

In Chapter One we saw that a **chargeable accounting period** (CAP – the period that we must use for Corporation Tax purposes) is the same as the period that the accounts have been prepared for, but only if that period is for 12 months or less. Where the company produces its financial accounts for a period exceeding 12 months, this will be divided into two CAPs (and require two Corporation Tax computations) –

- one CAP for the first 12 months of the financial accounting period and
- one CAP for the balance of the financial accounting period

For example, if a company produces financial accounts for the 18 month period 1/7/2006 to 31/12/2007, there will be two CAPs:

- a 12 month CAP: 1/7/2006 to 30/6/2007, and
- a 6 month CAP: 1/7/2007 to 31/12/2007

The mechanism for dealing with the two Corporation Tax computations for these periods is:

- the financial accounts for the long period are adjusted in one operation, with the exception of the capital allowances deduction
- the adjusted profits (before the deduction of any capital allowance) are then time-apportioned into the two CAPs
- capital allowances are calculated separately for each CAP (as we will see in the next chapter)
- each CAP's adjusted trading profit is then finalised by deducting the capital allowances that have been calculated for the specific period

We will now use a Case Study to illustrate this principle.

Case Study

THYME LIMITED: ACCOUNTS FOR A LONG PERIOD

Thyme Limited is changing its accounting dates, and to accommodate this has produced one long set of financial accounts, from 1/10/2006 to 31/3/2008.

Capital allowances have already been calculated for each of the two CAPs as follows:

CAP 1/10/2006 to 30/9/2007 £15,000

CAP 1/10/2007 to 31/3/2008 £6,000

The financial accounts for the 18 months to 31/3/2008 are as follows:

	£	£
Sales		237,000
less cost of sales		103,000
Gross profit		134,000
less expenses:		
Salaries and wages	43,500	
Rent, rates, and insurance	8,700	
Depreciation etc	11,000	
Selling expenses	15,780	
General expenses	15,630	
Bad Debts	19,400	
		114,010
Net Profit		19,990

The following information is also provided:

- Salaries and wages relate to the two directors, who are the only employees.
- Depreciation etc is made up as follows:
  - Depreciation £35,000
  - Loss on sale of motors £9,500
  - Profit on sale of building £33,500
- Selling expenses include:
  - Entertaining customers £4,700
  - Gifts of wine to customers £1,900
  - Gifts of calendars to customers (£10 each, with company advert) £500
- General expenses include accountancy fees of £2,800
- Bad debts are made up of:
  - Increase in specific provision £8,000
  - Bad debts written off £23,600
  - Bad debts recovered (£12,200)

Required

1 Adjust the financial accounts for the 18-month period, before deduction of capital allowances.

2 Time-apportion the adjusted profit figure into CAPs.

3 Calculate the trading income assessment for each CAP.

Solution

1

	£	£
Net Profit for 18-month period per accounts		19,990
Add back non-allowable expenditure:		
Depreciation		35,000
Loss on sale of motors		9,500
Entertaining customers		4,700
Gifts of wine		1,900
		71,090
Deduct income that is not taxable as trading income		
Profit on sale of building	33,500	
		(33,500)
Adjusted profit before capital allowances		37,590

Notes

- The profit on the sale of the building is not taxable as trading income, and is therefore deducted. An alternative approach would be to add back the net £11,000 that relates to the three items under the heading of 'depreciation'.
- The calendars are allowable under the gift rules.
- All the items under the bad debts heading are allowable/taxable, and therefore do not require adjustment.

2 The adjusted profit for the 18-month period is time-apportioned as follows:

CAP 1/10/2006 to 30/9/2007 £37,590 x 12/18 = £25,060

CAP 1/10/2007 to 31/3/2008 £37,590 x 6/18 = £12,530

3 Capital allowances are then deducted from the adjusted profit for each CAP:

	1/10/06 – 30/9/07	1/10/07 – 31/3/08
	£	£
Adjusted profit	25,060	12,530
Capital allowances	15,000	6,000
Trading Income	10,060	6,530

DEALING WITH TRADE LOSSES

If, once profits have been tax-adjusted and any capital allowances deducted, the result is a minus figure, a 'trading loss' will have arisen. This will have two implications:

- The trading income assessment for the chargeable accounting period will be zero (not the negative profit figure).
- The amount of the negative profit figure will form the trading loss, and the company can choose how to deal with it.

How does one deal with this situation? The options are as follows:

1 The trading loss can be carried forward to reduce trading income from the same trade in the future. If this option is chosen the loss must be used up as quickly as possible. If the following year's profit from the same trade is less than the loss, then that profit will be reduced to nil and the balance of the loss carried on forward. This will occur as many times as is necessary to offset the whole loss.

2 The trading loss can be used to reduce (or eliminate) all of the profits chargeable to Corporation Tax (PCTCT) in the same CAP that the loss arose. This set off would be against all taxable investment income and chargeable gains for the period.

3 Only if option (2) above is chosen, the loss can then be carried back against the PCTCT of the CAP in the 12 months immediately before the one in which the loss occurred. If there were two CAPs partly falling into that 12-month period, then both could be used.

The diagram at the top of the next page illustrates these options, using as an example a company making up accounts to the 31 December each year. A loss arises in the year ended 31/12/2007.

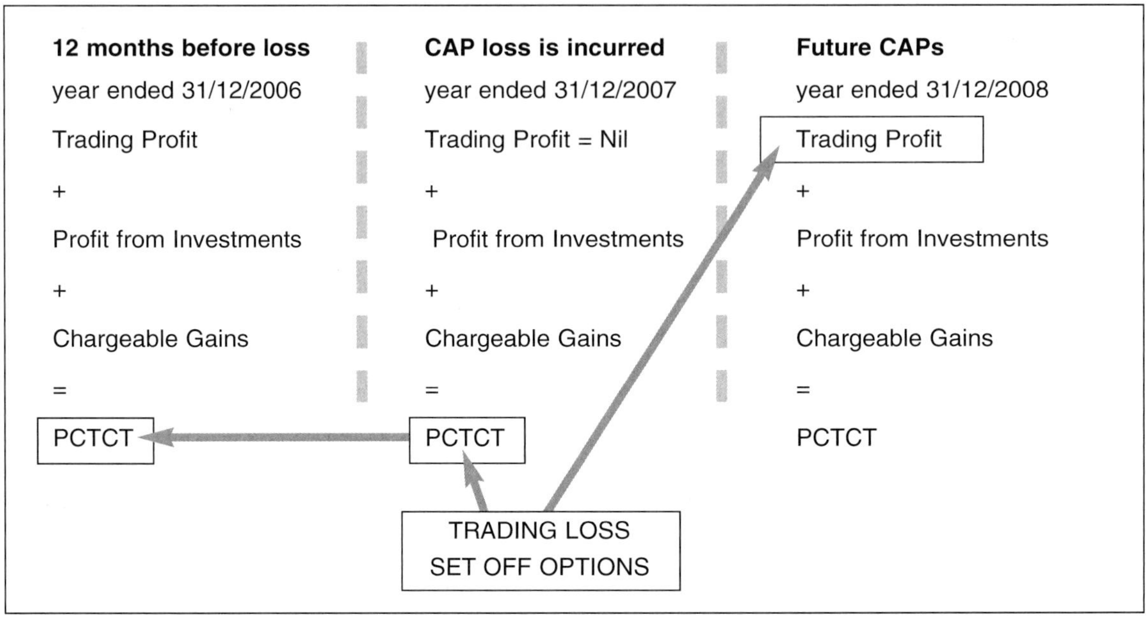

Where option (2) has been used, or option (2) followed by option (3), and the whole loss has still not been offset, any balance will follow option (1).

We can now revise our diagram (see page 2.3) illustrating the Corporation Tax Computation procedures to incorporate possible trading loss set off. The dark boxes are additions to the diagram.

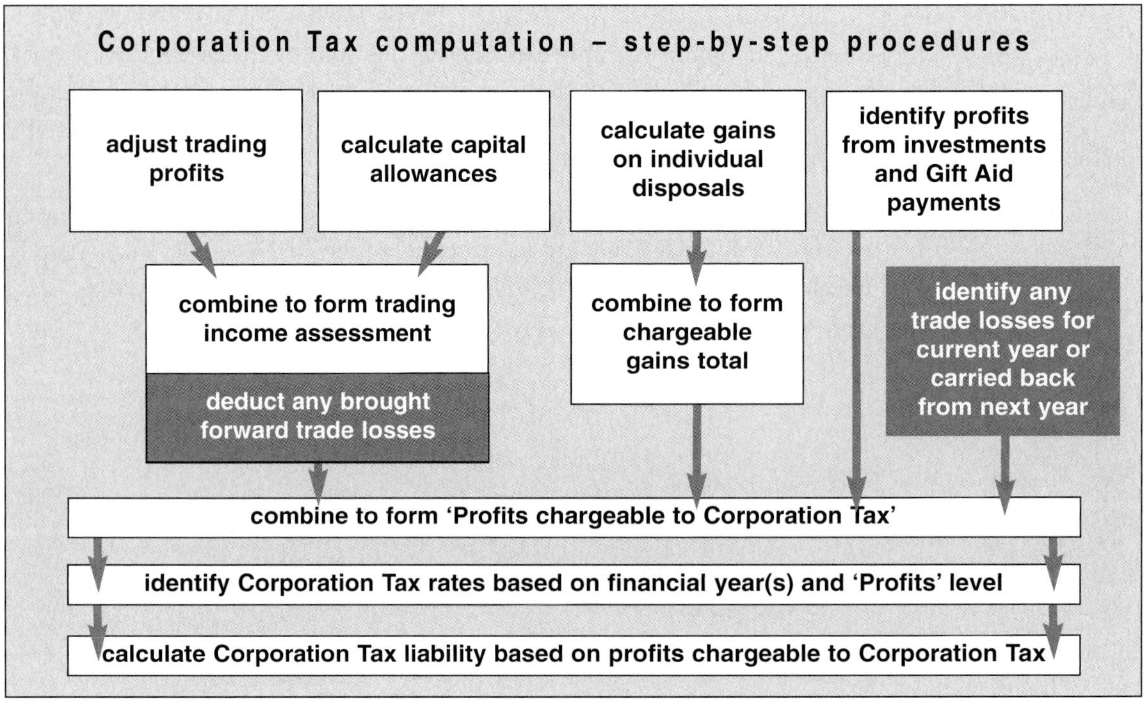

We will now use a Case Study to illustrate these options. We will also return to this topic in later chapters when we have studied the build-up of the PCTCT in more detail.

Case Study

DOWNSEA PANS LIMITED: TRADING LOSS OPTIONS

Downsea Pans Limited has the following tax-adjusted results for the three chargeable accounting periods to 31/12/2007.

CAP	**year ended 31/12/05**	**year ended 31/12/06**	**year ended 31/12/07**
	£000	*£000*	*£000*
Trading Profit/(Loss)	120	(150)	160
Profits from investments	40	50	55
Chargeable gains	75	15	80

Required

State the options available for offsetting the £150,000 trading loss incurred in the CAP year ended 31/12/2006.

Demonstrate the effects on the relevant PCTCT figures by showing Corporation Tax computation extracts.

Solution

We will show the options one by one, but with all the three years' details shown in columnar form for reference.

Option One

The trading loss could be carried forward and set against the trading income of y/e 31/12/2007. Since this profit is larger than the loss the whole loss could be offset in this way. The Corporation Tax computation extract for y/e 31/12/2007 would be affected, and the three years would look as follows:

	y/e 31/12/05	**y/e 31/12/06**	**y/e 31/12/07**
	£000	*£000*	*£000*
Trading Income	120	0	160
***less* loss relief**			(150)
			10
Profits from Investments	40	50	55
Chargeable Gains	75	15	80
PCTCT	235	65	145

Option Two

The trading loss could be set against the other profits and chargeable gains of the CAP y/e 31/12/2006 (the CAP in which the loss was incurred). Due to the size of the loss this will not be sufficient to offset the whole loss. The balance of the loss could then be carried back to the CAP y/e 31/12/2005 and set against the total PCTCT in that period as well. This would give the following Corporation Tax computation extracts:

	y/e 31/12/05	y/e 31/12/06	y/e 31/12/07
	£000	*£000*	*£000*
Trading Income	120	0	160
Profits from Investments	40	50	55
Chargeable Gains	75	15	80
	235	65	295
less **loss relief**			
first set off		**(65)**	
second set off	**(85)**		
PCTCT	150	0	295

Note that the loss can only be carried back after the current year set-off has been carried out to its full extent.

Option Three

Following the current year set-off as in option two, the previous year PCTCT need not be utilised. In that case the balance of the loss would be carried forward under S393(1) against the trading income only of y/e 31/12/2007. This would give the following figures for the three years.

	y/e 31/12/05	y/e 31/12/06	y/e 31/12/07
	£000	*£000*	*£000*
Trading Income	120	0	160
less **loss relief**			**(85)**
			75
Profits from Investments	40	50	55
Chargeable Gains	75	15	80
	235	65	210
less **loss relief**		**(65)**	
PCTCT	235	0	210

The actual choice of option would depend on factors such as the tax rates that would apply to the levels of PCTCT in each year. We will examine this issue in Chapter 5.

Chapter Summary

- The profits chargeable to Corporation Tax (PCTCT) include trading income, profits from investments, and chargeable gains. To arrive at the trading income, the profits based on the financial accounts must be adjusted, and capital allowances calculated and deducted from the adjusted profit figure.

- To adjust the profit based on the financial accounts, any income shown in the accounts that is not taxable as trading income is deducted, and any expenditure that is not allowable is added. The capital allowances that will have been calculated separately are then deducted to arrive at the assessable trading income.

- To be allowable, expenditure must be revenue (not capital), and wholly and exclusively for the purpose of the trade. There are also detailed rules about whether certain items of expenditure are allowable.

- Where the financial accounts are prepared for a period exceeding twelve months, the period will form two chargeable accounting periods. One CAP will be for the first twelve months, and the other for the balance of the financial accounting period. To deal with this situation, the financial accounts are adjusted as a whole, apart from the capital allowances. The adjusted profit is then time-apportioned into the two CAPs, and separate capital allowance figures deducted from each to form two trading income assessments.

- Where the adjusted trading profits (after capital allowances) result in a negative figure, the trading income assessment is zero, and a trading loss is formed that can be relieved in several ways. It may be carried forward and set off against the first available profits of the same trade. It may alternatively be set against the PCTCT of the CAP in which the loss was incurred. Where this happens and not all the loss is used up, the balance can be carried back against the PCTCT arising in the preceding twelve months.

Key Terms

Profits Chargeable to Corporation Tax (PCTCT)

The figure used as the basis for calculation of Corporation Tax for a limited company. It includes trading profits, profits from investments, and chargeable gains. It is calculated for each chargeable accounting period (CAP) that the company operates in.

Chargeable Accounting Period (CAP)

The period for which the PCTCT must be calculated. It is the same as the period for which the company produces financial accounts, unless that period is for more than twelve months. In that case the financial accounting period is divided into two CAPs.

Adjusted Trading Profits

The trading profits that have been adjusted for tax purposes by excluding income not taxable as trading income, and non-allowable expenditure.

Trading Income Assessment

The taxable trading profits for the CAP. It is made up of adjusted trading profits, after deducting any capital allowances.

Trading Loss

This occurs when the adjusted trading profits after deducting capital allowances produces a negative figure. The negative figure is the trading loss, whilst the trading income assessment is zero.

Loss Relief

The offsetting of the trading loss against profits, according to legislation. This may be against future profits from the same trade, or against certain PCTCTs.

Student Activities

Answers to the asterisked (*) questions are to be found at the back of this book.

2.1* The numbered items listed below appear in a profit and loss account (before the net profit figure).

If you are adjusting the trading profit for tax purposes, state whether each item should be:

- added to the net profit
- deducted from the net profit
- ignored for adjustment purposes

1 accountancy fees payable

2 amortisation of lease

3 non–trade interest received

4 dividends received

5 employees' travel expenses payable

6 gain on sale of fixed asset

7 decrease in specific provision for bad debts

8 gifts of cigars (with company adverts) to customers, costing £40 per recipient.

9 increase in general bad debt provision

10 donation to political party

11 employers' National Insurance contributions

12 charitable donation under the Gift Aid scheme

2.2* Ahoy Trading Limited is a company that specialises in selling yachting equipment.

The unadjusted profit and loss account for the accounting year is as follows:

	£
Sales	500,000
less cost of sales	220,000
Gross profit	280,000
Interest received	20,000
Dividends received	70,000
	370,000

	£	£
less expenses:		
Salaries and wages	99,000	
Depreciation	42,000	
Loss on sale of fixed assets	5,000	
Administration expenses	19,600	
Advertising	18,000	
Interest payable	22,000	
Travel and entertaining	19,100	
Bad debts and provisions	15,000	
		239,700
Net Profit		130,300

Notes:

- Administration includes £350 employees' parking fines incurred while on company business.
- Advertising includes:
  - gifts of chocolates with company logos to 100 top customers £4,900
  - gifts of sailing books with company logos to 200 other customers £5,000
- Travel and entertaining is made up as follows:

	£
– Employees' travel expenses	3,400
– Employees' subsistence allowances	5,600
– Entertaining customers	6,000
– Entertaining staff at Christmas	4,100
	19,100

- Bad debts and provisions is made up of:

	£
– Trade bad debts written off	18,400
– Decrease in general bad debt provision	(5,000)
Increase in specific bad debt provision	1,600
	15,000

Capital allowances for the period have been calculated at £23,000.

Required:

Adjust the net profit shown to arrive at the trading income assessment for Corporation Tax purposes.

2.3* All I Need Trading Limited has an unadjusted profit and loss account for the accounting year as follows:

	£	£
Sales		770,000
less cost of sales		420,000
Gross profit		350,000
Interest received		40,000
Gains on disposal of fixed assets		50,000
Rental income received		60,000
		500,000
less expenses:		
Discounts allowed	10,000	
Salaries and wages	80,500	
Depreciation	51,000	
Bad debts written off	12,000	
Rates and insurance	12,500	
Postage and stationery	11,050	
Administration expenses	12,600	
Advertising	14,000	
Travel and entertaining	19,750	
		223,400
Net Profit		276,600

Notes:

- Administration includes £2,000 directors' speeding fines incurred while on company business.
- Advertising consists of:
  - gifts of CDs with company logos to 1000 customers £9,000
  - gifts vouchers with company logos to 200 other customers £5,000
- Travel and entertaining is made up as follows:

	£
Employees' travel expenses	6,400
Employees' subsistence allowances	5,600
Entertaining customers	4,000
Entertaining staff on company trip to races	3,750
	19,750

Capital allowances for the period have been calculated at £31,500.

Required:

Adjust the net profit shown to arrive at the trading income assessment for Corporation Tax purposes.

2.4 Mint Limited is changing its accounting dates, and to accommodate this has produced a set of financial accounts over an extended period, from 1/12/2006 to 31/3/2008.

Capital allowances have already been calculated for each of the two CAPs as follows:

CAP 1/12/2006 to 30/11/2007	£8,000
CAP 1/12/2007 to 31/3/2008	£2,500

The financial accounts for the 16 months to 31/3/2008 are as follows:

	£	£
Sales		293,000
less cost of sales		155,000
Gross profit		138,000
add:		
Bad debts recovered		3,100
Discounts received		2,000
		143,100
less expenses:		
Salaries and wages	68,500	
Rent, rates, and insurance	9,200	
Depreciation etc	10,000	
General expenses	15,630	
Interest payable	8,300	
Bad debts written off	12,400	
Selling expenses	15,000	
		139,030
Net Profit		4,070

The following information is also provided:

- Depreciation etc is made up as follows:

Depreciation	£45,000
Loss on sale of computer	£19,500
Profit on sale of Building	£54,500

- General expenses include debt recovery fees of £800
- Selling expenses include:

Entertaining customers	£1,930
Gifts of diaries to customers (£6 each, with company advert)	£600

Required:

- Adjust the financial accounts for the 16-month period, before deduction of capital allowances.
- Time-apportion the adjusted profit figure into CAPs.
- Calculate the trading income assessment for each CAP.

2.5 The published accounts of Doormat Company Limited for the year ended 31 March 2008 are shown below, together with notes that provide some analysis of the summarised data. Capital allowances have already been calculated, and amount to £153,000.

	£000
Revenue	743
Cost of Sales	(302)
Gross Profit	441
Other Income	290
Distribution Costs	(144)
Administrative Expenses	(243)
Finance Costs	(50)
Profit before Tax	294
Tax	(71)
Profit for the Year	223

Notes

- Cost of Sales includes depreciation of £20,000
- Administrative Expenses include the following:

Loan to employee written off	£8,000
Increase in Specific Bad Debt Provision	£2,800
Increase In General Bad Debt Provision	£7,700
Entertaining Customers	£9,100

- Other Income consists of:

Rental Income	£200,000
Discounts received from trade suppliers	£12,000
Interest Received from Investments	£30,000
Profit on Sale of Fixed Assets	£33,000
Dividends Received	£15,000

- Finance Costs relates to bank overdraft interest.

Required:

- Calculate the trading income assessable figure as adjusted for tax purposes, and the amount of any trading loss.
- State how the trading loss could be relieved without carrying it forward to future periods.

3 Corporation tax – capital allowances

this chapter covers . . .

In this chapter we examine:

- *an introduction to Capital Allowances*
- *what 'Plant & Machinery' is*
- *Plant & Machinery allowances*
- *the Plant & Machinery capital allowances computation*
- *what 'Industrial Buildings' are*
- *Industrial Buildings Allowances*
- *how short Chargeable Accounting Periods are dealt with*

PERFORMANCE CRITERIA COVERED

unit 18: PREPARING BUSINESS TAXATION COMPUTATIONS

element 18.1

prepare capital allowances computations

A *classify expenditure on capital assets in accordance with the statutory distinction between capital and revenue expenditure*

B *ensure that entries and calculations relating to the computation of capital allowances for a company are correct*

D *ensure that computations and submissions are made in accordance with current tax law and take account of current Inland Revenue practice*

INTRODUCTION TO CAPITAL ALLOWANCES

As we saw in the last chapter, depreciation of fixed assets is not an allowable expense for Corporation Tax purposes, but **capital allowances** are often provided instead.

A **capital allowance** reduces the taxable profit for a chargeable accounting period. It results from the acquisition and use of certain fixed assets.

Capital allowances are not, however, automatically available for any fixed asset owned and depreciated by a company. Although many categories of fixed asset do attract capital allowances, there are some that do not. The company's own depreciation policy is also irrelevant when calculating the amount of capital allowance that can be claimed – the same HM Revenue & Customs rules apply for all companies.

To be eligible for capital allowances, the expenditure on the fixed assets must firstly be defined as **capital expenditure**, rather than revenue. Here the definition of capital is generally the same as in financial accounting – expenditure on assets that will benefit the business over several accounting periods.

Secondly, the expenditure must be on assets that attract specific capital allowances. There are several categories of capital allowances, but in this unit we will be examining the two most important ones:

- Plant and Machinery
- Industrial Buildings

Capital allowances are claimable for each Chargeable Accounting Period (CAP) separately, based on expenditure incurred in that period and any balances of expenditure brought forward. We will see exactly how this works shortly.

For all expenditure on fixed assets that attract capital allowances, it does not matter how the funding is obtained, whether from

- cash reserves and money in the bank
- a loan
- hire purchase
- finance leases of at least 5 years

In all these cases capital allowances are available on the full capital cost as soon as the expenditure is incurred – not when all payments have finally been made. Any interest on loans or hire purchase agreements etc is not capital expenditure, but forms allowable revenue expenditure.

If however an asset is leased on an operating lease then no capital allowances are available as the expenditure is treated as revenue.

WHAT IS 'PLANT AND MACHINERY'?

Plant and machinery capital allowances form a major area of study in this unit, and a large number of assets come under this category. As we will see, 'plant and machinery' covers not only items that most of us would expect to be classified in this way, but also a number of unexpected types of asset.

The exact definition of 'plant and machinery' has been subject to debate and modification through statute and case law over the years. One idea that may be useful as a starting point is that plant and machinery covers 'apparatus with which' the business operates, rather than assets 'in which' the business operates. This excludes assets which are simply part of 'the setting' of the business (eg buildings) from being plant and machinery. Examples of plant and machinery are listed below. Both new and second-hand items qualify.

- **Plant or machinery** in the normal use of the phrase. This includes moveable and fixed items and their installation costs, and ranges from factory conveyor equipment to cement mixers.
- **Vans, lorries, and other commercial vehicles**. This category also includes tractors, trailers and other specialist vehicles.
- **Cars** owned by a limited company and used by the employees (including for private use) are included as plant and machinery.
- **Furniture, carpets and other moveable items**. Equipment such as specialist lighting used for shop displays or to create atmosphere have been classed as plant and machinery.
- **Computers and other electronic equipment**. This includes 'information and communications technology'. Software is also eligible expenditure where it is a capital purchase.
- **Lifts and central heating systems**. Also included is thermal insulation expenditure in industrial buildings, and expenditure to meet fire regulations.

CAPITAL ALLOWANCES FOR PLANT AND MACHINERY

Some capital allowances that are available depend on the size of the company. Where this applies, the smaller the company, the more generous the capital allowances given. To qualify as being **small/medium-sized** the company must satisfy at least two of the three following conditions:

- annual turnover should be not more than £22.8 million
- assets not more than £11.4 million
- not more than 250 employees

The companies that we will come across in this unit will normally satisfy this definition, or can be assumed to do so. In the explanations of allowances that follow we will note those that depend on the business meeting these criteria.

Further criteria are used to define a business as '**small**'. These are

- annual turnover of not more than £5.6 million
- assets not more than £2.8 million
- not more than 50 employees

In an examination you would be informed if necessary if a company is 'small' where it is unclear from the data provided.

capital allowances

Before we examine the practicalities of calculating capital allowances for plant and machinery we will now explain the **types of allowance**. There are three basic types of capital allowance that can apply to plant and machinery. Note that these allowances are not time-apportioned on the basis of the date of purchase within the CAP. The amount of the allowance is the same if the plant and machinery is bought at the start or at the end of the CAP.

a note on 'asset pools'

When explaining the types of allowances, we will refer to **'pools'** of assets. This term describes the way in which assets are either grouped together (the **main pool**) or kept separate (**single asset pools**). We will see shortly which type of asset goes into which type of pool.

types of capital allowance

- **First Year Allowances (FYA).**
  These apply only in the CAP in which certain assets are bought.
  Current rates are 100% or 40%. 50% rates are also currently available for small businesses.

  100% First Year Allowances are available for **all businesse**s on

  – <u>new</u> cars that are electric powered, or have low Co2 emissions (not more than 120 g/km)

  – certain 'energy efficient' new plant

  50% First Year Allowances are available to **small businesses only** for expenditure between **1/4/2006 and 31/3/2008.** This applies to virtually all expenditure **except cars.**

  40% First Year Allowances are available for expenditure on most plant and machinery **except cars** for medium-sized businesses for all recent dates

Plant & Machinery – First Year Allowances Summary (1/4/2006 – 31/3/2008)		
Type of asset acquired	**Size of business**	**FYA available**
New 'low emission' cars and certain 'energy efficient' plant	All sizes	100%
All other cars	All sizes	No FYA available
Other plant & machinery (except cars)	Medium	40%
	Small	50%

- **Writing Down Allowances (WDA)**
  These are available for the balance of each 'pool' (ie a group of assets or a single asset), as we will see shortly. The rate is 25%. This is a similar principle to the 'reducing balance' depreciation calculations with which you may be familiar. Assets that receive first year allowances (FYAs) cannot also obtain writing down allowances (WDA) in the CAP of acquisition.
- **Balancing Allowances or Charges**
  Balancing allowances or balancing charges (effectively the opposite to an allowance) can arise when the asset in a single asset pool is disposed of. They can also arise in the main pool when the business ceases.

For example, suppose an item in a 'single asset pool' had been bought for £10,000, and then sold for £1,000 two years later. This could apply, for example, to a computer bought by a medium-sized company. The capital allowances calculation would be:

	£
Cost of computer	10,000
First Year Allowance (FYA) 40% (claimed in CAP when purchased)	(4,000)
	6,000
Writing Down Allowance (WDA) 25% of £6,000 (claimed in next CAP)	(1,500)
	4,500
Proceeds of sale	(1,000)
Balancing allowance available (claimed in CAP of disposal)	3,500

By keeping the computer separate in a single asset pool the company is able to claim the balancing allowance when then computer is sold. We will look in more detail at 'short life assets' like this in the next section of this chapter.

PLANT AND MACHINERY CAPITAL ALLOWANCE COMPUTATION

We will start by using a simple example to outline the way that capital allowances can work.

example – plant and machinery capital allowance computation

The Simple Company Limited is classed as a 'small' company. It started trading on 1/1/2007, and produced its first set of accounts for the year ended 31/12/2007. During that CAP it bought:

- a van for £10,000 on 1/1/2007
- machinery for £20,000 on 1/5/2007
- a car for £11,000 on 1/6/2007

The capital allowances that can be claimed for the CAP would be:

	£
50% First Year Allowance on the van (£10,000 x 50%)	5,000
50% First Year Allowance on the machinery (£20,000 x 50%)	10,000
Writing Down Allowance on the car (£11,000 x 25%) (1)	2,750
	17,750

(1) Cars are not eligible for FYAs, but WDAs can be claimed.

The £17,750 capital allowances would then be deducted from the adjusted trading profit for the CAP.

While this example is accurate, we have not laid it out in a way that will provide us with the data for the next CAP, nor work with more complex problems. To do this we will use a standard format for a plant and machinery capital allowances computation (see bottom of the next page).

We will now explain how a computation is laid out so that we can easily calculate the correct plant and machinery capital allowances. Note that most expenditure is shown in the same column (the 'main pool'), but some assets are kept separate – shown in their own column ('single asset pools').

The following types of asset require a separate 'single asset pool' for **each asset**:

- **cars costing over £12,000 when bought by the company**
  Here 'car' does **not** include commercial vehicles such as vans, trucks and lorries. The writing down allowance (normally 25%) is restricted to

a maximum of £3,000 a year for each of these 'expensive' cars. Each car will remain in its own pool, even when the pool balance drops below £12,000. This does not apply to new electric or 'low emission' cars that attract 100% first year allowance. You can assume that cars do not qualify for this 100% allowance unless specific information is provided.

- **short life assets**
  These are assets that the company believes it will dispose of within five years. The company can choose to treat assets in this way, and items that quickly become obsolete would make most sense. For example, a company may choose to treat computer equipment as a short life asset. If it is then sold for less than its written-down value (unrelieved expenditure) a balancing allowance is claimed. If the proceeds were more a balancing charge arises. Where an asset in the short life asset pool has not been disposed of within four years of the end of the CAP in which it was acquired, then it ceases to be a short life asset, and its pool balance will be transferred into the main pool.

plant and machinery capital allowance computation format

The format shown below allows us to calculate capital allowances quickly and will need to be learnt and used regularly. In an examination you will be expected to create and use this type of computation without further guidance. The number of single asset pools will depend on the assets bought or held. An explanation is given after the format.

		Main Pool	Single Asset Pools			Capital Allowances
			Exp Car 1	Exp Car 2	S/L Asset 1	
		£	£	£	£	£
WDV bf		X	X		X	
Additions without FYAs:		X		X		
Disposals		(X)	(X)			
Sub totals		X	X	X	X	
WDA 25%		(X) →		→ (X)	→ (X)	→ X
Balancing Allowance			(X) →			→ X
Additions with FYAs:	X					
FYAs	(X) →					→ X
		X				
WDV cf		X	-	X	X	
Total Capital Allowances						X

explanation of format:

- There are columns for the main pool of assets and a separate single asset pool for each expensive car ('exp' car) and each short-life asset (s/l asset). Here we have used two expensive cars and one short-life asset as examples. There is a final column on the right for the capital allowances.
- **WDV bf** stands for 'Written Down Value brought forward' and is the balance of each pool that is brought forward from the previous CAP. It represents the unrelieved expenditure on the asset(s).
- **Additions without FYAs** is any expenditure within the CAP on plant and machinery not eligible for first year allowances. These are mainly cars. They are added to the main pool, or (as here) to a newly created single asset pool if the car costs over £12,000 and is classed as 'expensive'.
- **Disposals** are the proceeds of any plant and machinery sold. The only situation where proceeds are not used is when the proceeds exceed the original cost, when the cost is entered instead. This is not a common occurrence! The amount is deducted from the pool that the asset was originally entered into. In the case of assets where 100% FYA had been claimed (for example low-emission cars) the disposal amount is deducted from the main pool.
- **WDAs** (writing down allowances) of 25% are then calculated, based on the preceding sub-total of each pool. To qualify for a WDA, the asset in a 'single asset pool' must still be owned by the company at the end of the CAP. Where the asset has been disposed of, a balancing allowance or charge (see below) will apply instead of a WDA. Remember that the WDA is limited to £3,000 a year in 'expensive' car single asset pools.
- A **balancing allowance** (or balancing charge) applies to single asset pools in the CAP in which the asset was disposed of. If the asset is sold for less than its written down value (unrelieved expenditure) a balancing allowance is claimed. If the proceeds were greater, a balancing charge arises. Balancing charges reduce total capital allowances.
- **Additions with FYAs** (first year allowances) are dealt with towards the bottom of the computation. This is because expenditure that qualifies for FYAs does not also qualify for WDAs in the same CAP. The FYAs are calculated at the appropriate rates, and the balance(s) of expenditure (where applicable) added to the appropriate pool(s).
- The **WDV cf** (carried forward) represents the new sub-total of unrelieved expenditure in each pool after all the allowances have been calculated. These figures will be used in the next CAP as the opening balances (WDV bf).
- **Capital allowances** are recorded in the right-hand column so they can be readily totalled. The column is totalled when the computation is completed, and it is this total that is deducted in the final stages of the Trading Income computation.

Before we use a Case Study to demonstrate how this computation works, we will summarise the main points that we have covered so far in a table.

The principles outlined here must be memorised so they can be applied in problems.

PLANT AND MACHINERY CAPITAL ALLOWANCE SUMMARY

	eligible for FYA? what rate?	which pool does balance of expenditure enter?	WDA claimable in future periods?	are balancing allowances possible?
Cars costing £12,000 or less	No	Main Pool	25% as part of main pool	No
Cars costing over £12,000	No	Single asset pools	25%, restricted to £3,000 pa	Yes
New low emission and electric cars (irrespective of size of business)	100%	Main pool, but no balance of expenditure after FYA	not applicable	No
Most assets (except cars) acquired by small businesses	50%	Main pool	25% as part of main pool	No
Most assets (except cars) acquired by medium businesses	40%	Main pool	25% as part of main pool	No
Computers etc	40%* or 50%*	Usually SLA, otherwise main pool	25%	Yes if SLA

note:

Where the % FYA is shown with an asterisk in the above table, this assumes that the business is medium sized (40%) or small (50%).

Before we carry out a computation in a comprehensive Case Study, we will go back to the straightforward example illustrated on page 3.7, to see how the format would work to obtain a solution.

example – a worked computation

The Simple Company Limited is classed as a 'small' company. It started trading on 1/1/2007, and produced its first set of accounts for the year ended 31/12/2007. During that CAP it bought:

- a van for £10,000 on 1/1/2007
- machinery for £20,000 on 1/5/2007
- a car for £11,000 on 1/6/2007

The computation, using the format on page 3.8 is as follows:

		Main Pool	Capital Allowances
		£	£
WDV bf		0	
Additions without FYAs:			
Car		11,000	
WDA 25%		(2,750)	2,750
Additions with FYAs:			
Van	10,000		
FYA 50%	(5,000)		5,000
		5,000	
Machinery	20,000		
FYA 50%	(10,000)		10,000
		10,000	
WDV cf		23,250	
Total Capital Allowances			17,750

The £17,750 capital allowances would then be deducted from the adjusted trading profit for the CAP. The parts of the format that were not applicable have been omitted in this example for clarity. Seeing this format used with familiar figures should reassure you that it is not as difficult to use as it may first appear.

We will now use a more comprehensive Case Study to demonstrate the type of situation that you may be presented with. Although it is quite complex, you should follow the calculations and format carefully so that you can carry out a similar computation in an examination.

Case Study

THE PM COMPANY LIMITED: PLANT AND MACHINERY CAPITAL ALLOWANCES

The PM Company Limited has a twelve month chargeable accounting period running from 1/4/2007 to 31/3/2008.

It is classed as a small company for capital allowance purposes.

The adjusted trading profit for this CAP has already been calculated at £189,000 before deduction of capital allowances for plant and machinery.

The capital allowance computation for the last CAP closed with written down values as follows:

• main pool	£40,000
• expensive car single asset pool (BMW)	£15,000
• short life single asset pool (machine bought to use for temporary contract)	£16,000

During the CAP the following assets were acquired or disposed of:

30/4/2007	a new pick-up truck was bought for £20,000
31/5/2007	the BMW was sold for £19,000
31/5/2007	a new electric car was bought for £24,000
31/5/2007	a used Audi car was bought for £22,000
31/7/2007	a computer system was bought for £25,000
31/10/2007	the machine in the short life pool was sold for £10,000
31/12/2007	a machine in the main pool was sold for £2,000
31/1/2008	a Ford car was bought for £8,000

All disposal proceeds were less than original cost.

The company does not wish to class the computer system as a short life asset.

Required

- Using a plant and machinery capital allowance computation, calculate the allowances for the CAP y/e 31/3/2008.
- Calculate the assessable trading income for the CAP y/e 31/3/2008.

Solution

The capital allowance computation is as follows. The notes below give explanations.

		main pool	Single Asset Pools exp car BMW	exp car Audi	S/L Asset	capital allowances
	£	£	£	£	£	£
WDV bf		40,000	15,000	-	16,000	
Additions without FYAs:						
Audi Car				22,000		
Ford Car		8,000				
Disposals:						
BMW			(19,000)			
SL machine					(10,000)	
Machine		(2,000)				
Sub totals		46,000	(4,000)	22,000	6,000	
WDA 25%		(11,500)		(3,000)		14,500
Balancing Allowance					(6,000)	6,000
Balancing Charge			4,000			(4,000)
Additions with FYAs:						
Computer	25,000					
FYA (50%)	(12,500)	12,500				12,500
Electric Car	24,000					
FYA (100%)	(24,000)					24,000
Pick-up	20,000					
FYA (50%)	(10,000)	10,000				10,000
WDV cf		57,000	-	19,000	-	
Total Capital Allowances						63,000

Notes

- The only additions that do not attract FYAs are the two normal cars. The Audi is classed as expensive, while the Ford joins the main pool.
- The two machines that are disposed of are deducted from the pools where their costs were originally added.

- The WDA in the main pool is calculated as 25% of £46,000. The WDA on the Audi is restricted to £3,000.
- The disposal of the short life asset results in a balancing allowance since the subtotal left after deducting the proceeds is positive. This means that more allowances can be claimed to bring the balance to zero.
- The disposal of the BMW was for more than the WDV brought forward. There is therefore a balancing charge (the opposite to an allowance) required to bring the pool balance to zero.
- The electric car attracts a 100% FYA (irrespective of company size). The computer system and the pick-up truck attract 50% since this is a small company. The balance after the deduction of FYA from the expenditure is added to the main pool.
- The total capital allowance is made up of the WDAs plus the balancing allowance and FYA, less the balancing charge.
- The written down values of £57,000 (main pool) and £19,000 (Audi) will be used as the opening figures at the start of the next CAP.

The trading income figure for the CAP y/e 31/3/2008 will be:
£189,000 – £63,000 = £126,000.

INDUSTRIAL BUILDINGS ALLOWANCE

The second capital allowance category that we are going to deal with in this unit is **Industrial Buildings Allowance** (IBA). This capital allowance system is quite different to the one for plant and machinery, and is generally simpler, especially since the number of transactions related to buildings is usually much smaller than those for plant and machinery.

what is an industrial building?

Only certain buildings qualify for Industrial Buildings Allowance. The main type of building for which a company can claim IBA is a building of an **industrial nature**, used in an **industrial trade**. The type of building, and the use to which it is put, are both important if IBA is to be claimed.

Examples of buildings that would usually satisfy these rules include:

- factories used for manufacturing or processing
- buildings used for storage before or after manufacture (ie used for raw materials or finished goods by a manufacturing company)
- design offices, drawing offices and staff canteens within a factory building

Note that shops, offices and wholesale warehouses do not fall within this definition. In most cases there are no capital allowances for such buildings.

what is the eligible cost of an industrial building?

When an industrial building is first constructed and brought into use for a qualifying purpose, the IBA will be based on the eligible cost of the building. This cost includes site preparation costs as well as the cost of constructing the building. The cost of the land is not an eligible part of the cost.

Where an industrial building is constructed to include some non-industrial parts (eg offices) then this can be considered as eligible provided it accounts for less than 25% of the cost of the whole building.

For example, if £1 million was spent on constructing a building that cost

- £780,000 for the industrial part (eg factory), and
- £220,000 for the general offices in the building

Then the whole £1 million would qualify as cost, since £220,000 is less than 25% of £1 million. Note that the percentage relates to the whole, including the non-industrial part.

Where the cost of the non-industrial part (eg offices) exceeds 25% of the total cost of the property then the non-industrial part will not qualify for IBA.

how much IBA can be claimed?

In the chargeable accounting period (CAP) in which a new industrial building is first brought into use for a qualifying purpose, a **writing-down allowance** (WDA) can be claimed.

This allowance is **4% of the eligible cost**, provided the CAP is for 12 months, and is deducted in the trading income computation in the same way as capital allowances for plant and machinery.

The date within the CAP that the building is brought into use is irrelevant; what matters is that the building is used for a qualifying purpose on the last day of the CAP.

Each subsequent year that the building is used by the company for a qualifying purpose, a further WDA of 4% of the original eligible cost can be claimed, until allowances have been claimed for 25 years, and the whole cost has been used up. This 25-year period is known as the 'tax-life' of the building. Note that the WDA is the same for each 12 month CAP (like straight line depreciation), unlike plant and machinery allowances that use the reducing balance principle.

We will look at how IBAs work on disposal next, but before we do so, we will use a short Case Study to illustrate what we have learned so far about IBAs.

Case Study

THE INDUSTRIAL MANUFACTURING COMPANY LTD: INDUSTRIAL BUILDINGS ALLOWANCE

This company has been operating a manufacturing business (a qualifying trade) for several years, using an accounting year ending on 31 March.

On 1 June the operation moved from rented premises into two separate new purpose-built factories, which had costs as follows:

	Factory One	Factory Two
Cost of land	£80,000	£100,000
Land Preparation	£20,000	£10,000
Main Factory Building	£150,000	£190,000
Sales Office	£40,000	-
Admin Offices	£40,000	£60,000
Drawing Office	-	£40,000
Staff Canteen	£ 50,000	-
Total Cost	£380,000	£400,000

Required

- Calculate the eligible cost of each separate factory for IBA purposes.
- Calculate the total IBA writing down allowance available for the current CAP for each factory.
- If the company's adjusted profits for the current CAP were £155,000 before deducting any capital allowances, and there were plant & machinery capital allowances of £15,000 claimable, calculate the assessable trading income for the CAP.

Solution

The first procedure is to calculate the cost of each factory that is eligible for IBA because it relates to industrial purposes.

Next the cost of the non-industrial part (the offices) in each building is checked to see if it amounts to less than 25% of the whole (including the offices). If it is less than 25% then the office cost is added; if it is more than 25% of the whole, it is ignored.

	Factory One	Factory Two
Land Preparation	£20,000	£10,000
Main Factory Building	£150,000	£190,000
Drawing Office	-	£ 40,000
Staff Canteen	£50,000	-
Definitely eligible for IBA	£220,000	£240,000
Office cost eligible for IBA	nil (1)	£60,000 (2)
Total eligible cost	£220,000	£300,000

(1) Office cost is £80,000. Total cost of Factory One is therefore £220,000 + £80,000 = £300,000, of which the offices account for £80,000 / £300,000 = 26.6%. The whole sales and admin office cost is not therefore eligible for this factory.

(2) Office cost is £60,000. Total cost of Factory Two is therefore £240,000 + £60,000 = £300,000, of which the offices account for £60,000 / £300,000 = 20%. The admin office cost is therefore eligible for this factory.

Note also that:

- The land cost was excluded throughout.
- The drawing office is considered a building used for an industrial purpose, and is included throughout. It is not subject to the 25% test.

The WDA for the current CAP for each factory is:

Factory One	£220,000 x 4%	=	£8,800
Factory Two	£300,000 x 4%	=	£12,000
			£20,800

The assessable trading income will be:

£155,000 – £15,000 – £20,800 = £119,200

plant. IBA.

DEALING WITH DISPOSALS OF INDUSTRIAL BUILDINGS

If an industrial building is disposed of after the end of its 25-year 'tax life' then there are no IBA implications for the company that disposes of the building, and no IBA claimable by the business acquiring the property.

The industrial buildings allowance implications for both the seller and the buyer of an industrial building during its 25 year 'tax life' was changed radically in the 2007 budget. With effect from 21 March 2007 any such disposals will be dealt with as follows:

- There will be no industrial buildings allowances for the seller. There will be no balancing allowances, nor balancing charges. The company simply ceases claiming any writing down allowances. Since the building will not be used by the seller for an industrial purpose on the last day of the CAP in which it was sold, no WDA will be available for that CAP.
- The writing down allowances that will be available to the buyer will be identical to the amounts previously available to the seller (i.e. 4% of the *original* eligible amount). This is regardless of the amount paid for the building by the buyer. The new owner will be entitled to this amount for each 12 month CAP providing the building is in industrial use on the last day of that CAP, for the remainder of the 25 year 'tax life' of the building.

Note that if the industrial building is disposed of for more than cost there may be chargeable gains implications for the company that sold it. We will examine this in the next chapter.

CAPITAL ALLOWANCES FOR SHORT CAPS

So far in this chapter we have examined the way that capital allowances for plant and machinery and for industrial buildings are calculated for chargeable accounting periods of twelve months.

It is, however, possible to have CAPs for less than twelve months, and this can arise either

- if the accounts are prepared for a period of less than twelve months, or
- where accounts are prepared for a period exceeding twelve months, and are divided into two CAPs, one for the first twelve months, and another for the balance

In each of these situations, the impact on capital allowances for both plant and machinery and industrial buildings in the short CAP is the same:

- First Year Allowances, Balancing Allowances and Balancing Charges are unaffected and are calculated as normal.
- Writing Down Allowances are time-apportioned based on the short CAP. This time apportionment is carried out on:
  - the 25% WDA relating to Plant and Machinery
  - the £3,000 limit relating to expensive cars
  - the 4% WDA relating to Industrial Buildings

DEALING WITH THE ACCOUNTS FOR A LONG PERIOD

As we saw in the last chapter, where we have accounts that are prepared for a long period, the procedure is:

- the accounting profits for the long period are adjusted in one operation, with the exception of the capital allowances deduction
- the adjusted profits (pre capital allowance deduction) are then time-apportioned into the two CAPs
- capital allowances are calculated separately for each CAP
- each CAP's adjusted profit is then finalised by deducting the capital allowances that have been calculated for the specific period

We can now examine the issues involved in creating two capital allowance computations, one for each CAP within a long period for which accounts were prepared. The points to note are:

- each acquisition and disposal of assets needs to be allocated to the correct CAP, and incorporated in the appropriate computation
- the written-down values (for plant and machinery) at the end of the first CAP will become the brought forward amounts at the start of the second CAP
- the rules regarding time apportionment of WDAs for short CAPs as described above need to be used in the second CAP

Now that we have seen all the principles explained, we can use a Case Study to illustrate the way they work.

Case Study

CHOPPITT PLC:
DEALING WITH ACCOUNTS FOR A LONG PERIOD

Choppitt plc (a medium-sized company) has produced a set of accounts for the period 1/1/2007 to 30/4/2008. The adjusted trading profit for the 16-month period has already been produced from the accounts, and provides a profit of £320,000, before any capital allowances are taken account of.

The company has owned and used a factory for a qualifying trade since it was bought new for £300,000 in 1991. It continues in qualifying use throughout 2007 and 2008.

The plant and machinery capital allowance computation for the CAP y/e 31/12/2006 provided carried forward written down values as follows:

- general pool £50,000
- expensive car (Ford) £18,000

Analysis of the accounts reveals that the following assets were acquired or disposed of during the 16-month period:

1/11/2007	disposal of plant for £2,000 (original cost £20,000).
1/12/2007	acquisition of second-hand BMW car for £17,000
1/3/2008	acquisition of plant costing £20,000.
1/4/2008	disposal of Ford car for £8,000 (original cost £24,000)

Required

1 State the periods for the two CAPs that need to be formed.

2 Calculate the Industrial Buildings Allowances for each of the two CAPs.

3 Calculate the Plant & Machinery capital allowances for each of the two CAPs.

4 Calculate the trading income assessments for each of the two CAPs.

Solution

1 The CAPs will be:

1/1/2007 – 31/12/2007	(12 months)
1/1/2008 – 30/4/2008	(4 months)

2 The IBA claimable will be:

For CAP 1/1/2007 – 31/12/2007	4% x £300,000 = £12,000
For CAP 1/1/2008 – 30/4/2008	4% x £300,000 x 4/12 = £4,000

3 To calculate the Plant and Machinery capital allowances we will need to prepare two computations, one for each CAP.

Each one will incorporate the acquisitions and disposals that occur in that CAP.

CAP FOR THE YEAR ENDING 31/12/2007

		Single Asset Pools		Capital
	Main Pool	Exp Car (Ford)	Exp Car (BMW)	Allowances
	£	£	£	£
WDV bf	50,000	18,000		
Additions without FYAs:				
BMW Car			17,000	
Disposals:				
Plant	(2,000)			
Sub Total	48,000	18,000	17,000	
WDA 25%	(12,000)	(3,000)*	(3,000)*	18,000
WDV cf	36,000	15,000	14,000	
Total Capital Allowances				18,000

*limited to £3,000

CAP FOR THE 4 MONTHS TO 30/4/2008

		Main Pool	Single Asset Pools: Exp Car (Ford)	Single Asset Pools: Exp Car (BMW)	Capital Allowances
	£	£	£	£	£
WDV bf		36,000	15,000	14,000	
Disposals:					
Ford car			(8,000)		
Sub Total		36,000	7,000	14,000	
WDA 25% x 4/12		(3,000)		(1,000) *	4,000
Balancing Allowance			(7,000)		7,000
Additions with FYAs:					
Plant	20,000				
FYA 40%	(8,000)				8,000
		12,000			
WDV cf		45,000	0	13,000	
Total Capital Allowances					19,000

*limit £3,000 x 4/12

4 Calculation of trading income assessments.

Firstly the adjusted trade profits are time-apportioned:

CAP 1/1/2007 to 31/12/2007 £320,000 x 12/16 = £240,000

CAP 1/1/2008 to 30/4/2008 £320,000 x 4/16 = £80,000

Capital allowances are then deducted from the adjusted profit for each CAP:

	1/1/07 – 31/12/07	1/1/08 – 30/4/08
	£	£
Adjusted profit	240,000	80,000
Capital allowances:		
IBA	(12,000)	(4,000)
P & M	(18,000)	(19,000)
Trading Income	210,000	57,000

Chapter Summary

- Capital allowances are available on certain fixed assets, and act for tax computation purposes as an alternative to depreciation, which is never allowable as tax-deductible (set off against tax).

- The two main types of capital allowances are for 'plant and machinery' and 'industrial buildings'.

- Plant and machinery includes vehicles, computers, and various other assets. Allowances include first year allowances at 100%, 50% or 40% for certain assets for some companies, as well as writing down allowances at 25% on a reducing balance basis.

- Many assets are merged together or 'pooled' in the capital allowance computation, but some need to be kept separately in 'single asset pools'. Single asset pools are used for cars costing over £12,000 and short-life assets. Balancing allowances and charges occur in single asset pools when the asset has been disposed of, and also in the general pool when the business ceases.

- Industrial buildings allowance is available on industrial buildings used for a qualifying purpose. The writing down allowance for each twelve month CAP is 4% of the eligible cost. Eligible cost excludes land and excludes non- industrial parts over a 25% cost threshold. The allowance is available throughout the building's tax life of 25 years provided it continues to be used for a qualifying purpose.

- No balancing allowance or charge occurs on the sale of the building if sold within its tax life. The new owner will be able to claim the same writing down allowances as the previous owner.

- When capital allowances are calculated for a chargeable accounting period of less than twelve months any writing down allowances are time-apportioned. This applies to both plant and machinery and industrial buildings.

- First year allowances and balancing allowances and charges are unaffected by short CAPs. Where the accounts for a company have been prepared for a period of over 12 months, the two CAPs that result will each require a separate capital allowance computation. Fixed asset acquisitions and disposals will need to be allocated to the correct CAP before these capital allowance computations are carried out.

Key Terms

Capital allowance The term used for allowances that reduce taxable profit for a chargeable accounting period, resulting from the acquisition and use of certain fixed assets.

Chargeable Accounting Period (CAP) The period for which the profits chargeable to Corporation Tax must be calculated. It is the same as the period for which the company produces financial accounts, unless that period is for more than twelve months. In that case the financial accounting period is divided into two CAPs.

Plant and Machinery One of the major fixed asset categories for capital allowance purposes. It includes vehicles and computers.

Industrial Buildings Allowance This is a capital allowance (IBA) available for this category of fixed assets, provided the building is used for a qualifying purpose.

First Year Allowances These allowances (FYA) are available on certain plant and machinery in the CAP in which the acquisition takes place. The rates currently available are 100%, 50% and 40%. There are no first year allowances currently available for industrial buildings.

Writing Down Allowances These allowances (WDA) are available at 25% of the pool value for plant and machinery, and at 4% of the eligible cost for industrial buildings. Both these figures relate to twelve month CAPs, and are time-apportioned for shorter periods.

Written Down Value (Plant and Machinery)

This term relates to the balance at the end of a CAP that remains in a plant and machinery pool. It represents thc part of the pool value that has not yet been claimed as allowances, and is carried forward to the next CAP.

Balancing Allowance (Plant and Machinery)

This allowance can be claimed when an asset is sold for less than the written-down value (unrelieved expenditure) in a single asset pool.

Balancing Charge (Plant and Machinery)

This charge is the opposite of an allowance, and occurs when the disposal proceeds of an asset in a single asset pool are more than the written-down value (unrelieved expenditure). It is in effect a reclaiming of allowances previously obtained.

Student Activities

Answers to the asterisked (*) questions are to be found at the back of this book.

3.1* Complete the following table by inserting words and/or percentages to denote the plant and machinery computation procedure and allowances available for each asset when acquired by a 'small' company after 1/4/2006. The first item is completed to show you what is required.

	Eligible for FYA? What rate?	**Which pool does balance of expenditure enter?**	**WDA claimable in future periods?**	**Balancing Allowances possible?**
Van costing £9,000	50%	Main pool	25% as part of main pool	No
Lorry costing £25,000				
Car costing £10,000				
Computer costing £12,000				
Machinery costing £20,000				
Car costing £25,000				
Equipment with short life costing £1,000				
'Low emission' car costing £18,000				

3.2* The Capital Company Limited has a twelve month chargeable accounting period running from 1/4/2007 to 31/3/2008. It is classed as a small company for capital allowance purposes. The adjusted trading profit for this CAP has already been calculated at £154,000 before deduction of capital allowances for plant & machinery.

The capital allowance computation for the last CAP closed with written down values as follows:

main pool	£60,000
expensive car single asset pool (VW)	£13,000
short-life single asset pool (machine bought to use for temporary contract)	£10,000

During the CAP the following assets were acquired and disposed of:

30/4/2007	a new fork-lift truck was bought for £30,000.
31/7/2007	the VW was sold for £10,000.
31/7/2007	a new BMW car was bought for £24,000.
31/7/2007	a computer system was bought for £5,000 (not a short life asset).
31/10/2007	the machine in the short life pool was sold for £3,000.
31/12/2007	a machine in the main pool was sold for £3,000.

All disposal proceeds were less than original cost.

Required:

- Using a plant and machinery capital allowance computation, calculate the allowances for the CAP year ended 31/3/2008.
- Calculate the assessable trading income for the CAP year ended 31/3/2008.

3.3* The 2P Company Limited has been operating a manufacturing business (a qualifying trade) for several years, using an accounting year to 31 March.

On 1 September 2007 the operation moved from rented premises into two separate new purpose-built factories, which had costs as follows:

	Factory One	**Factory Two**
Cost of land	£90,000	£100,000
Land Preparation	£40,000	£10,000
Main Factory Building	£250,000	£170,000
Sales Office	£40,000	-
Admin Offices	£70,000	£60,000
Design Office	-	£40,000
Warehouse	£150,000	£80,000
Total Cost	£640,000	£460,000

The warehouse sections were for the storage of raw materials prior to production, and finished goods.

The company's adjusted profits for the CAP y/e 31/3/2008 were £280,000 before deducting any capital allowances, and there were plant & machinery capital allowances of £38,000 claimable for the CAP.

Required:

- Calculate the eligible cost of each separate factory for IBA purposes.
- Calculate the total IBA writing down allowance available for the CAP y/e 31/3/2008 for each factory.
- Calculate the assessable trading income for the CAP.

3.4 Solvitt plc (a medium-sized company) has produced a set of accounts for the period 1/1/2007 to 31/3/2008. The adjusted trading profit for the 15-month period has already been produced from the accounts, and provides a profit of £480,000, before any capital allowances are taken account of.

The company has owned and used a factory for a qualifying trade since it was bought for £200,000 in 2000. It continues in qualifying use throughout 2007 and 2008.

The plant and machinery capital allowance computation for the CAP y/e 31/12/2006 provided carried forward written-down values as follows:

general pool	£60,000
expensive car (Citroen)	£14,000

Analysis of the accounts reveals that the following assets were acquired or disposed of during the 15-month period.

1/12/2007	Disposal of plant for £4,000 (original cost £30,000)
1/12/2007	Acquisition of second-hand Ford car for £16,000
1/3/2008	Acquisition of plant costing £20,000
1/3/2008	Disposal of Citroen car for £7,000 (original cost £20,000)

Required:

- State the periods for the two CAPs that need to be formed.
- Calculate the Industrial Buildings Allowances for each of the two CAPs.
- Calculate the Plant and Machinery capital allowances for each of the two CAPs.
- Calculate the trading income assessments for each of the two CAPs.

3.5 Tuffwun Limited has produced a set of accounts for the period 1/7/2007 to 30/4/2008. The adjusted trading profit for the 10-month period has already been produced from the accounts, and provides a profit of £295,000, before any capital allowances are taken account of. Tuffwun Limited is classed as a medium sized company.

Tuffwun Limited has previously rented its factory, but on 1/7/2007 it bought a second hand factory from Gladstone Limited for £400,000, and immediately moved in and started using it for a qualifying purpose. Gladstone had originally bought the factory new on 1/7/2001 for £440,000, and claimed industrial buildings allowance for each of its five 12-month CAPs since that time. The factory was still being used for a qualifying purpose by Tuffwun Limited on 30/4/2008.

Tuffwun Limited's plant and machinery capital allowance computation for the CAP y/e 30/6/2007 provided carried forward written down values as follows:

general pool	£90,000
expensive car (Toyota)	£13,000

Analysis of the accounts reveals that the following assets were acquired or disposed of during the ten month period:

1/9/2007	Acquisition of new BMW car for £27,000
1/10/2007	Disposal of plant for £1,000 (original cost £10,000)
1/3/2008	Acquisition of plant costing £15,000
1/4/2008	Disposal of Toyota car for £12,000

Required:

- Calculate the Industrial Buildings Allowances for Tuffwun Limited for the CAP to 30/4/2008.
- Calculate the Plant and Machinery capital allowances for Tuffwun Limited for the CAP to 30/4/2008.
- Calculate the trading income assessment for Tuffwun Limited for the CAP to 30/4/2008.

4 Corporation tax – chargeable gains

this chapter covers . . .

In this chapter we examine:

- *an introduction to chargeable gains*
- *chargeable and exempt assets*
- *how gains are charged to Corporation Tax*
- *the computation of each gain, and links with capital allowances*
- *how to deal with improvement expenditure, part disposals and chattels*
- *how to deal with shares and securities*
- *rollover relief*

PERFORMANCE CRITERIA COVERED

unit 18: PREPARING BUSINESS TAXATION COMPUTATIONS

element 18.3

prepare capital gains computations

A *identify and value correctly any chargeable assets that have been disposed of*

B *identify shares disposed of by companies*

C *calculate chargeable gains and allowable losses*

D *apply reliefs, deferrals and exemptions correctly*

E *ensure that computations and submissions are made in accordance with current tax law and take account of current Inland Revenue practice*

INTRODUCTION TO CHARGEABLE GAINS

A chargeable gain (or its opposite – a capital loss) occurs when a company disposes of certain assets that it has previously acquired. The gain is then brought into the Corporation Tax computation. It does not apply to a trading situation, where items are regularly bought and sold to make a profit. Such profits would be assessed as trading income, as we have already seen. The assets that can form chargeable gains will often be fixed assets or investments that the company has acquired outside of its trading activities. A chargeable gain often applies to the sale of an asset that may have been owned for quite some time.

In addition to applying to the business assets of companies, chargeable gains can also arise for individuals who are subject to capital gains tax on the disposal of both personal assets and business assets. In this book, however, we are only going to examine how disposals of business assets are taxed. In this chapter we will examine the way that companies' chargeable gains are subject to Corporation Tax, and later in this book we will look at how Capital Gains Tax applies to the disposal of business assets by sole traders.

Gains on the disposal of personal assets are dealt with in Osborne Books' *Personal Taxation,* a study text for Unit 19 'Preparing Personal Taxation Computations'.

a note for those familiar with Capital Gains Tax for individuals

Although there are similarities between Capital Gains Tax for individuals and the treatment of chargeable gains for companies under Corporation Tax, there are also significant differences. If you have already studied personal taxation you should be very careful to study the way in which the gains of companies are taxed. Do not be lulled into a false sense of security by the similarities to the system that you have already studied.

The following main differences between Capital Gains Tax for individuals and chargeable gains for companies will now be highlighted in advance so that you can appreciate their impact. In calculating the chargeable gains of companies

- there is no annual exempt amount
- there is no taper relief
- there is no restriction on the indexation allowance at April 1998, it is claimed up to the date of disposal
- the matching rules for shares are different from those for individuals

These are important differences, and can cause confusion.

basis of assessment

Chargeable gains are calculated according to the same Chargeable Accounting Periods (CAPs) as are used for the rest of the Corporation Tax computation. The basis of assessment is the chargeable gains less capital losses arising from disposals that occur during the CAP. We will look at how losses are dealt with a little later in this chapter. The main issue to understand at this point is that the chargeable gain that is brought into the Corporation Tax computation is based on the total (or aggregate) of gains that have occurred during the CAP, and that a gain can only arise when a disposal has taken place.

disposals

A disposal arises when an asset is

- sold (or part of it is sold), or
- given away, or
- lost, or
- destroyed

Most of the situations that we will deal with will be based on the sale of an asset.

CHARGEABLE AND EXEMPT ASSETS

For a chargeable gain or capital loss to arise, the asset that has been disposed of must be a 'chargeable' asset. Disposals of exempt assets cannot form chargeable gains or capital losses. Instead of there being a long list of the assets that are chargeable, there is a fairly short list of assets that are exempt. The simple rule is that if an asset is not exempt, then it must be chargeable!

Chargeable business assets that are popular in examination tasks include:

- land and buildings
- shares

You must remember that these are only examples – all assets are chargeable unless they are exempt.

exempt assets

The following is a list of the main **exempt assets** that relate to companies:

- trading stock (as discussed earlier, this is part of the trading profit)
- cars

- chattels bought and sold for £6,000 or less (chattels are tangible moveable property)
- Government Securities (also known as 'Gilts', these are a form of investment)

CHARGEABLE GAINS AND CORPORATION TAX

Where, during a CAP, there are several disposals that result in chargeable gains, these are aggregated and the result brought into the Corporation Tax computation. This total chargeable gain then forms part of the 'Profits Chargeable to Corporation Tax' (the PCTCT) along with trading profits as Trading Income and any income from investments. The Corporation Tax is then calculated on this total PCTCT, as we will see in the next chapter.

If any disposals result in capital losses, then these are set against any chargeable gains relating to the same CAP. Provided the net result is a chargeable gain, this amount is brought into the Corporation Tax computation as described above. If the losses exceed the chargeable gains of the same CAP, then the result is that:

- no chargeable gains are brought into the PCTCT computation, and
- the net capital loss is carried forward to be set against the chargeable gain that arises in the next CAP (and so on if necessary until all the loss is utilised)

Note that capital losses cannot be set against any other profits (eg from trading or investment) in the Corporation Tax computation, but must be carried forward against future chargeable gains.

We must now turn our attention to how to calculate the chargeable gain or loss on each separate disposal.

THE COMPUTATION OF EACH GAIN

Each disposal of a chargeable asset requires a calculation to determine the amount of any gain or loss. This computation follows a standard format that is in effect a 'mini' profit & loss account for the item disposed of.

There are some minor variations to this format in particular circumstances, as we will see later.

The basic format is shown on the next page:

computation of a chargeable gain

	£
Proceeds on disposal	X
less	
Incidental costs of disposal	(x)
Net proceeds	X
less:	
Original cost	(x)
Incidental costs of acquisition	(x)
Unindexed gain	X
less	
Indexation allowance	(x)
Chargeable Gain	X

We will now look at the components of the individual gain computation in more detail.

proceeds on disposal

This normally refers to the amount that the asset was disposed of for, ie the selling price. However there are some special situations where the figure used is different:

- If the asset is given away, or sold to a connected company or person at less than the market value, the market value is used in the computation instead of the actual amount received.
- If the asset is lost or destroyed then the asset will have been disposed of for zero proceeds, and zero will be used in the computation. The exception to this would be if an insurance claim had been made, in which case the claim proceeds would be used.

incidental costs of disposal

These are the costs incurred by the company in selling the asset. Examples include advertising expenses, auction costs, or estate agent's fees for selling a property.

original cost, and incidental costs of acquisition

These relate to the amount paid to acquire the asset in the first place, plus any other costs incurred to buy it. Examples of these costs include legal fees and auction costs. We will examine later on in this chapter how to deal with expenditure that is incurred after purchase to improve the asset.

indexation allowance

This is a deduction that is used to compensate for the impact of inflation on the value of the asset. It works by using figures from the Retail Price Index (RPI) to calculate an inflation factor to multiply by the original cost and any other acquisition costs. This allows for general inflation of the cost between the date of acquisition and the date of disposal.

The indexation factor is calculated as:

$$\frac{(\text{RPI at the date of disposal} - \text{RPI at the date of acquisition})}{\text{RPI at the date of acquisition}}$$

The result of this fraction is rounded to three decimal places before being multiplied by the historical cost figure.

Note that indexation for a company chargeable gain does not stop at April 1998 – unlike Capital Gains Tax for individuals.

Note also that the indexation allowance cannot either

- turn an unindexed gain into a loss, or
- increase the amount of an unindexed loss

This means that the indexation allowance cannot be a larger amount than the unindexed gain that it follows in the computation. If the figure before indexation is applied is a loss, then there can be no indexation allowance at all.

We will now use a Case Study to show how the computation is carried out.

Note that the RPI figures are shown in the Tax Data section at the beginning of this book. The figures that we need in this Case Study are, however, repeated here for convenience.You will normally be provided with the indexation factor itself in the examination.

Case Study

THE SIMPLE COMPANY LIMITED: CALCULATING A CHARGEABLE GAIN

The Simple Company Limited bought a retail shop in August 1990. The company paid £59,000 for the shop, and also paid legal fees of £1,000 at the same time to arrange the purchase. The shop was sold in February 2007. The company prepares its accounts annually to 31 December, and the sale of the shop was the only chargeable disposal that the company made in 2007. It had no capital losses brought forward.

We will assume three different selling prices for the sale of the shop. In each case the estate agent's fees for the sale were £3,000, and the company incurred further legal fees of £2,000.

1 Assume that the company sold the shop for £240,000

2 Assume that the company sold the shop for £75,000

3 Assume that the company sold the shop for £58,000

Required

Using the RPI figures of 128.1 for August 1990 and 203.1 for February 2007, calculate the chargeable gain or capital loss resulting from the disposal of the shop (to the nearest £) for each of the situations 1, 2 and 3.

Also state the amount of chargeable gain to be brought into the PCTCT for the CAP year ended 31/12/2007 for each situation, and explain how any capital loss should be dealt with.

Solution

Option 1

	£
Proceeds on disposal	240,000
less:	
Incidental costs of disposal	(5,000)
Net proceeds	235,000
less:	
Original cost	(59,000)
Incidental costs of acquisition	(1,000)
Unindexed gain	175,000
less:	
Indexation allowance*	(35,100)
Chargeable Gain	139,900

* the indexation factor is calculated as:

$$\frac{(203.1 - 128.1)}{128.1} = 0.585 \text{ (rounded to 3 decimal places)}$$

The indexation factor is multiplied by the costs incurred in August 1990 of £59,000 + £1,000 = £60,000:

0.585 x £60,000 = £35,100

The chargeable gain of £139,900 would form part of the PCTCT for the CAP for the year ended 31/12/2007.

Option 2

	£
Proceeds on disposal	75,000
less:	
Incidental costs of disposal	(5,000)
Net proceeds	70,000
less:	
Original cost	(59,000)
Incidental costs of acquisition	(1,000)
Unindexed gain	10,000
less:	
Restricted indexation allowance*	(10,000)
Chargeable Gain	Nil

*Here the indexation allowance that would be calculated as £35,100 (as in option 1) is restricted to the amount of the unindexed gain of £10,000, so that it will not turn an unindexed gain into a loss.

Since there is neither a gain nor a loss, there is no figure to form part of the PCTCT for the CAP for the year ended 31/12/2007.

Option 3

	£
Proceeds on disposal	58,000
less:	
Incidental costs of disposal	(5,000)
Net proceeds	53,000
less:	
Original cost	(59,000)
Incidental costs of acquisition	(1,000)
Unindexed loss	(7,000)
less:	
Indexation allowance*	Nil
Capital Loss	(7,000)

*Here there is no indexation allowance since there is an unindexed loss that cannot be increased through indexation.

Since there is a capital loss, and no chargeable gains in the CAP to set it against, there is no figure to form part of the PCTCT for the CAP y/e 31/12/2007. The capital loss of £7,000 will be carried forward to set against chargeable gains in the next CAP.

links with capital allowances

As we saw in the last chapter, capital allowances are available for 'Plant and Machinery' and 'Industrial Buildings'. The following rules apply to the disposal of fixed assets where capital allowances have been claimed on the asset:

- Where the asset is sold for less than it cost, the only tax implication is through plant and machinery or industrial buildings capital allowance computations. A capital loss will not arise.
- Where a chattel is sold for more than it cost, a chargeable gain can only arise if the proceeds exceed £6,000. If the proceeds do exceed £6,000 then a chargeable gain can arise, subject to the special chattel rule that we will look at shortly. This situation is rare, since items in this category do not usually appreciate in value.
- Where an industrial building is sold for more than it cost, a chargeable gain will arise, calculated in the normal way, as described in the last section.

DEALING WITH PART DISPOSALS

We saw earlier in the chapter that a disposal can relate to all or part of an asset. Although part disposal will not apply to many assets that are not divisible, it could apply, for example, to a piece of land.

If an asset was acquired as a whole, and then part of it is sold while the rest is retained we need to compute the gain (or loss) on the part that was disposed of. The difficulty is that although we know how much the proceeds are for that part of the asset, we probably do not know how much of the original cost of the whole asset relates to that portion.

The solution to this problem is to value the remaining part of the asset at the time of the part disposal. The original cost can then be apportioned by using these figures.

The formula for working out the cost of the part disposed of is:

$$\text{Original cost of whole asset} \times \frac{A}{(A + B)}$$

where A = proceeds (or market value) of the part disposed of

B = market value of the part retained

The following example will illustrate this type of calculation.

example of a gain computation involving part disposal

Fielding and Company Limited bought a piece of land for £4,000 in January 1991 to use as a car park. In February 2007 the company sold a part of the land for £3,000. At the same time the remainder of the land was valued at £9,000.

The indexation factor from January 1991 to February 2007 is 0.560.

The portion of the original cost relating to the part of the field that was sold can be calculated as:

$$£4,000 \times \frac{£3,000}{(£3,000 + £9,000)} = £1,000$$

The computation would then be carried out in the normal way:

	£
Proceeds	3,000
less cost (as calculated above)	(1,000)
indexation allowance:	
0.560 x £1,000	(560)
Chargeable Gain	1,440

IMPROVEMENT EXPENDITURE

Where expenditure after acquisition is used to enhance an asset, and the asset is then disposed of in this improved condition, the improvement expenditure forms an allowable cost in the computation.

The expenditure must be of a 'capital' nature, and examples of this could include extending a building or having an antique professionally restored. The improvement expenditure will also attract indexation allowance. This would run from the date the improvement expenditure was incurred until the date of disposal. A situation would therefore arise where two (or more) indexation allowances were deducted in the computation, each with different start dates, but all with the same end date. This is shown in the diagram that follows on the next page.

indexation allowances on an 'improved' asset

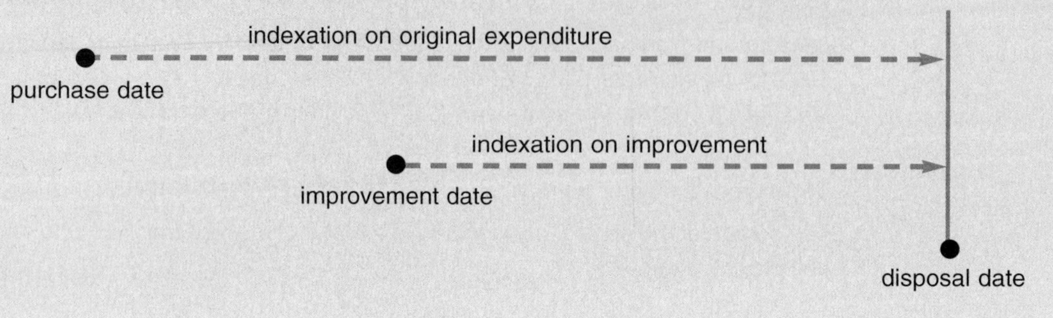

The following example illustrates how this works in practice:

example: chargeable gain involving improvement expenditure

Ledger and Company Limited bought an office building for £60,000 in September 1984. In January 1990 the company spent £40,000 extending the property. The company sold the building in February 2007 for £300,000.

The indexation factors are:

September 1984 to February 2007	1.254
January 1990 to February 2007	0.670

The calculation is as follows:

	£
Proceeds	300,000
less:	
original cost	(60,000)
improvement expenditure	(40,000)
Unindexed gain	200,000
less:	
indexation allowance on original cost	
1.254 x £60,000	(75,240)
indexation allowance on extension	
0.670 x £40,000	(26,800)
Chargeable Gain	97,960

SPECIAL RULES FOR CHATTELS

Chattels are tangible, moveable items such as furniture, portable equipment, works of art and vans.

Apart from the exemptions for all cars, and chattels bought and sold for less than £6,000, there are also some special rules about the amount of gain or loss that can occur when chattels are disposed of. Although these rules are not particularly complicated, they do need to be remembered.

chattels sold at a gain for over £6,000

In this situation the gain is limited to an amount of:

5/3 (Proceeds – £6,000)

Note that in this formula both the fraction of 5/3 and the amount of £6,000 are stated in the tax legislation and will be the same in all these calculations.

This restriction may, or may not, affect the chargeable gain. To give an illustration, suppose that gains (after any indexation) had been calculated on disposals in the following two examples:

Disposal A	Proceeds £9,000,	Gain £7,500
Disposal B	Proceeds £9,000,	Gain £2,500

In the case of Disposal A, the gain would be restricted to:

5/3 (£9,000 – £6,000) = £5,000

£5,000 would therefore be used as the chargeable gain figure. Using the same formula for Disposal B the gain would also be restricted to £5,000, but since the calculated gain is only £2,500 the restriction would be irrelevant and have no effect.

chattels sold at a loss for less than £6,000

If the chattel had been bought for less than £6,000 the transaction would be exempt from CGT.

If the chattel had cost more than £6,000 then the loss would be limited by using the figure of £6,000 in the gains computation **instead of the actual proceeds**. This will mean that the capital loss is smaller than it would be if the actual proceeds could be used.

We use the phrase 'deemed proceeds' to describe substituting the actual proceeds with another figure. £6,000 is always used as the 'deemed proceeds' where the actual proceeds are less than £6,000, but the chattel was bought for more than £6,000.

For example a chattel, such as furniture, bought for £8,000 and sold for £3,000 would result in a loss calculated as:

	£
Deemed proceeds	6,000
less actual cost	(8,000)
Loss	(2,000)

Make sure that you understand this process, and remember that it is the proceeds that are deemed to be £6,000. This is an area where it is easy to get confused if you are not careful.

We will now present a Case Study to consolidate an understanding of the main issues that we have covered in this chapter so far.

Case Study

INN CREASE LIMITED: USING SPECIAL RULES

Inn Crease Limited runs a chain of hotels and pubs. During the CAP y/e 31/12/2007 the company made the disposals listed below.

The company has capital losses brought forward from the previous CAP of £20,000.

disposals:

- The company sold an antique dresser in January 2007 for £7,500. The dresser had cost £3,200 when purchased in January 1996.
- The company sold part of a plot of land for £100,000 in February 2007. It had bought the whole plot in January 1990 for £80,000. In February 2007 the market value of the remaining part of the plot of land was £300,000.
- The company sold an office building in March 2007 for £150,000. The building was bought in September 1995 for £60,000, and extended in June 2000 at a cost of £40,000.
- The company sold ten identical shoe-cleaning machines from its hotels for £100 each in January 2007. The machines had been bought for £500 each in January 1996, and plant & machinery capital allowances had been claimed on them through the main pool.

- The company sold 1,000 ordinary shares in Gloxxo plc for a total of £10,000 in March 2007. The shares had been bought for £6.00 each in September 1995. These had been the only shares that it owned in Gloxxo plc.

indexation factors

The indexation factors have been calculated as follows:

January 1990 – February 2007	0.687
September 1995 – March 2007	0.357
January 1996 – January 2007	0.342
June 2000 – March 2007	0.195

Required

- Calculate the chargeable gain or capital loss on each applicable disposal.
- Calculate the total chargeable gain that will be used in the PCTCT computation for the CAP y/e 31/12/2007.

Solution

Antique Dresser

	£
Proceeds	7,500
less cost	(3,200)
less indexation (0.342 x £3,200)	(1,094)
Chargeable Gain	3,206

but gain restricted to:

5/3 (£7,500 – £6,000) = £2,500

Land

Proceeds	100,000
less apportioned cost:	
£80,000 x £100,000 / £400,000	(20,000)
less indexation:	
0.687 x £20,000	(13,740)
Chargeable gain	66,260

Office building

	£
Proceeds	150,000
less cost	(60,000)
Improvement expenditure	(40,000)
less:	
indexation on cost	
£60,000 x 0.357	(21,420)
indexation on improvement	
£40,000 x 0.195	(7,800)
Chargeable gain	20,780

Shoe cleaning machines

The shoe cleaning machines are sold at a loss, and are therefore dealt with entirely through the Plant and Machinery capital allowances computation.

Shares

Proceeds	10,000
less cost	(6,000)
less indexation (0.357 x £6,000)	(2,142)
Chargeable Gain	1,858

calculation of chargeable gain for PCTCT computation

We can now bring the chargeable gains together, and deduct the capital loss brought forward.

	£
Antique dresser	2,500
Land	66,260
Office building	20,780
Shares	1,858
	91,398
Less capital loss brought forward	(20,000)
Chargeable gain to be used in PCTCT computation	71,398

MATCHING RULES FOR SHARES

In the Case Study on the previous page, shares are shown as chargeable assets, and the computation for the acquisition and subsequent disposal of a block of shares is the same as for other assets.

A complication can arise when various quantities of the same type of share in the same company are bought over a period of time and then sold. The problem faced is similar to that in any stock valuation situation – how to determine which of the shares that were bought are deemed to be the ones that were sold.

The problem is solved in this situation by the application of strict **matching rules**, in other words, matching up the shares that have been sold with the shares originally held.

When shares are sold the **matching process** is carried out by working through, in order, the following categories of acquisition, missing out any that do not apply, until all the shares sold have been matched. A separate chargeable gains computation is then used for each separate match.

- Firstly, any shares bought on the **same day** that the disposal occurs are matched with that disposal.
- Secondly, any shares bought in the **nine days before the disposal** are matched with those disposed of. When this occurs no indexation allowance is available.
- Finally any remaining shares not yet matched are deemed to have come from the **'FA 1985 pool'** of shares. This is a device for merging and indexing shares. ('FA 1985' stands for the 'Finance Act 1985' which established this procedure, explained on the next page).

The matching process process is a little complicated, but forms a possible examination task. The most likely questions will involve shares matched to the FA 1985 pool because there are no very recent acquisitions.

Note that these matching rules for companies are different from the ones that relate to individuals that you may have studied in the Personal Taxation unit. The matching rules for individuals are outside the scope of this Business Taxation unit.

Remember that this matching process only applies where there have been several purchases of the same type of shares in the same company. It does not apply to a mixture of different company's shares, nor is it needed where a shareholding is bought and sold intact.

using the 'FA 1985 pool'

This device was introduced in the 1985 Finance Act, and merges (or 'pools') shares in the same company and of the same type together, and applies indexation allowances at the same time. As explained on the last page, it forms the last of the matching rules, and is used to calculate the cost of shares acquired earlier than nine days before disposal.

The pooling process is similar to the calculation of weighted average stock valuations (as you have probably studied in Costing), but with the additional complication of indexation allowance.

The 'pool' needs to record accurate data:

- the number of shares in each transaction
- actual costs
- indexed costs

These form the three main columns of the pool working.

The pool commences with the first shares bought. The cost of these is then indexed up to the time when other shares are bought (or sold). These are added in, and the cumulative indexed cost is then re-indexed up to the date of the next share transaction. This process is repeated as often as necessary, with the last indexation occurring up to the disposal date of the shares for which we are working out the gain. The indexed balance in the pool is then used to calculate the cost of shares from the pool that are sold, by apportionment based on the number of shares.

We will now demonstrate how this works, using a numerical example.

example: using the FA 1985 pool

On 1/1/2007 Jay Limited sold 10,000 ordinary shares in WyeCo Ltd for £12 each, from its shareholding of 25,000. The shareholding had been built up as follows:

1/1/1988 bought 17,000 shares for £5.00 each

1/1/1993 bought 8,000 shares for £7.00 each

The relevant indexation factors are:

January 1988 to January 1993	0.335
January 1993 to January 2007	0.462

Since there are no acquisitions on the day of disposal, nor the nine days before that, the whole of the disposal of 10,000 shares will be matched with the pool. The pool will be built up as follows, with the disposal deducted as the latest transaction:

	Number	Cost	Indexed Cost
		£	£
1/1/1988 Purchase	17,000	85,000	85,000
Indexation to Jan 1993:			
£85,000 x 0.335			28,475
			113,475
1/1/1993 Purchase	8,000	56,000	56,000
			169,475
Indexation to January 2007:			
£169,475 x 0.462			78,297
Pool Totals:	25,000	141,000	247,772
Less Disposal	(10,000)	(56,400)	(99,109)
Pool Balance after disposal	15,000	84,600	148,663

You should examine these workings carefully, and note the following:

- Indexation is applied to consecutive periods based on transaction dates. Here the periods were:
  – January 1988 to January 1993
  – January 1993 to January 2007
- Purchases at cost are added to the cumulative indexed cost figure, and the combined amount is then re-indexed to the date of the next transaction.
- The cost figures for the disposal are a proportional amount of the pool costs before disposal, based on the number of shares.
  (eg £247,772 x 10,000 / 25,000 = £99,109)

The computation for the disposal will now be as follows:

	£
Proceeds (10,000 x £12)	120,000
less cost	(56,400)
less indexation (£99,109 - £56,400)	(42,709)
Chargeable Gain	20,891

The cost and indexation figures are shown here separately, but would total the indexed cost amount shown in the pool workings (£56,400 + £42,709 = £99,109). This is shown this way in case the indexation needs to be restricted to avoid creating a loss.

If at some future date there was another disposal of shares from the pool then the pool balances remaining (indexed as appropriate) would be used to determine the cost of the shares in the further disposal.

BONUS AND RIGHTS ISSUES

dealing with bonus shares

Bonus shares are additional shares given free to shareholders, based on their current shareholding. This is sometimes called a 'scrip issue' and this process may be carried out as part of a capital restructuring of a company.

For chargeable gains purposes, the bonus shares are treated as if they were acquired at the same time as the original shares that generated the issue. For example a company that owned 1,000 shares that were bought in January 2001 would be entitled to a further 200 shares if there were a bonus issue of 'one for five' shares. The total of 1,200 shares would be treated as bought in January 2001 for the amount paid for the 1,000 shares.

Bonus shares are added to the pool when they are received. Since no payment is made, there is no adjustment to the cost or indexed cost figures. The bonus share transaction date is not relevant for indexation purposes.

dealing with rights issues

A rights issue is when additional shares are sold to existing shareholders, usually at a special discounted price. For matching purposes, the shares that are bought in this way are treated as if they were bought with the original shares. However, any indexation that applies to rights issue shares will only apply from the date that they were paid for. Rights issue shares will join the pool and be treated like any other share purchase. Their cost will be added into the pool, and the date they were bought will be treated as a date to index to and from as usual.

Dealing with share transactions is one of the most complicated areas of study in this unit, yet it is a likely examination task. We will therefore use a further case study to consolidate understanding.

Case Study

CHER THYME LIMITED: MATCHING AND POOLING SHARES

Cher Thyme Limited has acquired the following quoted ordinary shares in AbCo Plc:

1/5/1985	1,000 shares at £4.00 each	£4,000
1/1/1990	Bonus issue of 1 for 4	
1/1/1992	1,750 shares at £4.20 each	£7,350
1/1/1995	Rights issue of 1 for 2 at £4.10 each	
1/12/2001	1,800 shares at £5.10 each	£9,180

On 8/12/2001 the company sold 1,000 of its shareholding of AbCo Plc

On 15/3/2007 the company sold a further 2,500 ordinary shares in AbCo Plc for £8.00 each.

Required

1 Identify which shares would have already been matched against the disposal that took place on 8/12/2001.

2 State how the disposal of shares on 15/3/2007 will be matched against the acquisitions.

3 Calculate the total gain arising from the sale of shares that took place on 15/3/2007.

Indexation factors have already been calculated, and are as follows:

May 1985 – Jan 1992	0.424
Jan 1992 – Jan 1995	0.077
Jan 1995 – Dec 2001	0.188
Dec 2001 – March 2007	0.179

Solution

1 The disposal of 1,000 shares on 8/12/2001 would have been matched with 1,000 of the 1,800 shares that were bought on 1/12/2001 for £5.10 each. This leaves 800 of that purchase to join the pool at that time.

2 Matching of the 15/3/2007 disposal of 2,500 shares will be against the pool, since there are no acquisitions on the same day, or any in the previous nine days.

3 To carry out the computation we must first build up the FA 1985 pool:

	Number	Cost	Indexed Cost
		£	£
1/5/1985 Purchase	1,000	4,000	4,000
1/1/1990 Bonus Issue	250		
Indexation May 1985 to Jan 1992:			
£4,000 x 0.424			1,696
	1,250	-	5,696
1/1/1992 Purchase	1,750	7,350	7,350
	3,000	11,350	13,046
Indexation Jan 1992 to Jan 1995			
£13,046 x 0.077			1,005
1/1/1995 Rights issue 1 for 2	1,500	6,150	6,150
	4,500	17,500	20,201
Indexation Jan 1995 to Dec 2001:			
£20,201 x 0.188			3,798
1/12/2001 Purchase (Balance)	800	4,080	4,080
	5,300	21,580	28,079
Indexation Dec 2001 to March 2007:			
£28,079 x 0.179			5,026
Pool Totals	5,300	21,580	33,105
Less Disposal	(2,500)	(10,179)	(15,616)
Pool Balance after disposal	2,800	11,401	17,489

	£
Proceeds (2,500 x £8)	20,000
Less cost	(10,179)
Less indexation (£15,616 - £10,179)	(5,437)
Chargeable Gain	4,384

ROLLOVER RELIEF

Rollover relief applies when one business asset is sold, and another is bought. It is a deferral relief, which means that it postpones the impact of a chargeable gain. Since a gain can be deferred more than once, provided the rules don't change in the future, gains can sometimes be postponed almost indefinitely.

Where one business asset is replaced with another, then the gain of the first may be rolled over (deferred) into the second, so that any eventual gain on the replacement asset would include the gain deferred from the first asset.

For example, (ignoring indexation for simplicity), suppose a qualifying asset, such as a warehouse, is sold for £200,000, incurring a gain of £50,000. Another qualifying asset is then bought for £220,000, and the gain on the first asset is rolled over into the second, which means no tax is payable on the gain at this time.

If the second asset is sold some time later, and incurs a 'normal' chargeable gain of £100,000, the deferred gain from the first asset will increase the total chargeable gain to £150,000.

Full deferral can only occur when all the proceeds of the first asset are invested in the replacement asset(s). Any part of the proceeds that are not reinvested in the second asset will form a chargeable gain immediately.

The replacement asset must be acquired between one year before and three years after the sale of the first asset.

Both assets must be in the categories listed below, but do not have to be like-for-like replacements for each other, nor even in the same category.

This is an abbreviated list based on the type of assets involved:

- land & buildings
- immovable plant & machinery
- ships, aircraft & hovercraft

A company could, for example, sell an aircraft, and invest the proceeds in an office building and roll over the gain.

The most common examination tasks involving rollover relief relate to land and buildings. You may be expected to recognise that rollover relief would benefit a company in a given situation, and calculate the position accordingly.

Companies can choose whether or not to use rollover relief.

The example on the next page illustrates how the system works.

example: rollover relief

Rollo and Company Limited purchased an office building in January 1992 for £300,000. The company sold the building in January 2007 for £800,000. A shop had been purchased for £950,000 in August 2006.

The indexation factor from January 1992 to January 2007 is 0.487.

The chargeable gain on the office building would be calculated as follows (initially ignoring any rollover relief).

	£
Proceeds	800,000
less cost	(300,000)
less indexation	
0.487 x £300,000	(146,100)
Chargeable Gain	353,900

Using rollover relief, all of this gain of £353,900 can be deferred, because all of the proceeds were invested in the shop – the shop was bought for more than £800,000. This means that there is no gain on the office building chargeable in the current CAP.

The deferral works by deducting the deferred gain of £353,900 from the purchase cost of the shop in the chargeable gains computation when the shop is ultimately disposed of.

This would make the revised 'cost' figure (£950,000 – £353,900) = £596,100. Any gain at disposal of the shop would therefore consequently be greater than if rollover relief had not been used.

If the shop had been purchased for less than £800,000, not all of the gain on the office building could have been deferred. For example, if the shop had been bought for £700,000 only £253,900 of the gain could be deferred and a £100,000 gain would be chargeable immediately.

Chapter Summary

- Chargeable gains for companies are part of the profits chargeable to Corporation Tax (PCTCT). Such gains arise when chargeable assets are disposed of during the chargeable accounting period (CAP). A disposal usually takes the form of the sale of the asset. All assets are chargeable unless they are exempt. Exempt assets include cars, government securities (gilts), and certain chattels.

- Each disposal uses a separate computation that compares the proceeds or market value with the original cost of the asset. Indexation allowance is also deductible based on inflation from the time of acquisition up to disposal. Losses are set off against gains before bringing the net figure into the PCTCT computation. Where the net result is a capital loss, the amount is carried forward to set against chargeable gains arising in the next CAP. Where capital allowances have been claimed on an asset that is disposed of, capital losses cannot arise.

- The cost of a part disposal is calculated by apportioning the cost of the whole asset. This is carried out by using the proceeds of the part disposed of as a proportion of the value of the whole asset at the time of disposal.

- Improvement expenditure that is reflected in the asset when disposed of is an allowable cost. It also attracts indexation allowance from the date of expenditure up to the date of disposal.

- Chattels that are acquired and sold for under £6,000 are exempt. Where they are sold at a gain for over £6,000 the gain is restricted to 5/3 of the proceeds minus £6,000. Where sold at a loss for under £6,000, the loss is restricted by substituting £6,000 for the actual proceeds in the computation.

- When shares of the same type in the same company are bought and sold at different times matching rules are used to identify the shares disposed of. Firstly shares bought on the day of disposal are matched. Secondly those bought in the 9 days before disposal are matched. Thirdly acquisitions are pooled (including indexation) and matched. This is known as the FA 1985 (Finance Act 1985) pool.

- Bonus and rights issues are treated as acquired at the time of the shares that they are derived from for matching purposes. They can both appear as part of the FA 1985 pool.

- Rollover relief relates to certain categories of assets. It can defer a chargeable gain where the company reinvests all or part of the proceeds of disposal in further assets. The full deferral of a gain can only occur when all of the proceeds are reinvested.

Key Terms

Chargeable Gains
These can arise when companies dispose of chargeable assets. Chargeable Gains form part of the profits chargeable to Corporation Tax (PCTCT).

Capital Loss
This is effectively a negative chargeable gain. It results when the allowable costs of an asset exceed the sale proceeds (or market value). Indexation cannot be used to increase a loss. A capital loss is used by setting it against a gain in the same CAP, or if this is not possible, by carrying it forward to set against chargeable gains in the next available CAP.

Disposal
A disposal for Capital Gains Tax purposes is the sale, gift, loss or destruction of an asset.

Chargeable Asset
This term is used to describe assets, the disposal of which can result in a chargeable gain or capital loss. All assets are chargeable unless they are exempt.

Exempt Asset
This is an asset that is not a chargeable asset. Exempt assets include cars, Gilts, and some chattels.

Chattel
A tangible, moveable asset.

Net Proceeds
The proceeds from the sale of an asset, less any incidental costs of selling the asset.

Unindexed Gain
The net proceeds (or market value in some situations) less the original cost of the asset and any other allowable costs incurred. It is the subtotal of the gain computation before indexation allowance is deducted.

Indexation Allowance
An amount that is deductible in the gain computation that compensates for the effect of inflation on the asset between acquisition and disposal. It uses the Retail Price Index to calculate a factor that is multiplied by the historical cost of the asset.

Part Disposal

This occurs when part of an asset is disposed of, but the remainder is retained.

Improvement Expenditure

This term relates to capital expenditure that enhances an asset. If the enhancement is still evident at disposal then the improvement expenditure is an allowable cost.

Matching Rules for Shares

These rules determine which acquisitions of shares are identified with each disposal.

Bonus Shares

Shares issued at no cost to shareholders, the number of shares being based on their current shareholding.

Rights Issue

Shares issued by a company to its existing shareholders at a special price.

Rollover Relief

A deferral relief available to businesses (including companies). It has the effect of postponing a chargeable gain when the proceeds of disposal have been reinvested in further assets.

Student Activities

Answers to the asterisked (*) questions are to be found at the back of this book.

4.1* Analyse the following list of assets into those that are chargeable assets and those that are exempt.

(a) Antique painting sold for £10,000

(b) An office block

(c) Shares in CIC plc

(d) An industrial building

(e) A portable machine, sold at a profit for under £6,000

(f) A plot of land

(g) A car

(h) Government securities

(i) Trading stock

4.2* April Limited bought an office block in May 1995 for £600,000 and sold it in January 2007 for £1,300,000. The company had no other disposals in the CAP y/e 31/12/2007. April Limited had a capital loss brought forward from the previous CAP of £15,000.

The indexation factor from May 1995 to January 2007 is 0.348.

Calculate the chargeable gain that will form part of the PCTCT for April Limited for the CAP y/e 31/12/2007.

4.3* Cee Limited bought 200 ordinary shares in Zedco plc in August 1998 for £50,000 and sold them in March 2007 for £145,000. It had no other disposals in the CAP y/e 31/12/2007.

Cee Limited had a capital loss brought forward from the previous CAP of £25,000.

The indexation factor from August 1998 to March 2007 is 0.249.

Calculate the chargeable gain that will form part of the PCTCT for Cee Limited for the CAP.

4.4 Aye Limited made the following disposals in March 2007. These were its only disposals during CAP y/e 31/12/2007.

It sold a factory for £500,000 that had been used for a qualifying purpose since it was bought new for £300,000 in September 1986. IBA had been claimed in each CAP since that time.

It sold part of a piece of land for £30,000 that it had bought in January 1992. The whole piece of land had cost £50,000 at that time. At the time of the sale the remaining land was valued at £120,000.

Required:

- Calculate any impact on industrial buildings allowances of the sale of the factory.
- Calculate the total chargeable gains arising from the two disposals.

The relevant indexation factors are:

September 1986 to March 2007	1.079
January 1992 to March 2007	0.507

4.5 Dee Limited made the following disposals in its CAP y/e 31/12/2007.

It sold 10,000 of its ordinary shares in Zydeco Ltd on 30/03/2007 for £50,000 in total. The shareholding in this company had been built up as follows:

1/1/1992	Bought 3,000 shares for £3.00 each.
1/1/1995	Bought 12,000 shares for £3.50 each
1/1/1999	Received bonus shares on the basis of I for 5
1/1/2000	Sold 5,000 shares

It sold a portable antique machine to a local museum for £6,900 on 31/3/2007. The machine had been bought for £3,000 in January 2000, and capital allowances had been claimed on it since through the main pool.

Required:

- Calculate any chargeable gain made on
  - the disposal of shares in March 2007, and
  - the disposal of the machine in March 2007.
- State how the disposal of the machine will be dealt with for capital allowances.

The relevant indexation factors are:

January 1992 to January 1995	0.077
January 1995 to January 2000	0.141
January 2000 to March 2007	0.227

5 Corporation Tax – calculating the tax

this chapter covers . . .

In this chapter we examine:

- *the Corporation Tax computation*
- *rates of Corporation Tax and marginal relief*
- *the effect of associated companies and short CAPs*
- *how to deal with different types of losses*
- *the impact of Income Tax on limited companies*
- *the impact of National Insurance on limited companies*
- *payment dates for Corporation Tax*
- *completion of the Corporation Tax self-assessment return*
- *interest and penalties for late payments and returns*
- *maintaining appropriate records*

PERFORMANCE CRITERIA COVERED

unit 18: PREPARING BUSINESS TAXATION COMPUTATIONS

element 18.4

prepare Corporation Tax computations

A *enter adjusted trading profits and losses, capital allowances, investment income and capital gains in the Corporation Tax computation*

B *set-off and deduct loss reliefs and charges correctly*

C *calculate Corporation Tax due, taking account of marginal relief*

D *identify and set-off Income Tax deductions and credits*

E *identify the National Insurance Contributions payable by employers*

F *identify the amount of Corporation Tax payable and the due dates of payment, including payments on account*

G *complete Corporation Tax returns correctly and submit them, together with relevant claims and elections, within statutory time limits*

I *give timely and constructive advice to clients on the maintenance of accounts and the recording of information relevant to tax returns*

THE CORPORATION TAX COMPUTATION

structure of the computation

As discussed in earlier chapters, the Corporation Tax computation starts with a summary of profits from various sources that are chargeable to Corporation Tax (PCTCT). The computation then goes on to calculate the amount of Corporation Tax that is payable.

A separate computation will need to be carried out for each Chargeable Accounting Period (CAP), which will result in a tax liability for the period. A separate CT600 return form will also need to be completed for each CAP. A simple version of this computation is repeated here:

Trading Income		X
+	Profits from Investments	X
+	Chargeable Gains	X
=	Profits Chargeable to Corporation Tax (PCTCT)	X
	Corporation Tax on PCTCT	X

revision – what we have covered so far

In Chapters 2 and 3 we examined in detail how the 'Trading Income' figure is calculated, including the calculation of capital allowances for plant & machinery and industrial buildings. In Chapter 4 we saw how chargeable gains are calculated on individual chargeable disposals and combined ready for inclusion in the Corporation Tax computation.

where we go from here

In this chapter we will be looking at the final stage of the Corporation Tax computation – bringing all the income together and working out the Corporation Tax liability. We will then go on to look at the impact of Income Tax and National Insurance on companies, before seeing how the tax return is completed and the dates for payment. Finally we will look briefly at the sort of records that should be kept to show how the figures in the computation have been arrived at.

You may recall the summary diagram from Chapter 2, reproduced at the top of the next page. We have now looked in detail at the elements in the first three of the boxes along the top of the diagram, and will now follow the rest of the procedures over the next few pages.

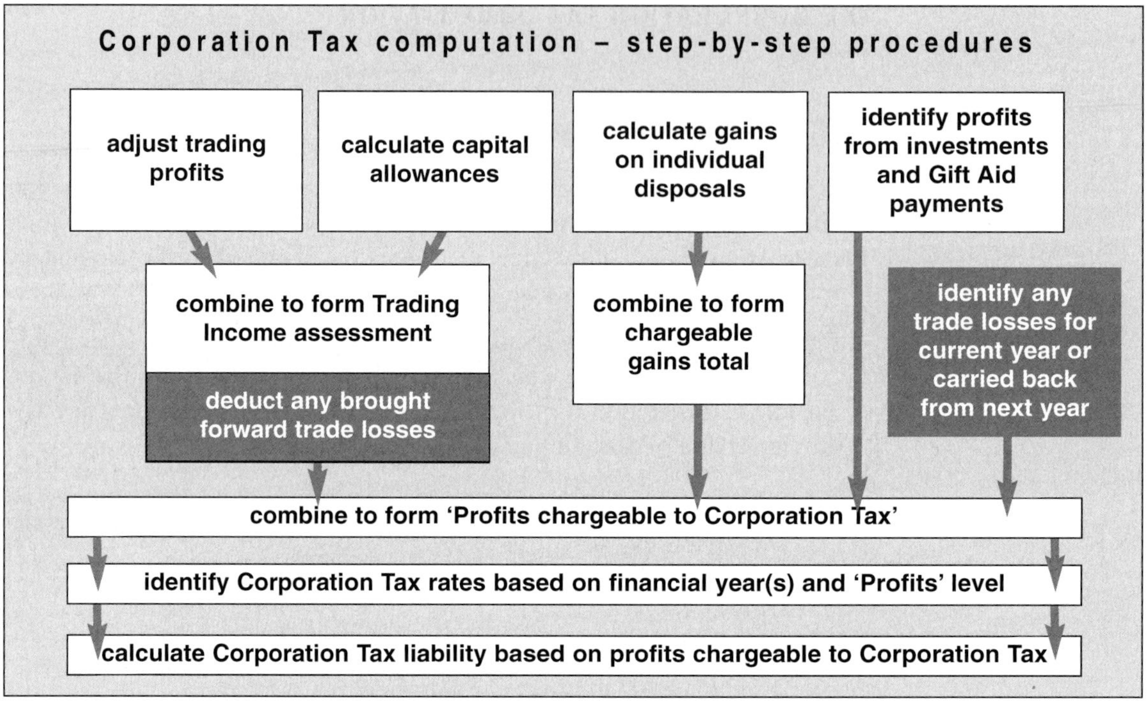

profits from investments

You will see from the above diagram that profits from investments need to be identified so that they can be incorporated into the computation. These profits could include:

- **Interest received from non-trade investments**

  The gross amount of any interest receivable (ie on an accruals basis) during the CAP forms an investment income assessment that is brought into the main computation. Examples of the sources of interest include bank and building society deposits, debentures and Government securities ('gilts'). You can assume that any such interest in an examination task is non-trade, and should therefore be treated in this way. You would not be asked to make any adjustments to interest received amounts in an examination.

- **Profits from renting out property**

  The tax-adjusted profits from rental income are assessed as 'property income'. You would not be expected to carry out adjustments to such figures, and would just need to incorporate the profit figure into the main computation. A little later in this chapter we will see how to deal with any losses that may arise from this type of income.

You should note that **dividends received** from other UK companies are **not** brought into the Corporation Tax computation, and are not taxed. This is because the profits from which they derive have already been taxed through the other company's computation. However, such dividends received can have an impact on the rate of Corporation Tax that is applied, as we shall see shortly.

gift-aid payments

Companies are entitled to make gifts to charities under the gift-aid scheme, and obtain tax relief on their payments. This operates simply by allowing the company to deduct the amount of the payment from the total profits in the Corporation Tax computation. This is carried out as the final stage in the calculation of the Profits Chargeable to Corporation Tax (PCTCT). The payment date determines which CAP the gift-aid payment falls into, for example if the payment was made during a 'long' accounting period. Unlike the gift-aid scheme for individuals (that you may have come across in the personal taxation unit), the company makes the payment to the charity as a gross amount, with no adjustment for tax. As we saw in Chapter 2, the company cannot use a gift-aid payment as an allowable deduction in the calculation of Trading Income profits, since this would form a duplication of tax relief.

If there are insufficient total profits to set a gift-aid payment against in the final calculation of PCTCT, then the tax relief on the balance of the payment is lost, since it cannot be carried forward. Where trading losses are set against the PCTCT, (as outlined in Chapter 2) this is carried out in priority to gift-aid payments, so again there is a possibility of losing the tax relief on the gift-aid payment.

We will now use a Case Study to demonstrate how the various elements are combined into a Corporation Tax computation, before looking at the tax calculation itself.

Case Study

THE BASIC COMPANY LIMITED: CALCULATING CORPORATION TAX

The Basic Company Limited has produced accounts for the year ended 31/3/2008. The accounts have been adjusted for tax purposes, and the following figures have been established:

	£
Adjusted Trading Profit (before capital allowances)	1,000,000
Capital Allowances – Plant & Machinery	123,000
Capital Allowances – Industrial Buildings	40,000

	£
Payment to Charity under Gift-Aid scheme	28,000
Non-Trade Interest Receivable	55,000
Dividends Received from UK Company	90,000
Chargeable Gains	34,000
Rental Income	48,000

Required

Using a Corporation Tax Computation, calculate the Profits Chargeable to Corporation Tax (PCTCT) for the CAP y/e 31/3/2008.

Solution

In order to complete the computation, the trading income assessment must first be established:

		£
Adjusted Trading Profits		1,000,000
less	Plant & Machinery capital allowances	(123,000)
	Industrial Buildings capital allowances	(40,000)
Trading Income assessment		837,000

Building on the outline computation shown at the start of this chapter, we can now combine the figures that make up the Profits Chargeable to Corporation Tax (PCTCT).

Corporation Tax Computation

	£
Trading Income	837,000
Profits from Investments:	
Non-Trade Interest Receivable	55,000
Property Income	48,000
Chargeable Gains	34,000
	974,000
less Gift-Aid payments	(28,000)
Profits Chargeable to Corporation Tax ('PCTCT')	946,000

Note the structure of the computation, since you will need to use this in an examination without further guidance. Note also that the dividends received of £90,000 are left out of the PCTCT calculation entirely.

In the next section we will see how the tax itself is calculated.

CALCULATING THE CORPORATION TAX LIABILITY

Once the PCTCT has been established for a chargeable accounting period (CAP) the next step is to calculate the tax itself. The tax rate to be applied, and any further calculation will depend on the size of the company – decided by a special 'profit' figure – and the financial year or years into which the accounts fall. We will be mainly using the tax rates that apply to the financial year 2007 (the period 1 April 2007 to 31 March 2008). Later on we will also see how to deal with a company whose CAP is partly in the previous financial year – 2006, when some rates were different.

The 'profits' figure referred to above is calculated as:

		£
	PCTCT for the CAP (as calculated)	X
add	the amount of any dividends received from UK companies plus the associated tax credit	X
	'Profits' for the purpose of determining the tax rate	X

The dividends received plus the associated tax credit is also known as **Franked Investment Income** (FII). The tax credit is equal to 10/90 of the dividend amount itself, and therefore the FII figure can be calculated as:

Dividend + (10/90 x Dividend)

or simply as 100/90 x Dividend

This is the same calculation that is carried out for individuals when working out the amount of dividend income that is assessable to Income Tax.

Corporation Tax 'bands' and marginal relief

There are currently three 'bands' for Corporation Tax purposes, and the first step is to establish into which band the 'profits' figure falls. This will determine the rate of tax that will be applied to the PCTCT, and whether there is any **marginal relief** available. Marginal relief is a deduction in the calculation of the Corporation Tax amount. It is calculated by formula and has the effect of smoothing the transition from one tax rate to the next.

For those who have already studied Income Tax you will find that, unlike Income Tax, the Corporation Tax calculation does not involve working up through the bands, nor does the PCTCT have to be analysed into different categories of income.

The table on the next page shows the bands and the tax rates that apply within each band, based on a twelve month CAP.

Corporation Tax rates

'Profit' range	Corporation Tax 1/4/2006 – 31/3/2007	Corporation Tax 1/4/2007 – 31/3/2008
£0 – £300,000	Small Companies Rate (19%)	Small Companies Rate (20%)
£300,001 – £1,500,000	Full Rate (30%) less marginal relief	Full Rate (30%) less marginal relief
£1,500,001 and over	Full Rate (30%)	Full Rate (30%)

calculations without marginal relief

Where there is no marginal relief available, the Corporation Tax is calculated simply by multiplying the PCTCT (Profits Chargeable to Corporation Tax) by the appropriate percentage. Note that it is the PCTCT that we are using here, not the 'profits' figure that was used to determine the band.

For example, suppose a company has the following results for a twelve month CAP (Chargeable Accounting Period) to 31/3/08:

	Profits Chargeable to Corporation Tax (PCTCT)	£200,000
+	Franked Investment Income (FII)	£20,000
=	'Profits'	£220,000

The 'profits' figure falls into the small companies rate band of £0 to £300,000 (see table above) and therefore the Corporation Tax will be calculated as:

£200,000 x 20% = £40,000.

There are additional calculations required where the CAP falls into two financial years where different rates apply. We will examine these a little later.

calculations using marginal relief

Marginal relief is a deduction in the calculation of the Corporation Tax amount. It is calculated by formula. It has the effect of smoothing the transition from one tax rate to the next. Where **marginal relief** is available, the tax is calculated by firstly multiplying the PCTCT by the appropriate rate, and then deducting the marginal relief, which is calculated using the following formula.

Marginal Relief Fraction x (Maximum of Band – 'Profits') x (PCTCT / 'Profits')

This formula is sometimes abbreviated to:

Fraction x (M – P) x (I / P)

where

M = **M**aximum of Band (normally £1,500,000)

P = '**P**rofits'

I = PCTCT (or **I**ncome)

In the financial year 2007, where marginal relief is to be deducted from Full Rate Corporation Tax the fraction is **1/40**. The fraction in the financial year 2006 is **11/400**.

If there are no dividends received, then the final fraction in the formula (PCTCT / 'Profits') will equal 1 (since the PCTCT = 'Profits'). This will make the calculation easier. Note also that this fraction can never exceed 1 since PCTCT will never be greater than 'Profits'.

Both the abbreviated formula and the marginal relief fractions will be provided for you in an examination, but you would still be advised to learn the formula in a form that you can use. It would not be much use if, when given the abbreviated formula, you could not remember what the letters stood for.

We will now use the data from the last Case Study on pages 5.5 and 5.6 to demonstrate how the tax calculation is carried out.

Case Study

THE BASIC COMPANY LIMITED: CALCULATING THE CORPORATION TAX

The Basic Company Limited has produced a Corporation Tax computation for the CAP year ended 31/3/2008.

This shows PCTCT of £946,000. It is also noted that the company received dividends from another UK company of £90,000 during the CAP (see page 5.6).

Required

Calculate the Corporation Tax liability of the Basic Company Limited for the CAP y/e 31/3/2008.

Solution

The first stage is to calculate the 'profits' figure, that will determine the rate of tax and whether marginal relief is available.

		£
	PCTCT for the CAP (as calculated)	946,000
add	the amount of any dividends received from UK companies plus the associated tax credit (£90,000 x 100/90)	100,000
	'Profits' for the purpose of determining the tax rate	1,046,000

Using the table (on page 5.8) we can see that the Basic Company Limited will pay Corporation Tax at the full rate of 30%, less marginal relief for this CAP. The calculation is as follows:

		£
	PCTCT at full rate: £946,000 x 30%	283,800
less	marginal relief:	
	1/40 x (£1,500,000 – £1,046,000) x (£946,000 / £1,046,000)	(10,265)
	Corporation Tax Liability	273,535

Note

The marginal relief calculation is best carried out in stages:

- the contents of the first bracket is calculated as £454,000
- this is divided by 40 to give £11,350
- this is multiplied by 946 and divided by 1046 to give the final result (the three zeros can be omitted from both parts of the final fraction like this to avoid exceeding the capacity of the calculator)

Note again that the Corporation Tax is calculated on the PCTCT, not on the 'profits' figure.

effective rates of Corporation Tax

One impact of the way in which the tax bands work is that the effective rate of Corporation Tax within the marginal relief is even higher than the full rate. This can be demonstrated with a simple example.

If we look at the difference in Corporation Tax in financial year 2007 at two profit levels for a company (with no FII for simplicity), we get the following comparison.

	PCTCT	Rate	Corporation Tax
	£300,000	20%	£60,000
	£1,500,000	30%	£450,000
Difference:	£1,200,000		£390,000

The £1,200,000 PCTCT between £300,000 and £1,500,000 creates additional tax of £390,000. This band is therefore effectively being taxed at

£390,000 / £1,200,000% = 32.5%.

You should not use this percentage in your calculations, but you should be aware of the fact that extra profits within this band are taxed more severely than those outside it.

DEALING WITH ASSOCIATED COMPANIES

Where a company is either one of a group of companies, or one of a number of companies that are all controlled by the same person, then the companies are said to be 'associated' for tax purposes. The impact of this is that the limits of £1,500,000 and £300,000 for each band are scaled down, by dividing them by the total number of associated companies.

Therefore a company that was one of three associated companies (itself and two others) would pay Corporation Tax at the full rate if its 'profits' were over £1,500,000 / 3 = £500,000. The same would apply to each of the other two associated companies, and the other band limit of £300,000 would also be similarly scaled down. This would also mean that if marginal relief were available the band upper limit in the formula would also be the scaled down figure. The 'profits' in this situation only include dividends from companies that are not associated.

The example on the next page will demonstrate how this works . . .

example: computations for associated companies

One of Three Limited has two associated companies. Its PCTCT for the CAP for the year ended 31/3/2008 is £250,000. It also received dividends during the CAP of £45,000 from another UK company (not an associate).

As there are three associated companies in total, the band limits are scaled down by dividing by three. The 'profits' would be £250,000 + (£45,000 x 100/90) = £300,000. This is between the scaled down limits of

- £1,500,000 / 3 = £500,000, and
- £300,000 / 3 = £100,000

Therefore the company pays Corporation Tax at full rate, less marginal relief.

The Corporation Tax calculation would be:

	£
PCTCT at full rate: £250,000 x 30%	75,000
less marginal relief: 1/40 x (£500,000 - £300,000) x (£250,000 / £300,000)	(4,167)
Corporation Tax Liability	70,833

DEALING WITH SHORT CHARGEABLE ACCOUNTING PERIODS

Where the CAP is less than twelve months the band limits are time-apportioned. This has the same impact as the scaling down of bands to deal with associated companies.

For example, if the CAP were for nine months, the limits would become:

- £1,500,000 x 9/12 = £1,125,000
- £300,000 x 9/12 = £225,000

The limit figure used in the marginal relief formula would also be the time-apportioned one.

If there were a situation where there were both

- associated companies, and
- a short CAP

then the limits would be scaled down twice.

For example a company with one associate, and a four-month CAP would have an upper limit of:

- (£1,500,000 / 2) x 4/12 = £250,000

dealing with financial years with different tax rates

You may have noticed from the table shown earlier that the financial years 2006 and 2007 both use the same full Corporation Tax rate of 30%, but have different small companies rates and different marginal relief fractions. The band limits of £1,500,000 and £300,000 are however the same for both years.

This means that we must be particularly careful if the CAP for a company does not fall entirely into either the financial year 2006 or the financial year 2007. If the CAP does straddle the 1st April 2007, this is the procedure that we should adopt:

- Using the 'profits' figure for the whole CAP, see which tax band will apply to the company.
  - If it is to pay tax at the full rate (with no marginal relief) then the tax calculation will simply be the whole PCTCT x 30%.
  - If it is to pay at small companies' rate or at full rate less marginal relief then the following must be carried out.
- Time-apportion the PCTCT into the part falling into the FY 2006 and that falling into the FY 2007.
- Calculate the tax separately for each of these parts of the CAP, using the appropriate tax rates and marginal relief calculations.
- Add together the two tax figures.

If the company is to pay tax at full rate less marginal relief then the limits used in the formulas will need to be time-apportioned based on the length of that part of the CAP.

The procedure outlined above could apply to any two adjacent financial years where the tax rates differ.

We will now use a case study to demonstrate this technique in full.

Case Study

THE COMPLEX PRACTICE: DEALING WITH DIFFERENT FINANCIAL YEARS

situation

The Complex Practice specialises in producing tax computations for limited company clients. There are currently four (unconnected) clients with adjusted tax data as follows:

- The Alpha Company Limited has a twelve month CAP running from 1st January 2007 to 31st December 2007. It has PCTCT for this period of £2,100,000, and did not receive any dividends.
- The Beta Company Limited has a twelve month CAP running from 1st November 2006 to 31st October 2007. It has PCTCT for this period of £120,000, and received dividends from UK companies of £54,000.
- The Delta Company Limited has a twelve month CAP running from 1st February 2007 to 31st January 2008. It has PCTCT for this period of £1,200,000, and received dividends from UK companies of £108,000.
- The Gamma Company Limited has a ten month CAP running from 1st September 2006 to 30th June 2007. It has PCTCT for this period of £500,000, and received dividends from UK companies of £9,000.

required

Calculate the Corporation Tax for each of the four companies.

solution

- The Alpha Company Limited has a 'profits' figure of £2,100,000 (the same as the PCTCT since there are no dividends received). This means that the company will pay Corporation Tax for this CAP at the full rate. Since this rate is 30% for the whole of the CAP, the tax calculation is simply:

  PCTCT of £2,100,000 x 30% = £630,000.

- The Beta Company Limited has a 'profits' figure for the CAP of £120,000 + (£54,000 x 100/90) = £180,000. As this figure is below £300,000 the small companies' rate of Corporation Tax is payable for the CAP. Since the rate is different for each of the financial years that the CAP falls into we will need to time-apportion the PCTCT and calculate each part of the tax separately, as follows:

  PCTCT falling into the financial year 2006 is based on the five month period 1/11/2006 to 31/3/2007 (i.e. 5/12 x £120,000 = £50,000).
  Corporation Tax on this amount is £50,000 x 19% = £9,500.

PCTCT falling into the financial year 2007 is based on the seven month period 1/4/2007 to 31/10/2007 (i.e. 7/12 x £120,000 = £70,000).
Corporation Tax on this amount is £70,000 x 20% = £14,000.

The total Corporation Tax for the CAP is therefore:
£9,500 + £14,000 = £23,500.

- The Delta Company Limited has a 'profits' figure for the CAP of £1,200,000 + (£108,000 x 100/90) = £1,320,000.

  As this figure is between £300,000 and £1,500,000 the company must pay Corporation Tax at the full rate less marginal relief. Although the full rate is 30% for both financial years, the marginal relief fraction is different, so we will need to carry out a time-apportionment calculation. Since we will be using the marginal relief formula for each part of the CAP, we will have to calculate both the PCTCT and the 'profits' figures relating to each financial year, as well as the time-apportioned band maximum of £1,500,000.

Financial Year	Time Apportionment	PCTCT	'Profits'	Max of Band
2006	2/12	£200,000	£220,000	£250,000
2007	10/12	£1,000,000	£1,100,000	£1,250,000

The tax calculation for each part of the CAP is then:

Financial Year 2006:

Corporation Tax at Full Rate	£200,000 x 30% =	60,000
Less marginal relief		
11/400 x (£250,000 – £220,000) x (£200,000 / £220,000)		(750)
		59,250

Financial Year 2007:

Corporation Tax at Full Rate	£1,000,000 x 30% =	300,000
Less marginal relief		
1/40 x (£1,250,000 – £1,100,000) x (£1,000,000 / £1,100,000)		(3,409)
		296,591

The total Corporation Tax for the CAP is:
£59,250 + £296,591 = £355,841.

- The Gamma Company Limited has a 'profits' figure for the CAP of £500,000 + £9,000 x 100/90) = £510,000. Since this is a ten-month CAP we must compare this figure with 10/12 of the normal limits. The 'profits' figure falls between the time-apportioned limit figures of 10/12 x £300,000 = £250,000 and 10/12 x £1,500,000 = £1,250,000. This confirms that the company will pay tax for this CAP at full rate less marginal relief. The calculation will therefore be similar to the Delta Company Limited, although we must take care with the time-apportionment calculations.

  The data that we will need is as follows:

Financial Year	Time Apportionment	PCTCT	'Profits'	Max of Band
2006	7/10	£350,000	£357,000	£875,000
2007	3/10	£150,000	£153,000	£375,000

  The tax calculation for each part of the CAP is then:

  Financial Year 2006:

Corporation Tax at Full Rate	£350,000 x 30% =	105,000
Less marginal relief		
11/400 x (£875,000 – £357,000) x (£350,000 / £357,000)		(13,966)
		91,034

  Financial Year 2007:

Corporation Tax at Full Rate	£150,000 x 30% =	45,000
Less marginal relief		
1/40 x (£375,000 – £153,000) x (£150,000 / £153,000)		(5,441)
		39,559

  The total Corporation Tax for the CAP is:
  £91,034 + £39,559 = £130,593.

The tax calculations in this case study have become progressively more difficult with each example. Make sure that you can follow the logic and carry out the calculations yourself.

DEALING WITH A VARIETY OF LOSSES

Over the last few chapters we have seen how different sorts of losses can be relieved against profits.

- in Chapter 2 we saw that trading losses can be
  - carried forward against future trading profits, or
  - set against the current period PCTCT, and if this has been done,
  - then set against the PCTCT of the previous twelve months
- in Chapter 4 we saw that capital losses on a disposal are first set against chargeable gains arising in the same CAP, and then carried forward against chargeable gains in the future
- rental losses can be set against the current period PCTCT and any amount not used carried forward and set against future property income

We must therefore be careful if presented with a variety of losses to deal with each one correctly. Although the above rules are fairly straightforward, they must be learnt, since it would be easy to get confused.

It is also worth remembering that Corporation Tax at full rate less marginal relief is effectively the highest rate for the profits within that band. This means that any reduction of such profits by offsetting losses would be particularly advantageous. This would apply where the 'profits' were between £300,000 and £1,500,000.

If you are asked to recommend how trade losses should be offset (the only losses where there is a choice), you should remember to try to reduce the amount of tax paid in the marginal relief band.

We will use a Case Study now to illustrate how to deal with a variety of losses.

Case Study

LOSER PLC: DEALING WITH DIFFERENT LOSSES

Loser plc has the following actual and projected adjusted results for the CAPs y/e 31/3/2008, and y/e 31/3/2009.

	Actual y/e 31/3/2008	Projected y/e 31/3/2009
	£	£
Trading Profit / (Loss)	(100,000)	500,000
Rental Profit / (Loss)	(15,000)	45,000
Non-Trade Interest Receivable	225,000	210,000
Chargeable Gains / (Capital Loss)	(50,000)	120,000

The company has not received dividends from other UK companies.

Assume that tax rates for the financial year 2008 are the same as for the financial year 2007.

Required

1. Explain how the rental losses and capital losses must be offset, and describe the alternative ways in which the trading loss could be offset.
2. Calculate the Corporation Tax liability for the CAPs y/e 31/3/2008 and y/e 31/3/2009, based on each alternative.
3. Recommend how the trading loss should be offset, based on the amount of tax payable.

Solution

1 The rental loss of £15,000 is set against the PCTCT for the year ended 31/3/2008, giving a net figure of £210,000. The capital loss must be carried forward to the next CAP, to reduce the Chargeable Gains amount. This will give a chargeable gains assessment of £120,000 – £50,000 = £70,000 in the CAP to 31/3/2008.

The trading loss could either be:

(a) set against the PCTCT of the CAP y/e 31/3/2008; since the only profits in that period are from interest receivable less the rental loss, the trade loss would reduce the PCTCT of the CAP to £210,000 – £100,000 = £110,000.

(b) carried forward and set against the trading profits of the CAP y/e 31/3/2009; this would reduce the trading income amount for that period to £500,000 – £100,000 = £400,000

2 The tax computations are as follows:

Option (a)

	CAP y/e 31/3/2008	CAP y/e 31/3/2009
	£	£
Trading Income	0	500,000
Property Income	0	45,000
Interest Receivable	225,000	210,000
Chargeable Gains	0	70,000
Less Loss on Property Income	(15,000)	-
Less Trading Loss of the year	(100,000)	-
PCTCT	110,000	825,000
Corporation Tax	(1) 22,000	(2) 230,625

Corporation Tax Workings:

		£
(1)	Taxed at small companies rate:	
	£110,000 x 20% =	22,000
(2)	Taxed at full rate, less marginal relief:	
	£825,000 x 30% =	247,500
	1/40 x (£1,500,000 – £825,000) x (£825,000 / £825,000)	(16,875)
		230,625

Option (b)

	CAP y/e 31/3/2008	CAP y/e 31/3/2009
	£	£
Trading Income	0	500,000
Less trading loss bf	-	(100,000)
		400,000
Property Income	0	45,000
Interest Receivable	225,000	210,000
Chargeable Gains	0	70,000
Less Loss on Property Income	(15,000)	-
PCTCT	210,000	725,000
Corporation Tax	(1) 42,000	(2) 198,125

Corporation Tax Workings:

	£
(1) Taxed at small companies rate:	
£210,000 x 20% =	42,000
(2) Taxed at full rate, less marginal relief:	
£725,000 x 30% =	217,500
1/40 x (£1,500,000 - £725,000) x (£725,000 / £725,000)	(19,375)
	198,125

3 By adding together the tax liabilities for each CAP under each option, we can see which produces the lower amount.

Option (a)	£22,000 + £230,625 =	£252,625
Option (b)	£42,000 + £198,125 =	£240,125
Difference		£12,500

Option (b) – carrying the trading loss forward – produces the lower total tax amount.

This is because in this situation option (a) simply reduces the tax payable at 20%, whereas option (b) reduces the amount of tax payable at the marginal tax rate (effectively 32.5%).

The difference in total tax payable of £12,500 is equal to the loss of £100,000 x (32.5% – 20% = 12.5%).

INCOME TAX AND LIMITED COMPANIES

Before April 2001 companies had to deduct Income Tax from a variety of payments. This system has been amended, so that the following situations are now the only ones where companies can become involved with Income Tax:

- Paying to HM Revenue & Customs amounts that have been deducted from employees under the PAYE scheme. These Income Tax deductions are payable to HM Revenue & Customs on a monthly basis, along with National Insurance payments.
- Paying to HM Revenue & Customs amounts that have been deducted from payments of interest to individuals, such as debenture interest. These interest payments must have Income Tax deducted at 20%. This is accounted for on a quarterly basis, using form CT 61. Payment of interest to other companies does not require any Income Tax deduction.

NATIONAL INSURANCE AND LIMITED COMPANIES

As we saw in Chapter 1, a limited company is treated as an employer for National Insurance purposes, and therefore has to make payments to HM Revenue & Customs of:

- employees' contributions, that have been deducted from employees' pay under PAYE, and
- the employer's NI contributions that form a cost to the company

The employer's contributions are separated into Class 1 contributions and Class 1A contributions, as follows:

- Class 1 contributions are calculated as 12.8% of (gross pay less £100 per week), and
- Class 1A contributions are calculated as 12.8% of the assessable value of employee benefits in kind

The Class 1 employer's contribution is payable monthly, along with the employees' contributions through the PAYE system. The Class 1A contributions are payable to HM Revenue & Customs annually by the 19th July following the end of the tax year.

Remember also that the directors of a limited company are employees of the company.

WHEN TO PAY CORPORATION TAX

As we noted in Chapter 1, Corporation Tax is payable nine months and one day after the end of the chargeable accounting period to which it relates, unless payments by instalment are necessary.

Whether instalment payments need to be made depends on the rate of Corporation Tax that the company is paying. Instalments are only required where the company is paying at full rate (with no marginal relief). This means that only companies with 'profits' of £1,500,001 and over for a twelve month CAP will need to pay by instalments (assuming no associates).

For these 'large' companies, all of the company's estimated Corporation Tax liability must be paid in the following 4 instalments (25% in each instalment). The first instalment is due on day 14 of month 7 within the CAP. The next three instalments follow at 3 monthly intervals. Any remaining balance of Corporation Tax (since the instalments were based on an estimate) will be payable at the normal due date, nine months and one day after the end of the CAP.

example: payment of Corporation Tax by instalment

Largos Limited has an estimated PCTCT of £2,000,000 in the CAP y/e 31/12/2007.

The estimated Corporation Tax would be:

£2,000,000 x 30% = £600,000.

This would be payable in four instalments of £150,000 each on 14/7/2007, 14/10/2007, 14/1/2008 and 14/4/2008. Any remaining balance would be due on 1/10/2008.

The following 'time-line' diagram illustrates this:

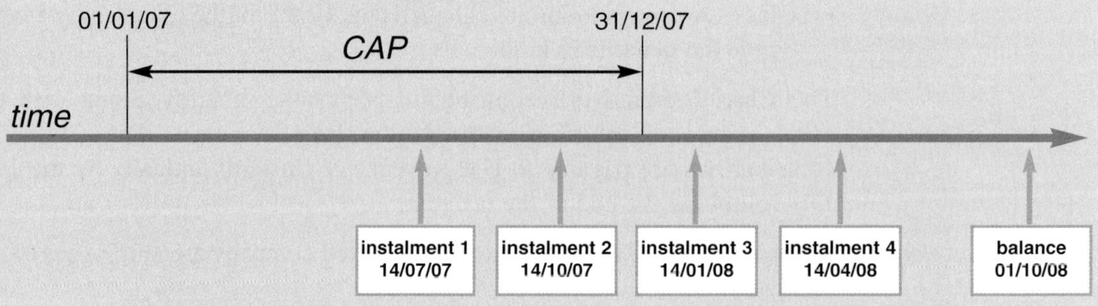

COMPLETION OF THE COMPANY TAX RETURN

The company tax return (the 'CT600') must be returned by twelve months after the end of the company's accounting period from which the CAP was derived. This will be the same date as twelve months after the CAP, unless the accounting period is over twelve months long, and had to be divided into two CAPs.

There is a full version of the CT600, and a shorter version - the 'short tax return form'. Although the full version CT600 is quite long, we should only need to be able to complete numerical information in the following sections of the 'short tax return form':

The company tax calculation (page 2)

Capital allowances, and losses (page 3)

We will now look at the company tax calculation to see what is required, before using a Case Study to demonstrate how to complete the form.

the company tax calculation

This page of the return is reproduced overleaf. It generally follows the same logic and order as a Corporation Tax computation, and is therefore relatively easy to fill in.

Notes on the completion of the main boxes in which you will need to make entries are set out opposite the page.

Boxes that are simply sub-totals have been excluded from these notes. Make sure that you read the instructions on the form relating to all the boxes carefully, so that you don't miss filling in any of the numerous sub-totals.

The top part of the page is a summary of the items making up the PCTCT.

The lower section of the page summarises the Corporation Tax itself.

Page 2 Boxes

Box 1 Total turnover from trade or profession. Enter the sales figure here.

Box 3 Trading and professional profits
The trading income amount will be inserted here.

Box 4 Trading losses brought forward claimed against profits
This is only for trading losses that are brought forward from an earlier period to be set against profits from the same trade.

Box 6 Bank, building society or other interest, and profits and gains from non-trading loan relationships
This is for non-trade interest receivable.

Box 11 Income from UK land and buildings. This is for property income.

Box 16 Gross chargeable gains
The total of chargeable gains on disposals in the CAP.

Box 17 Allowable losses . . .
Insert here any capital losses from the current CAP or previous CAPs to be offset against the above gains.

Box 30 Trading losses….
This is where a trading loss is set against the whole PCTCT.

Box 35 Charges paid. Gift aid payments are inserted here.

Box 37 Profits chargeable to Corporation Tax
This is the final PCTCT figure.

Box 38 Franked investment income
This is for UK dividends received, multiplied by 100/90

Box 39 The number of companies associated in this period. Note that this number of companies does not include the company itself.

Box 42 Marked with an 'X' if any rate less than the full rate is applicable.

Boxes 43-63 Corporation Tax chargeable
This is for tax before any marginal relief is deducted. It needs to be time-apportioned into financial years where the CAP crosses 1 April, even if the rate is the same.

Box 64 Marginal rate relief
This is for the total marginal relief that is to be deducted from the tax above.

Box 66 Underlying rate of corporation tax.
This is calculated by dividing the tax (after marginal relief) by the PCTCT. It is shown to 2 decimal places as a %.

Box 70 Corporation tax chargeable.

Page 2

Company tax calculation

Turnover

1	Total turnover from trade or profession		1 £

Income

3	Trading and professional profits	3 £	
4	Trading losses brought forward claimed against profits	4 £	
5	Net trading and professional profits		box 3 minus box 4 5 £
6	Bank, building society or other interest, and profits and gains from non-trading loan relationships		6 £
11	Income from UK land and buildings		11 £
14	Annual profits and gains not falling under any other heading		14 £

Chargeable gains

16	Gross chargeable gains	16 £	
17	Allowable losses including losses brought forward	17 £	
18	Net chargeable gains		box 16 minus box 17 18 £
21	**Profits before other deductions and reliefs**		sum of boxes 5, 6, 11, 14 & 18 21 £

Deductions and Reliefs

24	Management expenses under S75 ICTA 1988	24 £	
30	Trading losses of this or a later accounting period under S393A ICTA 1988	30 £	
31	*Put an 'X' in box 31 if amounts carried back from later accounting periods are included in box 30*	31	
32	Non-trade capital allowances	32 £	
35	Charges paid	35 £	
37	**Profits chargeable to corporation tax**		box 21 minus boxes 24, 30, 32 and 35 37 £

Tax calculation

38	Franked investment income	38 £	
39	Number of associated companies in this period or	39	
40	Associated companies in the first financial year	40	
41	Associated companies in the second financial year	41	
42	*Put an 'X' in box 42 if the company claims to be charged at the starting rate or the small companies' rate on any part of its profits, or is claiming marginal rate relief*		42

Enter how much profit has to be charged and at what rate of tax

Financial year *(yyyy)*	Amount of profit	Rate of tax	Tax
43	44 £	45	46 £ p
53	54 £	55	56 £ p

63	Corporation tax		total of boxes 46 and 56 63 £ p
64	Marginal rate relief	64 £ p	
65	Corporation tax net of marginal rate relief	65 £ p	
66	Underlying rate of corporation tax	66 • %	
67	Profits matched with non-corporate distributions	67	
68	Tax at non-corporate distributions rate	68 £ p	
69	Tax at underlying rate on remaining profits	69 £ p	
70	**Corporation tax chargeable**		*See note for box 70 in CT600 Guide* 70 £ p

CT600 (Short) (2006) Version 2

We will now use the data from the earlier Case Study, Loser plc (see pages 5.18 to 5.20) to show how the short calculation is completed.

Case Study

LOSER PLC: THE SHORT CALCULATION OF THE CT600

Loser plc has the following Corporation Tax computation for the CAP y/e 31/3/2009, following its decision to carry forward trading losses from y/e 31/3/2008. We will assume the tax rates and forms for the FY 2007 apply.

	£	£
Adjusted Trading Profits	500,000	
less trading loss brought forward	(100,000)	
Assessable Trading Income		400,000
Property Income		45,000
Interest Receivable		210,000
Chargeable Gains	120,000	
less capital loss brought forward	(50,000)	
		70,000
PCTCT		725,000
Taxed at full rate, less marginal relief: £725,000 x 30% =		217,500
1/40 x (£1,500,000 - £725,000) x (£725,000 / £725,000)		(19,375)
Corporation Tax		198,125

Required

Complete page 2 of the short company tax return form CT600 for Loser plc for the CAP y/e 31/3/2009. Round figures to nearest £.

State the date by which the Corporation Tax should be paid, and the date for submission of the form.

Solution

The completed form is shown on the next page.

The Corporation Tax must be paid by 1/1/2010 (no instalments are required), and the CT600 submitted by 31/3/2010.

Company tax calculation

Turnover

1	Total turnover from trade or profession (not provided in this case study)		1 £

Income

3	Trading and professional profits	3 £ 500,000	
4	Trading losses brought forward claimed against profits	4 £ 100,000	
5	Net trading and professional profits		box 3 minus box 4 5 £ 400,000
6	Bank, building society or other interest, and profits and gains from non-trading loan relationships		6 £ 210,000
11	Income from UK land and buildings		11 £ 45,000
14	Annual profits and gains not falling under any other heading		14 £ -

Chargeable gains

16	Gross chargeable gains	16 £ 120,000	
17	Allowable losses including losses brought forward	17 £ 50,000	
18	Net chargeable gains		box 16 minus box 17 18 £ 70,000
21	**Profits before other deductions and reliefs**		sum of boxes 5, 6, 11, 14 & 18 21 £ 725,000

Deductions and Reliefs

24	Management expenses under S75 ICTA 1988	24 £	
30	Trading losses of this or a later accounting period under S393A ICTA 1988	30 £	
31	*Put an 'X' in box 31 if amounts carried back from later accounting periods are included in box 30*	31	
32	Non-trade capital allowances	32 £	
35	Charges paid	35 £	
37	**Profits chargeable to corporation tax**		box 21 minus boxes 24, 30, 32 and 35 37 £ 725,000

Tax calculation

38	Franked investment income	38 £	
39	Number of associated companies in this period or	39 0	
40	Associated companies in the first financial year	40	
41	Associated companies in the second financial year	41	
42	*Put an 'X' in box 42 if the company claims to be charged at the starting rate or the small companies' rate on any part of its profits, or is claiming marginal rate relief*		42 X

Enter how much profit has to be charged and at what rate of tax

Financial year *(yyyy)*	Amount of profit	Rate of tax	Tax
43 2008	44 £ 725,000	45 30%	46 £ 217,500 p
53	54 £	55	56 £ p

63	Corporation tax		total of boxes 46 and 56 63 £ 217,500 p
64	Marginal rate relief	64 £ 19,375 p	
65	Corporation tax net of marginal rate relief	65 £ 198,125 p	
66	Underlying rate of corporation tax	66 27.33 %	
67	Profits matched with non-corporate distributions	67	
68	Tax at non-corporate distributions rate	68 £ p	
69	Tax at underlying rate on remaining profits	69 £ p	
70	**Corporation tax chargeable**		*See note for box 70 in CT600 Guide* 70 £ 198,125 p

CT600 (Short) (2006) Version 2

COMPLETING THE REMAINDER OF THE CT600

The Case Study on the last few pages has explained how page 2 of the CT600 is completed. The top part of page 3 (shown opposite) is a continuation of the tax amount calculation on page 2, and is self-explanatory. We will now describe the completion of the sections on page 3 dealing with capital allowances and losses.

information about capital allowances and balancing charges

The following are the boxes that you are most likely to need to use.

Charges and allowances are inserted into boxes 107-114. Note that balancing charges are inserted into the boxes on the right, while both capital allowances and balancing allowances together are inserted into those on the left.

The boxes are:

Boxes 107 – 108 for plant & machinery in the general pool

Boxes 109 – 110 for 'expensive' cars

Boxes 111 – 112 for industrial buildings

The capital allowances and balancing charges are then totalled into boxes 115 and 116.

Box 118 Expenditure on machinery and plant on which first year allowance is claimed.

Note that it is the expenditure, not the allowance needed here.

Box 121 Qualifying expenditure on machinery and plant on other assets.

This is again for expenditure in the CAP (for example on motor cars), excluding that in box 118.

losses, deficits and excess amounts

This section is for completion where losses have been incurred in the CAP to which the return relates (and which exceed any profits that they can be set against). The only boxes that we may need to complete are:

Box 122 Trading losses

Box 127 Property Income losses ('Schedule A Losses')

Box 131 Capital losses

79 **Tax payable under S419 ICTA 1988**		79 £ p
80 *Put an 'X' in box 80 if you completed box A11 in the Supplementary Pages CT600A*	80	
84 **Income tax deducted from gross income included in profits**		84 £ p
85 **Income tax repayable to the company**		85 £ p
86 **Tax payable - this is your self-assessment of tax payable**		total of boxes 70 and 79 minus box 84 86 £ p

Tax reconciliation

91 **Tax already paid (and not already repaid)**	91 £ p
92 **Tax outstanding**	box 86 minus box 91 92 £ p
93 **Tax overpaid**	box 91 minus box 86 93 £ p

Information about capital allowances and balancing charges

Charges and allowances included in calculation of trading profits or losses

	Capital allowances	Balancing charges
105 - 106 **Machinery and plant - long-life assets**	105 £	106 £
107 - 108 **Machinery and plant - other (general pool)**	107 £	108 £
109 - 110 **Cars outside general pool**	109 £	110 £
111 - 112 **Industrial buildings and structures**	111 £	112 £
113 - 114 **Other charges and allowances**	113 £	114 £

Charges and allowances not included in calculation of trading profits or losses

	Capital allowances	Balancing charges
115 - 116 **Non-trading charges and allowances**	115 £	116 £
117 *Put an 'X' in box 117 if box 115 includes flat conversion allowances*	117	

Expenditure

118 **Expenditure on machinery and plant on which first year allowance is claimed**		118 £
119 *Put an 'X' in box 119 if claim includes enhanced capital allowances for designated energy-saving investments*	119	
120 **Qualifying expenditure on machinery and plant on long-life assets**		120 £
121 **Qualifying expenditure on machinery and plant on other assets**		121 £

Losses, deficits and excess amounts

122 **Trading losses Case I**	calculated under S393 ICTA 1988 122 £	124 **Trading losses Case V**	calculated under S393 ICTA 1988 124 £
125 **Non-trade deficits on loan relationships and derivative contracts**	calculated under S82 FA 1996 125 £	127 **Schedule A losses**	calculated under S392A ICTA 1988 127 £
129 **Overseas property business losses Case V**	calculated under S392B ICTA 1988 129 £	130 **Losses Case VI**	calculated under S396 ICTA 1988 130 £
131 **Capital losses**	calculated under S16 TCGA 1992 131 £	136 **Excess management expenses**	calculated under S75 ICTA 1988 136 £

INTEREST AND PENALTIES

interest

Where tax is paid after the due date (or a lower amount is paid than is due) interest is charged. This applies both to large companies that need to pay by instalments, and other companies that should pay nine months and one day after the end of the CAP. The interest rates are laid down by HM Revenue & Customs, although the rates that charge for underpaid instalments are lower than the rates applying in other situations.

If a company overpays its Corporation Tax (or pays early) interest is payable to the company (although the interest rates are generally lower than amounts charged on overdue tax). Interest that is paid to the Company is taxable, but interest payable is an allowable deduction against non-trading interest.

notification of trading

Companies must inform HMRC within three months that they started trading. There is an initial penalty of £300 for failing to do so, followed by a further £60 per day for continued failure to notify.

late payment penalties

Where a company pays its instalments late a penalty of up to twice the interest charge can also be levied, but this only occurs in exceptional circumstances.

late return penalties

There are also penalties for failure to submit a Corporation Tax Return on time. These are divided into flat amount and percentage penalties:

- the initial penalties are £100 for submitting up to three months late and £200 for submitting more than three months late. These can increase for repeated occurences.
- in addition 10% of the Corporation Tax relating to the return period can be charged where the return is 6-12 months late, increasing to 20% for over 12 months.

KEEPING RECORDS

general principles

Accounting records must be retained by a business, including a company, or its agent (for example an accountant) for at least six years after the end of the accounting period. This period is extended if an enquiry is taking place.

A business will normally archive appropriate accounting records automatically for six years to satisfy the requirements of a variety of statutes, including the Companies Acts and the Limitation Act (which allows legal action to be brought on a contract for up to six years after a breach of that contract). Documents such as invoices, for example, are evidence of contracts of sale.

These records will need to be made available for a number of interested parties – and particularly in the unfortunate event of an inspection or investigation being made:

- auditors (when an audit is required)
- HM Revenue & Customs for both Corporation taxes and VAT
- Department of Work & Pensions

Typical records include:

- ledger accounts and daybooks - manual or computerised
- financial documents, eg invoices, credit notes, bank statements, cheque book stubs
- payroll records
- VAT records

records relating to tax computations

A company will need to keep for at least six years, as part of the general archiving process, a number of records which specifically relate to Corporation Tax matters. These include:

- profit & loss accounts and balance sheets
- taxation working papers, including capital allowance computations
- copies of tax returns
- invoices relating to allowable expenses and the acquisition of fixed assets
- details of non-trade income
- fixed asset schedules

Chapter Summary

- The Corporation Tax computation for a chargeable accounting period (CAP) involves combining profits from various sources, and deducting any payments made to charity under the gift aid scheme.

- In order to establish the rate at which Corporation Tax is payable, a 'profits' figure is calculated by adding UK dividends (x 100/90) to the profits chargeable to Corporation Tax (PCTCT). Where this figure is £1,500,001 or over for a 12 month period Corporation Tax is payable at the full rate (currently 30%). Where it is below this figure, different rates or marginal relief applies, according to which band the 'profit' figure falls into, and the financial year the CAP is in.

- The band limits are scaled down where there are associated companies, and where the CAP is for less than 12 months.

- Property income losses are initially set against the PCTCT of the current period, with any remaining balance carried forward to be set against the first available property income. Capital losses can only be carried forward to offset against income of the same type. There are various options for dealing with trade losses. Since the marginal rate of Corporation Tax for a medium-sized company has the highest effective rate, profits within this band should be reduced by losses when possible.

- Companies are liable to pay employers' National Insurance contributions, and to deduct Income Tax and employees' National Insurance contributions and pay them to HM Revenue & Customs. If interest payments are made to individuals, then Income Tax must be deducted from these and paid to HM Revenue & Customs.

- Corporation Tax is payable a maximum of nine months and one day after the end of the CAP. For companies paying only at the full rate, instalments are paid, based on the estimated tax payable.

- The company tax return (CT600) is due to be submitted twelve months after the end of the accounting period.

- Appropriate records must be kept for at least six years from the end of the accounting period.

Key Terms

Profits Chargeable to Corporation Tax (PCTCT)
This is the figure used as the basis for calculation of Corporation Tax for a limited company. It includes trading income, profits from investments, and chargeable gains, and is charged after gift-aid payments have been deducted. It is calculated for each chargeable accounting period (CAP) within which the company operates.

Chargeable Accounting Period (CAP)
This is the period for which the PCTCT must be calculated. It is the same as the period for which the company produces financial accounts, unless that period is for more than twelve months. In that case the financial accounting period is divided into two CAPs.

Gift-Aid
A system which allows payments that companies have made to charity to be deducted in the final calculation of PCTCT. This provides the company with tax relief on the payment.

Franked Investment Income (FII)
This non-taxable income is calculated by multiplying UK dividends received by 100/90. The FII amount is added to the PCTCT to arrive at the 'profits' figure that is used to establish the rate of Corporation Tax that is payable.

'Profits'
This figure is the PCTCT plus FII. It is used to establish the size of the company, which in turn determines the rate of Corporation Tax that is payable.

Marginal Relief
A deduction from Corporation Tax calculated at the full rate that applies at some 'profit' levels.

Associated companies
Companies are associated for Corporation Tax purposes when they are part of a group of companies, or are all controlled by the same person. The Corporation Tax band limits are divided by the number of associated companies.

CT600
The self-assessment Corporation Tax return for limited companies. One form must be completed for each CAP.

Student Activities

Answers to the asterisked (*) questions are to be found at the back of this book.

5.1* The Management Company Limited has produced accounts for the year ended 31/3/08. The accounts have been adjusted for tax purposes, and the following figures have been established.

	£
Adjusted Trading Profit (before capital allowances)	1,120,000
Capital Allowances – Plant & Machinery	143,000
Balancing Charge – Industrial Buildings	80,000
Payment to Charity under Gift-Aid scheme	45,000
Non-Trade Interest Receivable	60,000
Dividends Received from UK Company	90,000
Chargeable Gains	48,000
Rental Income	23,000

Required

Using a Corporation Tax Computation, calculate the Profits Chargeable to Corporation Tax (PCTCT) for the CAP, and the Corporation Tax payable.

Carry out all calculations to the nearest £.

5.2* The Resource Company Limited has produced accounts for the year ended 31/3/08. The accounts have been adjusted for tax purposes, and the following figures have been established.

	£
Adjusted Trading Profit (before capital allowances)	1,420,000
Capital Allowances – Plant & Machinery	193,000
Capital Allowances – Industrial Buildings	12,000
Payment to Charity under Gift-Aid scheme	8,000
Non-Trade Interest Receivable	12,000
Dividends Received from UK Company	27,000
Chargeable Gains	88,000
Capital Loss brought forward from previous year	18,000
Rental Income	92,000

Required

Using a Corporation Tax Computation, calculate the Profits Chargeable to Corporation Tax (PCTCT) for the CAP, and the Corporation Tax payable.

Carry out all calculations to the nearest £.

5.3* The Quick Company Limited has the following tax-adjusted results for the CAP y/e 31/12/07.

	£
Trading Loss	120,000
Chargeable Gains	90,000
Non-trade Interest Receivable	40,000
Rental Income	35,000
Gift-Aid Payment	10,000

The company also has capital losses brought forward of £8,000, and rental losses brought forward of £13,000.

The company wishes to obtain any relief for the offset of its trading loss as quickly as possible, and will therefore set it against the PCTCT of the current CAP.

Required

Using a Corporation Tax Computation, calculate the Profits Chargeable to Corporation Tax (PCTCT) for the CAP, and the Corporation Tax payable.

Carry out all calculations to the nearest £.

State an alternative option that may be available to this company for offsetting its trading loss.

5.4 Trade Trader Ltd has an unadjusted profit and loss account for the year ended 31/3/2008 as follows:

	£	£
Sales		720,000
less cost of sales		400,000
Gross profit		320,000
Interest receivable		50,000
Profit on disposal of fixed assets		50,000
Rental income receivable		60,000
		480,000
less expenses:		
Discounts allowed	11,000	
Salaries and wages	70,000	
Depreciation	41,000	
Bad debts written off	12,000	
Rates and insurance	13,000	
Postage and stationery	10,000	
Administration expenses	14,000	
Advertising	18,000	
Travel and entertaining	20,000	
		209,000
Net Profit		271,000

Notes:

- Administration includes £1,000 directors' speeding fines incurred while on company business.
- Advertising consists of:
  - gifts of CDs with company logos to 1000 customers totalled £8,000
  - gifts of food hampers with company logos to 400 other customers totalled £10,000
- Travel and entertaining is made up as follows:

	£
Employees' travel expenses	7,400
Employees' subsistence allowances	3,600
Entertaining customers	6,000
Entertaining staff on company trip to theme park	3,000
	20,000

The interest receivable is non-trade, and the figure in the accounts can be used for tax purposes.

The profit on sale of fixed assets resulted in a chargeable gain of £41,000.

The rental income is assessable as Property Income, and the figure in the accounts can be used for tax purposes.

Capital allowances for the period have been calculated at £11,000.

Required

1 Adjust the net profit shown to arrive at the trading income assessment for Corporation Tax purposes.

2 Calculate the PCTCT.

3 Calculate the Corporation Tax payable.

4 Complete page 2 of tax return CT600.
(A blank form is reproduced in the Appendix of this book or may be downloaded from the Student Resource pages of www.osbornebooks.co.uk or from www.hmrc.gov.uk)

Carry out all calculations to the nearest £.

5.5 Mastermind Limited is changing its accounting dates, and to accommodate this has produced one long set of financial accounts, from 1/12/2006 to 31/3/2008.

Capital allowances have already been calculated for each of the two CAPs as follows:

CAP 1/12/2006 to 30/11/2007	£8,000
CAP 1/12/2007 to 31/3/2008	£2,500

The financial accounts for the 16 months to 31/3/2008 are as follows:

	£	£
Sales		293,000
less cost of sales		155,000
Gross profit		138,000
add		
bad debts recovered		3,100
discounts received		2,000
		143,100
less expenses:		
Salaries and wages	68,500	
Rent, rates, and insurance	9,200	
Depreciation	10,000	
General expenses	15,630	
Interest payable	8,300	
Bad debts written off	12,400	
Selling expenses	15,000	
		139,030
Net Profit		4,070

The following information is also provided:

- Depreciation etc is made up as follows:

– Depreciation	£45,000
– Loss on sale of computer	£19,500
– Profit on sale of Building	£54,500

- General expenses include debt recovery fees of £800

- Selling expenses include:

– Entertaining customers	£1,930
– Gifts of diaries to customers (£6 each, with company advert)	£600

The profit on the sale of the building resulted in a chargeable gain of £45,000 on 1/3/2008.

There were no other chargeable gains in either CAP.

Required

- Adjust the financial accounts for the 16-month period, before deduction of capital allowances.
- Time-apportion the adjusted profit figure into CAPs.
- Calculate the trading income assessment for each CAP.
- Calculate the PCTCT for each CAP.
- Calculate the Corporation Tax payable in respect of each CAP.

Carry out all calculations to the nearest £.

6 Income tax – trading profits

this chapter covers . . .

In this chapter we examine:

- *the basis of business taxation of individuals*
- *what 'trading' means*
- *the basis of assessment for trading profits under Income Tax*
- *the adjustment of trading profits for Income Tax purposes*
- *capital allowances for sole traders and partnerships*
- *relief for trading losses*

PERFORMANCE CRITERIA COVERED

unit 18: PREPARING BUSINESS TAXATION COMPUTATIONS

element 18.1

prepare capital allowances computations

A *classify expenditure on capital assets in accordance with the statutory distinction between capital and revenue expenditure*

C *make adjustments for private use by business owners*

D *ensure that computations and submissions are made in accordance with current tax law and take account of current Inland Revenue practice*

element 18.2

compute assessable business income

A *adjust trading profits and losses for tax purposes*

B *make adjustments for private use by business owners*

INTRODUCTION TO BUSINESS TAXATION OF INDIVIDUALS

In this book so far we have provided an introduction to the taxes that apply to business in the UK, and looked in detail at the way that Corporation Tax is applied to various types of profits of limited companies.

In the remaining chapters of this book we are going to examine how the trading profits and gains of business are subject to Income Tax and Capital Gains Tax. This applies to organisations that have not been formed as limited companies, but are operated by individuals who are sole traders or partners.

The business activities of these individuals are not legally separate from their personal financial interests, and therefore they are subject to Income Tax and Capital Gains Tax on their income and gains from all sources. Unit 19 'Preparing Personal Taxation Computations' (covered in Osborne Books' *Personal Taxation* text) examines how Income Tax and Capital Gains Tax is calculated. In this book we will examine the impact of these taxes on individuals' **business** profits and gains.

WHAT IS TRADING?

In order to appreciate the way that Income Tax applies to those who operate a trade, we must first understand exactly what constitutes **trading** from a tax point of view. Nearly all of us buy and sell things from time to time (for example we may change our cars regularly), but we usually wouldn't think of ourselves as traders. It is important to distinguish between a trading and non-trading situation, since

- trading carried out by an individual is assessable to Income Tax as 'Trading Income'
- non-trading activities may be subject to Capital Gains Tax, or may be outside the scope of all taxation.

HM Revenue & Customs use several tests known as 'the badges of trade' to help decide whether they believe an activity should be classed as trading. The result of each of these tests will provide evidence in one direction or the other, and the final decision will be judged on the overall weight of evidence. These tests are described below.

the badges of trade

- **profit motive**

  Where profit is clearly the driving force behind the activity, then this is a strong indicator that the activity may constitute trading.

- **subject matter of the activity**

  Where the items bought and sold are of no personal use to the individual then this is further evidence of trading, and this case is strengthened if the individual already works in a situation where such items are traded. Where, however the items are used by the individual or can provide personal pleasure then this would be evidence that the activity is not trading.

- **length of ownership**

  Where items are sold shortly after acquisition then this is an indicator of trading. Where they are held for a long period it may provide evidence that it is not trading.

- **frequency of transactions**

  Where there is a series of similar transactions, then this indicates trading. A single transaction is less likely to be considered as trading.

- **supplementary work**

  Where the individual carries out work on the items (eg repairs) to make them more saleable, this is evidence of trading.

- **reasons for acquisition and sale**

  An intentional purchase and planned sale will provide evidence of trading. An item that was given to the individual, or one that was sold quickly to raise money to pay personal debts is less likely to constitute trading.

We will now illustrate the use of these indicators with a Case Study.

Case Study

DAN THE BANGER MAN: BADGES OF TRADE

Dan works as an assistant accountant, but in his spare time will often be found working on one of his cars in his garage. He usually owns a couple of cars at the same time – one to drive around in and one that he is repairing. He goes to a car auction about once every six weeks and buys a car that needs a little work, provided it is at a good price. After he has repaired the car he usually keeps it for a few weeks to use, before advertising it in his local paper and selling it, so that he can obtain the best price. Dan regards this activity as his hobby.

Required

Using the badges of trade, identify:

- the points that indicate that Dan is trading
- the points that suggest non-trading

Explain what conclusion you would reach from the balance of evidence.

Solution

The badges of trade can be interpreted as follows:

- **Profit motive**

  Dan seems to deliberately buy and sell at a profit. He buys only at auction, and sets his own selling price through his adverts. This indicates trading.

- **Subject matter**

  Dan gets personal use from the cars that he buys, and this could indicate that he is not trading. The fact that he is not employed in the car trade helps this argument.

- **Length of ownership**

  After repairing the cars, Dan only keeps them for a few weeks. Such a short time indicates trading.

- **Frequency of transactions**

  The buying and selling of cars seems to be a regular activity, with purchases being made about every six weeks. This indicates trading.

- **Supplementary work**

  Repairing the cars counts as supplementary work, and Dan deliberately buys cars that need work carrying out. This indicates trading.

- **Reason for acquisition and sale**

  Acquisition appears to be planned with the ultimate sale in mind. This indicates trading.

In conclusion . . .

Overall, nearly all indicators point to trading. The only point that indicates the opposite is that Dan uses the cars before sale. The fact that he views his activity as a hobby is not relevant in the face of such evidence.

It is likely that HM Revenue & Customs would wish to assess his income from this activity as Trading Income.

notification of starting trading

When an individual starts trading he/she must notify HM Revenue and Customs within three months. HMRC will then arrange to tax the income as 'Trading Income' under the self-assessment system as described in the next section.

THE BASIS OF ASSESSMENT OF TRADING PROFITS

Trading profits (both for sole traders and those in partnership) and professional profits are assessed to Income Tax as 'Trading Income'.

The trading income assessment for a sole trader will form part of his/her income that is taxable under Income Tax, and will be incorporated into the personal Income Tax computation. We examined this briefly in Chapter 1, and you may also have studied it in the personal taxation unit.

The assessable trading profits of a partnership are divided between the partners according to the partnership agreement, and each partner's share then forms part of their individual Income Tax computation.

basis period for assessment

Sole traders and partnerships can produce their annual accounts up to any date in the year that they choose. Once the business is established, most accounting years will consistently follow the same pattern.

Income Tax is assessed based on tax years (6 April to the following 5 April), so that all income (both business and personal) can be brought together and the tax calculated. This means that a link must be established between the profits that are generated in an accounting period and a particular tax year. This mechanism is part of the basis of assessment, and is known as the **basis period**.

For a continuing business this link is very straightforward. The normal basis of assessment for trading income is the adjusted profits for the accounting period that ends in the tax year. So for a business that produces its accounts each year to 31 December, the basis period for the tax year 2007/08 would be the accounting period 1/1/2007 to 31/12/2007.

The term 'adjusted profits' refers to profits (on an accruals basis) that have been adjusted for tax purposes, and incorporate any capital allowances. This procedure is very similar to the one that we studied in Chapters 2 and 3 in connection with Corporation Tax for limited companies.

The procedure that we need to use is summarised in the diagram on the next page. This diagram will also be useful later on, when we examine the more complicated basis of assessments that apply to businesses when they are starting trading or ceasing trading.

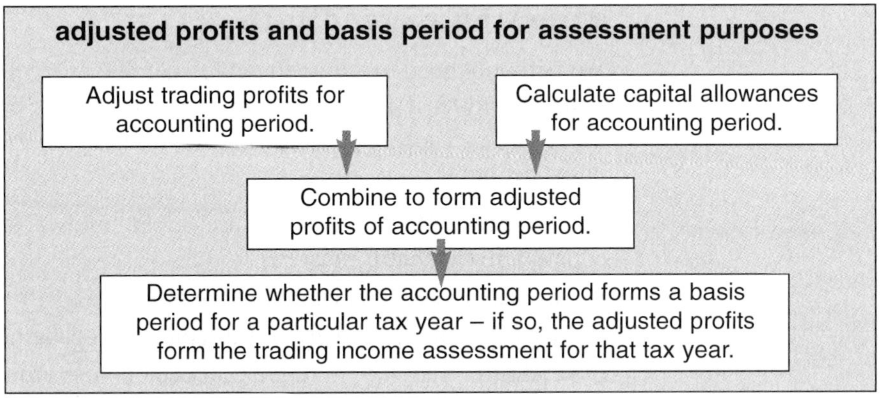

ADJUSTING THE TRADING PROFITS OF AN ACCOUNTING PERIOD

The procedure for adjusting profits for sole traders and partnerships is very similar to the one used for companies in Chapter 2. This means that you can use a lot of the knowledge gained in that area and apply it to this situation. We will firstly review the way that the procedure works, and then identify the main differences that you will encounter when dealing with trading under Income Tax rules in comparison with Corporation Tax.

review of adjusting profits

The object of adjusting the financial accounts is to make sure that:

- the only income that is credited is trading income
- the only expenditure that is deducted is allowable trading expenditure

When we adjust profits, we will start with the profit from the financial accounts, and

- deduct any income that is not trading income, and
- add back any expenditure that has already been deducted but is not allowable

adjusting income

Provided that the 'sales' amount relates entirely to trading, this figure will not need adjusting. Other income may or may not be taxable, but if it does not fall under trading income, then it will need to be adjusted for in the trading profit calculation. The following examples of non-trading income that were given in Chapter 2 are also valid in this situation:

- non-trading interest receivable
- rent receivable
- gains on the disposal of fixed assets
- dividends received

adjusting expenditure

We will only need to adjust for any expenditure accounted for in the financial accounts profit if it is not allowable. We do this by adding it back to the financial accounts profit. Expenditure that is allowable can be left unadjusted in the accounts.

The general rule for expenditure to be allowable in a trading income computation is that it must be:

- revenue rather than capital in nature, and
- 'wholly and exclusively' for the purpose of the trade

Expenditure that has a 'dual purpose' is therefore strictly speaking not allowable in its entirety (for example travel expenses for a trip combining a business conference and a holiday). However expenditure that can be divided into a part that was wholly business and a part that is wholly private could be apportioned and have the business portion allowed. This could apply to motoring expenses.

adjusting accounts of companies and individuals

- **issues not arising for sole traders and partnerships**

  The following items will not appear in the accounts that we will be adjusting for Income Tax purposes:

  - dividends payable
  - Corporation Tax
  - payments to directors

- **issues arising only for sole traders and partnerships**

  - private expenditure of the owner(s) – this is non-allowable expenditure.

    This could arise where entirely private expenditure had been paid through the business accounts (eg a personal electricity bill), or where certain expenditure needs to be apportioned between business and personal use. This latter situation is possible for expenditure such as motor expenses where business and private mileage could be used to apportion the total cost. As we will see later, there is a similar adjustment that is made to capital allowances on items with some private use.

  - drawings of the owner(s) – these are not allowable deductions.

    If the accounts have been produced following normal good accounting practice, then drawings will not appear before the net profit figure, and therefore no adjustment will be necessary. However some accounts may have been prepared to include drawing in the profit calculation, possibly under the heading of 'wages' and here the figure must be added back in the adjustment.

- taking trading goods out of the business for private use – this is also non-allowable, but requires particular care.

  In contrast to normal accounting practice, these goods need to be accounted for tax purposes at their normal selling price. This means that any profit that would have been made by selling the goods normally through the business is still assessable. If there is no other specific information to guide you, the normal mark-up profit percentage (from the accounts) should be added to the cost price when adjusting the accounts.

We will now summarise some common expenditure items that are allowable and non-allowable in the form of a table. We will then illustrate the points by means of a Case Study.

Allowable Expenditure	**Non-Allowable Expenditure**
Revenue expenditure wholly & exclusively for trade	Capital expenditure and private revenue expenditure
Cost of sales	Goods for private use
Staff salaries & wages (including employers' NIC)	Drawings of owner(s) (including self-employed NIC, pension payments and Income Tax)
Entertaining staff	Entertaining customers or suppliers
Certain gifts to customers (up to £50 each p.a., not food, drink, tobacco or vouchers)	All other gifts to customers
Trade bad debts written off	Non-trade bad debts written off
Increases in specific bad debt provisions	Increases in general bad debt provisions
Staff parking fines	All other fines for lawbreaking (owners and staff)
Capital allowances	Depreciation

Case Study

THE SOLE TRADER: ADJUSTING TRADING PROFITS

Rachel Sole is a fishmonger, operating under the trade name of 'The Sole Trader'.

Her draft accounts for the year are as follows:

	£	£
Sales		64,000
less cost of sales:		
Opening stock	6,000	
Purchases	30,000	
	36,000	
less closing stock	4,000	
		32,000
Gross profit		32,000
add: building society interest rec'd		600
		32,600
less expenses:		
Rent, Rates & Insurance	1,500	
Part Time Employee's Wages	5,500	
Employers' NIC for Part Time Employee	112	
Depreciation on Fittings	1,250	
Increase in General Provision for Bad Debts	550	
General Expenses	1,450	
Purchase of new Freezer Cabinet	1,000	
Wages drawn for self	15,100	
Personal pension contribution for self	400	
		26,862
Net Profit		5,738

Notes

1 Rachel pays the combined electricity bill for the shop and her private flat out of her personal bank account. The amount relating to the shop is calculated at £250.

2 Rachel took fish from her shop throughout the year to eat at home. The purchases figure in the accounts of £30,000 is after deducting the £1,000 cost price of this fish. Rachel's normal mark-up is 100% on cost.

3 Capital allowances have been calculated at £2,500 for the accounting period.

Required

Calculate the trading income assessment for Rachel.

Solution

		£
Net Profit per accounts		5,738
Add Back:		
Expenditure that is shown in the accounts but is not allowable		
Depreciation		1,250
Increase in General Bad Debt Provision		550
Capital expenditure (freezer)		1,000
Drawings		15,100
Personal pension contributions		400
Adjustment to reflect profit in goods taken for own use		1,000
		25,038
Deduct:		
Income that is not taxable as trading income	£	
Building Society Interest Received	600	
Allowable expenditure not shown in accounts		
Electricity for business	250	
Capital Allowances	2,500	
		(3,350)
Trading Income Assessment		21,688

Note

The adjustment for notional profit on the fish taken out of stock is based on the normal mark up of 100% of cost. This increases the value of the fish taken out of the business to its normal selling price. The mark up could also have been calculated from the accounts, where gross profit/cost of sales = 100%.

If the transaction deducting the fish at cost from the purchases had not been recorded in the accounts already, a total adjustment of £2,000 would have been required.

CAPITAL ALLOWANCES UNDER INCOME TAX

You will be relieved to learn that the calculation of capital allowances under Income Tax is nearly identical to the system under Corporation Tax, both for plant & machinery, and for industrial buildings.

Before you study this section, you may find it useful to revise capital allowances as they apply to Corporation Tax.

There are three main issues that are important regarding the capital allowances for a sole trader or partnership.

- Capital allowances are calculated for the accounting period, and are treated as allowable expenditure. If the accounting period is for less than 12 months, or between 12 months and 18 months, writing down allowances only are time apportioned. This includes the £3,000 restriction for expensive cars. This is consistent with the treatment under Corporation Tax, although you will recall that CAPs over 12 months long do not exist under that system.

- The same definitions of 'small' and 'small/medium' sized businesses apply to sole traders and partnerships as to limited companies. However, for practical purposes you can assume that all sole traders and partnerships that are used in examples are 'small' unless you are told otherwise. The 50% FYA (as noted in Chapter 3) applies under income tax to assets bought between 6/4/2006 and 5/4/2008.

- Assets that have some private use by the owner(s) of the business are treated in a special way for plant & machinery capital allowances purposes. Any asset with part private use must be held in a 'single asset pool', and the initial calculations of the allowances and balances carried forward are carried out as normal. However, only the business proportion of all allowances and charges that apply to that asset can be claimed. This is the main practical difference between preparing capital allowances under Income Tax and Corporation Tax, and can cause confusion. Remember that limited companies do not have private use, and therefore no private use adjustment applies.

We will now use a Case Study to illustrate some of the issues that we have discussed. When you are reading it, make sure, in particular, that you can understand how the private use of assets by the partners affects the computation.

Case Study

CAPITOL IDEAS: CAPITAL ALLOWANCES

Capitol Ideas is the trading name of a partnership owned and run by James and Jo Capitol. The business produces accounts to 30 June each year. It is classed as a small business for capital allowance purposes. The adjusted trading profit for the accounting period of 12 months to 30/6/2007 has already been calculated at £84,000 before deduction of capital allowances for plant & machinery.

The capital allowance computation for the last accounting period closed with written down values as follows:

- main pool £30,000
- single asset pool for car (a BMW) with 25% private use by Jo £15,000

During the accounting period the following assets were acquired and disposed of:

- On 30/11/2006 a new pick-up truck was bought for £20,000. This was to have 20% private use by James.
- On 31/12/2006 the BMW was sold for £14,000.
- On 31/12/2006 a used Audi car was bought for £25,000. This was to replace the BMW, and also had 25% private use by Jo.
- On 31/3/2007 a machine in the main pool was sold for £2,000.
- On 30/4/2007 a computer system was bought for £5,000.
- On 31/5/2007 a Ford car for staff use was bought for £11,000.

All disposal proceeds were less than original cost.

Required

- Using a plant & machinery capital allowance computation, calculate the allowances for the accounting period y/e 30/6/2007.
- Calculate the adjusted trading profits for the accounting period (after capital allowances), and state for which tax year these will form the trading income assessable profits.

Solution

The capital allowance computation is shown on the next page. The notes that follow provide explanations.

			Single Asset Pools			Capital Allowances
		Main Pool	Exp Car BMW (25% private)	Exp Car Audi (25% private)	Pick-up Truck (20% private)	
	£	£	£	£	£	£
WDV bf		30,000	15,000	-	-	
Additions without FYAs:						
Audi Car				25,000		
Ford Car		11,000				
Disposals:						
BMW			(14,000)			
Machine		(2,000)				
Sub totals		39,000	1,000	25,000	-	
WDA 25%		(9,750)		(3,000)x 75%		12,000
Balancing Allowance			(1,000) x 75%			750
Additions with FYAs:						
Pick-up	20,000					
FYA (50%)	(10,000) x 80%					8,000
					10,000	
Computer	5,000					
FYA (50%)	(2,500)					2,500
		2,500				
WDV cf		31,750	-	22,000	10,000	
Total Capital Allowances						23,250

Notes

- The only additions that do not attract FYAs are the two cars. The Audi has 25% private use (and is classed as expensive) so is kept separate, while the Ford joins the main pool.
- The disposal proceeds of the machine are deducted from the main pool.
- The WDA on the Audi is restricted to £3,000 x 75% business use. Note that the full £3,000 is used to calculate the WDV carried forward.
- The disposal of the BMW was for less than the WDV brought forward. There is therefore a balancing allowance, but this is restricted to the business use of 75%. If a balancing charge had arisen it would also have been restricted to the proportion of business use.

- The pick-up attracts a 50% FYA, but the amount claimable is 80% of this due to the private usage. The balance (after deducting the full 50%) is placed in a single asset pool due to the private usage. The computer also attracts a 50% FYA.

Calculation of trading income assessment:

	£
Adjusted trading profits (before capital allowances)	84,000
Capital allowances (as above)	(23,250)
Trading income assessment for tax year 2007/08	60,750

This amount will be then divided between the partners.

DEALING WITH TRADING LOSSES

In Chapters 2 and 5 we saw how trading losses for a limited company can be offset to reduce the amount of Corporation Tax that is payable. We will now examine the equivalent rules that apply to sole traders and partnerships under Income Tax. You will need to take particular care with loss provisions, since some rules under Income Tax and Corporation Tax are similar but not identical, and this can lead to confusion.

In this section we will examine losses that occur in continuing businesses that are using normal twelve month accounting periods. Later on when we look at the way that we deal with the commencement and cessation of a business we will also examine further loss options that can apply to those situations.

If, once profits for an accounting period have been tax-adjusted and any capital allowances deducted, the result is a minus figure a '**trading loss**' will have arisen. This will have two implications:

- The trading income assessment for the relevant tax year will be zero (not the negative profit figure). This is the tax year in which the accounting period ends – ie the basis period.
- The amount of the negative profit figure will form the trading loss, and the individual can choose how to set it off.

The choices available are as follows:

1 The trading loss can be carried forward to reduce profits from the same trade in the future. If this option is chosen the loss must be used up as quickly as possible. If the following year's profit from the same trade is less than the loss, then that profit will be reduced to nil and the balance of the loss carried on forward. This will occur as many times as is necessary to offset the whole loss.

2 The trading loss can be used to reduce (or eliminate) the total taxable income in the tax year of the loss. This set-off would be against taxable income from all sources for the relevant tax year.

3 Whether or not option (2) above is chosen, the loss can be carried back against the total taxable income from all sources in the tax year preceding the tax year of the loss. If the tax payer has sufficient loss and wishes to set against both these tax years, he/she can choose which year to set-off the loss first.

Note that one important difference between Income Tax loss set-off and the rules under Corporation Tax is that here the order of options 2 and 3 are entirely the taxpayer's choice.

Since the set offs under all the options take place before the personal allowance (currently £5,225) is deducted, there is a danger that this tax-free amount will be wasted in some situations.

The following diagram illustrates the options, using as an example a sole trader making up accounts to the 31st December each year. A loss arises in the year ended 31/12/2007, which forms the basis period of the tax year 2007/08.

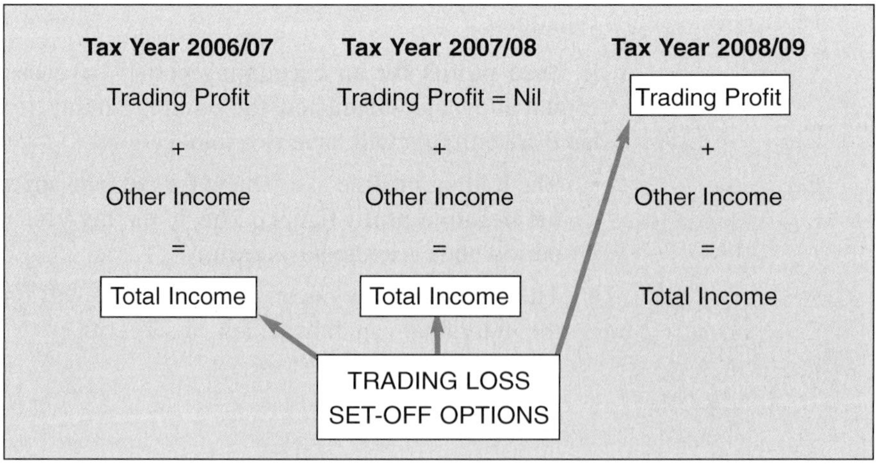

'Other Income' could include property income, employment income, savings income, and dividend income.

Case Study

DOWNHILL TRADING: TRADING LOSS OPTIONS

Downhill Trading is a business operated by Dawn Hill, who sells skiing equipment. The business has the following tax-adjusted trading results for the three twelve month accounting periods to 31/12/2008. Dawn also has other taxable income for the tax years 2006/07 – 2008/09 as stated below.

Accounting periods	**y/e 31/12/06**	**y/e 31/12/07**	**y/e 31/12/08**
	£	£	£
Trading Profit/(Loss)	12,000	(15,000)	16,000
Tax Years	**2006/07**	**2007/08**	**2008/09**
	£	£	£
Other Income	4,000	5,000	5,500

Required

State the options available for offsetting the £15,000 trading loss incurred in the y/e 31/12/2007. Demonstrate the effects on the relevant total income figures, and comment briefly on the implications of each option.

Solution

The tax year of the loss will be 2007/08, since the accounting period y/e 31/12/2007 ends in (i.e. is the basis period for) this tax year. The other two accounting periods (y/e 31/12/2006 and y/e 31/12/2008) form the basis periods for 2006/07 and 2008/09 respectively.

We will show the options one by one, but with all the three tax years' details shown in columnar form for reference. There are four options in this situation.

Option A

The trading loss could be carried forward and set against the trading income assessment of 2008/09. Since this profit is larger than the loss the whole loss could be offset in this way. The three years would look as follows:

	2006/07	**2007/08**	**2008/09**
	£	£	£
Trading Profits	12,000	0	16,000
less loss relief			(15,000)
			1,000
Other Income	4,000	5,000	5,500
Total Income	16,000	5,000	6,500

An advantage of this option is that there is sufficient total income in each tax year to utilise nearly all Dawn's personal allowances. However Dawn would have to wait until the tax for 2008/09 was payable until she felt the tax benefit of the loss in cash saved.

Option B

The trading loss could be set against the other income of the tax year of the loss (2007/08). Due to the size of the loss this will not be sufficient to offset the whole loss. The balance of the loss could then be carried back to the previous tax year and set against the total income. This would give the following figures.

	2006/07	**2007/08**	**2008/09**
	£	£	£
Trading Profits	12,000	0	16,000
Other Income	4,000	5,000	5,500
	16,000	5,000	1,500
less loss relief	**(10,000)**	**(5,000)**	
Total Income	6,000	-	21,500

A disadvantage of this approach would be that the personal allowance in 2007/08 is wasted, since there is no income in that tax year. However, Dawn would get a tax refund for 2006/07 almost immediately, assuming that she had already paid Income Tax based on total income of £16,000.

Option C

The trading loss could be set against the other income of the tax year of the loss (2007/08), as in option B. The balance of the loss could then be carried forward to the next tax year and set against the profits of the same trade only. This would give the following figures.

	2006/07	**2007/08**	**2008/09**
	£	£	£
Trading Profits	12,000	0	16,000
less loss relief			**(10,000)**
			6,000
Other Income	4,000	5,000	5,500
	16,000	5,000	11,500
less loss relief	**-**	**(5,000)**	
Total Income	16,000	-	11,500

A disadvantage of this approach would be that the personal allowance in 2007/08 is wasted, since there is no income in that tax year. Dawn would pay no tax for that year, but would have to wait to feel any further tax effect of the loss until payment of the 2008/09 tax.

Option D

The trading loss could be set against the other income of the previous tax year (2006/07). This would accommodate the whole loss. This would give the following figures:

	2006/07	**2007/08**	**2008/09**
	£	£	£
Trading Profits	12,000	0	16,000
Other Income	4,000	5,000	5,500
	16,000	5,000	21,500
less loss relief	**(15,000)**	-	
Total Income	1,000	5,000	21,500

A disadvantage of this approach would be that most of the personal allowance in 2006/07 is wasted, since there is only £1,000 of income in that tax year. However Dawn would get a tax refund for the tax paid for 2006/07 almost immediately, assuming she had already paid Income Tax based on a total income of £16,000.

Chapter Summary

- Trading profits of sole traders and partners are subject to Income Tax, and are included in their computations along with personal income. Evidence indicators called 'badges of trade' are used to establish whether an individual is trading or not.

- The normal basis of assessment for the trading income of a business is the adjusted profits (after capital allowances) of the accounting period that ends in the tax year. The accounts of sole traders and partnerships are tax-adjusted in a similar way to those of a limited company. Specific expenditure that is non-allowable in arriving at trading profit includes owners' drawings, private expenditure, and trading goods taken from the business for private use.

- Capital allowances for both plant & machinery and industrial buildings can be claimed by the self-employed in a similar way to companies. Assets that have a private use element by the business owners need to be kept in a single asset pool, and only the business proportion of the capital allowances can be claimed.

- Where the adjusted trading profits (after capital allowances) result in a negative figure, the trading income assessment is zero, and a trading loss is formed that can be relieved in several ways. It may be carried forward and set-off against the first available profits of the same trade. It may alternatively be set against the total income of the tax year in which the loss was incurred, and / or the previous tax year.

Key Terms

Badges of Trade — Indicators that are used to determine whether an activity constitutes trading, and should therefore be taxed as such.

Basis Period — The term that describes the link between accounting periods and tax years. For a continuing business, the basis period for a particular tax year is the 12-month accounting period that ends in that tax year.

Adjusted Trading Profits — Trading profits that have been adjusted for tax purposes by excluding income not taxable as trading income and non-allowable expenditure.

Trading Income Assessment — The taxable trading profit for the tax year. It is made up of adjusted trading profits for the basis period, after deducting any capital allowances.

Plant & Machinery One of the major fixed asset categories for capital allowance purposes. It includes vehicles and computers.

Industrial Buildings Capital allowances are available for this category of fixed assets provided the building is used for a qualifying purpose.

First Year Allowances Allowances are available on certain plant and machinery in the CAP in which the acquisition takes place. The rates available are 100%, 50% and 40%. There are no first year allowances currently available for industrial buildings.

Writing Down Allowances Allowances are available at 25% of the pool value for plant and machinery, and at 4% of the eligible cost for industrial buildings, Both these figures relate to 12-month accounting periods, and are time-apportioned for shorter periods and longer periods up to 18 months.

Written Down Value (Plant & Machinery)
This term relates to the balance at the end of an accounting period that remains in a plant & machinery pool. It represents the part of the pool value that has not yet been claimed as allowances, and is carried forward to the next accounting period.

Balancing Allowance (Plant & Machinery)
This allowance can be claimed when an asset is sold for less than the written down value (unrelieved expenditure) in a single asset pool.

Balancing Charge (Plant & Machinery)
This is the opposite of an allowance, and occurs when the disposal proceeds of an asset in a single asset pool are more than the written down value (unrelieved expenditure). It is in effect a reclaiming of allowances previously obtained.

Trading Loss This occurs when the adjusted trading profits after deducting capital allowances produces a negative figure. The negative figure is the trading loss, whilst the trading income assessment is zero.

Loss Relief The offsetting of the trading loss against profits or total income, according to legislation. This may be against future profits from the same trade, or against total income of the current and / or previous tax year.

Student Activities

Answers to the asterisked (*) questions are to be found at the back of this book.

6.1* Michelle Flatley has moved home seven times in the last five years, and currently lives in a house valued at £500,000. Her first property was a small studio apartment that she was left by her uncle. It was valued at £40,000. After carrying out some renovations she moved in, and stayed three months before selling the property for £60,000 and investing the proceeds in her next flat. She has continued this procedure with all the properties that she has owned, always renovating with a view to a prospective buyer, and always making a profit by timing the sale carefully.

Required

Using each of the 'badges of trade', explain the issues that provide evidence that she is trading, and those that point to non-trading.

6.2* The following items appear in a sole trader's profit and loss account (before the net profit figure). You are calculating an adjusted trading profit for tax purposes. State in each case whether:

- the item should be added to the net profit, or
- the item should be deducted from the net profit, or
- the item should be ignored

1. depreciation of vehicles
2. loss on sale of fixed assets
3. building society interest received
4. dividends received
5. owner's drawings
6. profit on sale of fixed asset
7. increase in general provision for bad debts
8. gifts of food hampers (with company adverts) to customers, costing £45 per recipient.
9. decrease in specific bad debt provision
10. owner's self-employed national insurance contribution
11. employers' national insurance contributions regarding employees
12. owner's private expenses

6.3* Vikram Singh is in business as a sole trader. The unadjusted profit and loss account for the year ended 31/1/2008 is as follows:

	£	£
Sales		700,000
less cost of sales		420,000
Gross profit		280,000
Bank interest received		12,000
Rental income		10,000
		302,000
less expenses:		
Salaries and wages	78,000	
Depreciation	22,000	
Loss on sale of fixed assets	4,000	
Administration expenses	11,600	
Advertising	8,000	
Overdraft interest payable	2,000	
Travel and entertaining	10,000	
Pension contributions	7,400	
Bad debts and provisions	15,000	
		158,000
Net Profit		144,000

Notes

- Salaries and wages include £18,000 drawn by Vikram.
- Advertising includes:
  - gift-vouchers given to 100 top customers £3,000
  - gifts of diaries with company logos to 200 other customers £1,000
- Travel and entertaining is made up as follows:

	£
Employees' travel expenses	2,000
Vikram's business travel expenses	3,500
Entertaining customers	4,500
	10,000

- Pension contributions consist of:

Contribution regarding employees	5,000
Contribution regarding Vikram	2,400
	7,400

- Bad debts and provisions is made up of:

Trade bad debts written off	10,400
Increase in specific bad debt provision	4,600
	15,000

- Capital allowances for the accounting period have been calculated at £23,000.

Required:

Adjust the net profit shown to arrive at the trading income assessment for the tax year 2007/08.

6.4 Candies & Cakes is the trading name of a shop owned and run by John Candy. The business produces accounts to 30 June each year. It is classed as a small business for capital allowance purposes. The adjusted trading profit for the accounting period of twelve months to 30/6/2007 has already been calculated at £12,000 before deduction of capital allowances for plant & machinery.

The capital allowance computation for the last accounting period closed with written down values as follows:

• main pool	£25,000
• single asset pool for car with 40% private use by John	£10,000

During the accounting period the following assets were acquired and disposed of:

- On 30/11/2006 a new 'low emission' car was bought for £26,000. This was to have 40% private use by John.
- On 30/11/2006 the original car used partly privately by John was sold for £4,000.
- On 31/3/2007 a computer system was bought for £2,000.
- On 31/3/2007 a food processor was sold for £200.
- On 30/4/2007 a new shop counter was bought for £3,000.

All disposal proceeds were less than original cost.

Required:

- Using a plant & machinery capital allowance computation, calculate the allowances for the accounting period y/e 30/6/2007.
- Calculate the adjusted trading profit or loss for the accounting period (after capital allowances).
- Explain any alternative options that are available to John, following the results of the last task.

6.5 Stan and Anne have run their partnership manufacturing business for many years, producing accounts up to the 31 March each year. At the start of April 2007 the following written down balances were brought forward for Plant & Machinery capital allowance purposes:

Main Pool	£66,300
Electronic Machine (short life asset)	£2,000
Expensive Car (80% business use BMW)	£16,000

They had bought a new factory on 1/4/2003 for £200,000 (exc. land), and claimed WDAs each year since. On 1/4/2007 they sold that factory for £190,000 (exc. land), and moved into a larger factory costing a total of £350,000 made up as follows:

Land	£50,000
Land Preparation	£10,000
Admin Offices	£60,000
Warehouse	£60,000
Manufacturing	£170,000

The Profit & Loss Account for the year ended 31/3/2008 was as follows:

	£	£
Sales		1,200,000
less cost of sales:		
Raw materials	300,000	
Direct labour	450,000	
Factory overheads	200,000	
		950,000
Gross profit		250,000
less:		
Administration salaries	50,000	
Selling & distribution expenses	15,000	
Depreciation etc	40,000	
General expenses	35,000	
		140,000
Net profit		110,000

Notes

- The direct labour relates to 20 employees of the partnership, and includes £5,000 employers' national insurance contributions.
- The administration salaries include £20,000 drawn by Stan, and £25,000 drawn by Anne. All private motor expenses are included in these drawings.
- The 'depreciation etc' figure is made up as follows:

	£
Depreciation on plant & cars	32,000
Loss on sale of BMW car sold for £12,000	3,000
Depreciation on Factory One	6,000
Gain on sale of Vauxhall car, sold for £4,000 on 1/12/07	(1,000)

- A used Range Rover (80% business use) was bought on 1/5/07 for £28,000 to replace the BMW.
- A new Ford Focus was bought on 1/12/07 to replace the Vauxhall. It had 100% business use and cost £11,000.
- There were no other acquisitions or disposals of fixed assets.
- General expenses include the following items:

	£
Bad Debts written off	3,000
Reduction in General Bad Debt Provision from £12,000 to £8,000	(4,000)
Office Party for all 20 employees	1,500
Entertaining customers	2,000

You are required to calculate:

- The Industrial Building Allowance for the accounting period y/e 31/3/2008.
- The Plant & Machinery Capital Allowances for the same period.
- Trading Income assessment for the partnership for 2007/08, after incorporating the above capital allowances.

7 Income tax – further issues

this chapter covers . . .

In this chapter we examine:

- *what happens when businesses start trading*
- *what happens when businesses cease trading*
- *dividing trading profits between partners*
- *dealing with changes in a partnership*
- *a review of National Insurance for the self-employed*
- *dates of payment for Income Tax and interest & penalties chargeable*
- *completion of the tax return pages for the self-employed and partners*
- *the maintenance of appropriate records*

PERFORMANCE CRITERIA COVERED

unit 18: PREPARING BUSINESS TAXATION COMPUTATIONS

element 18.1

prepare capital allowances computations

F *give timely and constructive advice to clients on the maintenance of accounts and the recording of information relevant to tax returns*

element 18.2

compute assessable business income

C *divide profits and losses of partnerships amongst partners*

D *apply the basis of assessment for unincorporated businesses in the opening and closing years*

E *identify the due dates of payment of Income Tax by unincorporated businesses including payments on account*

F *identify the National Insurance Contributions payable by self-employed individuals*

G *complete correctly the self-employed and partnership supplementary pages to the Tax Return for individuals, together with relevant claims and elections, and submit them within statutory time limits*

I *give timely and constructive advice to clients on the maintenance of accounts and the recording of information relevant to tax returns*

WHEN BUSINESSES START TRADING

In the last chapter we saw that the basis of assessment that applies when businesses have been trading for some time is the profits of the twelve month accounting period that ends in the tax year. This normal basis is known as the 'current year basis'. We now need to examine the special rules that operate before the normal basis can apply – in the first years of a new business. These rules apply to both sole traders and partnerships, and are designed so that all the profits throughout the life of a business are certain to be assessed in at least one particular tax year. We do not have an equivalent situation for limited companies, since under Corporation Tax each chargeable accounting period is assessed separately, with no need for basis periods.

A major issue to note is that right from the start of the business, accounts will be produced for the accounting periods that the business owners decide upon. These accounts will then be adjusted for tax purposes, including calculating capital allowances for the accounting period. Only when that has been carried out does the procedure relating to basis periods that we will now examine come into play.

We must initially determine which is the tax year in which the new business will first be assessed to Income Tax. The rule for this is straightforward – the first tax year in which a new business' profits are assessed is the tax year in which the business starts. Starting with this tax year, there are rules about exactly what profits from what period of time will be assessed in each of the first tax years. Because different businesses will have different accounting periods we will need to apportion the tax-adjusted trading profits (after capital allowances) to match these basis periods.

basis periods in the opening years

In the following summary that covers the majority of situations, 'accounting date' refers to a date up to which accounts are produced.

	tax year	basis period
1	the tax year in which the business starts	from the start date to the next 5 April
2	the next (second) tax year	the 12 month period that ends on the accounting date in the second tax year or (if that's impossible because the accounting period isn't long enough) the first 12 months of the business
3	the third tax year	normal 'current year basis' - the 12 month accounting period that ends in the third tax year

For example, if a new business starts trading on 1 January 2007, and produces annual accounts each year to 31 December, the following would apply.

The first tax year – the tax year in which business starts – is 2006/07.

The basis period for the tax year 2006/07 will be 1/1/2007 – 5/4/2007.

The second tax year will be the next year, 2007/08.

The basis period for the tax year 2007/08 will be the 12 months to 31/12/2007.

This is the 12-month period ending on the accounting date in the second tax year.

The third tax year will be the next year, 2008/09.

The basis period for the tax year 2008/09 will be the 12 months to 31/12/2008.

This is the normal 'current year' basis – the 12-month accounting period that ends in the third tax year.

This is demonstrated on the following time-line diagram.

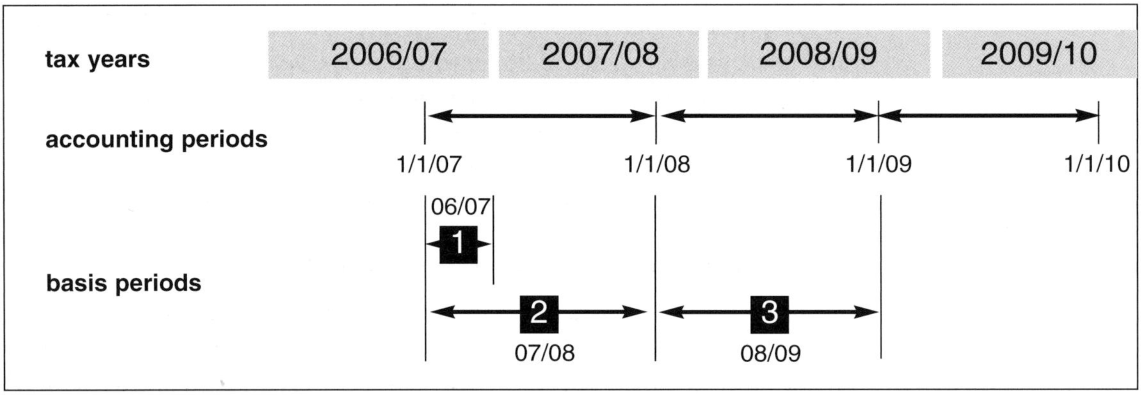

You can see that in this example there is a period of time that relates to two basis periods: the period 1/1/2007 to 5/4/2007 forms the basis period for 2006/07, but is also part of the year ended 31/12/2007 that forms the basis period for 2007/08. This is a common occurrence, and is known as an overlap period. The profits arising in that period are known as overlap profits. These profits are effectively assessed twice – once in each tax year. Only when the business ceases trading can such overlap profits reduce the final trading income assessment.

The rules and examples used so far will enable you to deal with the vast majority of situations for a new business. The only exception occurs when a business starts in one tax year and then produces a long first set of accounts that end in the third tax year. Since there is no accounting end date in the second tax year the previous summary does not apply. Instead, this is dealt with as follows:

- the basis period for the second tax year is 6th April to 5th April – i.e. the actual tax year
- the basis period for the third tax year is the 12 months leading up to the accounting date in the third tax year

The following diagram gives a comprehensive view of all possibilities for the second tax year in the form of a flowchart.

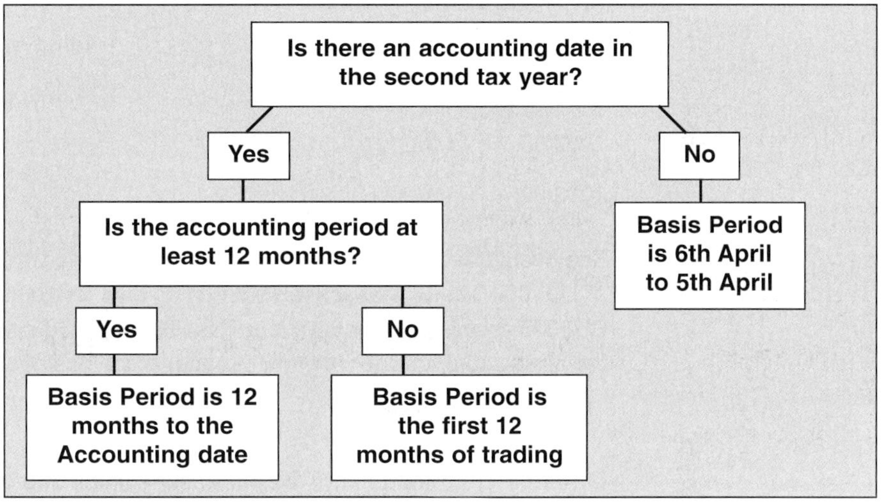

time-apportionment of trading profits

Each accounting period for the business will have adjusted trading profits. These profit figures will incorporate capital allowances that will have been worked out based on the same accounting period. The adjusted trading profits will then need to be matched to the basis periods that we have just examined, using time-apportionment where necessary. When carrying out time-apportionment, note that

- we will use whole months – each one assumed to be 1/12 of a calendar year
- the few days between 31 March and 5 April can be ignored – so for example the period 1 January to 5 April will be treated as exactly 3 months

We will follow both these practices in all examples and in the examination. These calculation methods are acceptable by HM Revenue & Customs.

example: time-apportionment of profits

Using the data from the previous example we will now show how the time-apportionment of profits is carried out.

The adjusted trading profits for the business (after capital allowances) have been calculated as:

1 January 2007 – 31 December 2007	£24,000
1 January 2008 – 31 December 2008	£30,000

Using the basis periods calculated earlier, these profits are used to form trading income assessments for the first few tax years of the business as follows:

Tax Year	Basis Period	trading income assessment	
2006/07	1/1/2007 – 5/4/2007	£24,000 x 3/12	= £6,000
2007/08	1/1/2007 – 31/12/2007		= £24,000
2008/09	1/1/2008 – 31/12/2008		= £30,000

The overlap profits are those arising from the period 1/1/2007 – 5/4/2007, and are £6,000, which is assessed both on its own for 2006/07, and as part of the £24,000 assessment for 2007/08. This £6,000 is deductible in the calculation of the assessable profit for the final tax year of the business when trading ceases.

Different combinations of business start dates and accounting periods will produce various basis periods and amounts of overlap profits. If accounts are always produced up to 31 March, there will not be any overlap profits. The key to accurate calculations is to learn and follow the rules outlined earlier in this chapter, being especially careful to identify each tax year accurately. Mistakes can also easily be made by incorrectly counting months when carrying out time-apportionment. If you find it helpful to sketch a time-line diagram, then this can form part of your workings.

The following Case Study illustrates a variety of possible situations. Examine it carefully to make sure that you could arrive at the same results without assistance.

Case Study

FRESHER AND CO: ASSESSING NEW BUSINESSES

Fresher and Company is an accountancy practice that has several new clients who have recently commenced trading.

John Able started trading on 1 July 2006. He produced accounts with adjusted trading profits (after capital allowances) as follows:

1/7/2006 – 30/6/2007	£18,000
1/7/2007 – 30/6/2008	£30,000
1/7/2008 – 30/6/2009	£33,000

The partnership of Joe and Jo Barclay started trading on 1 December 2006. They produced accounts with adjusted trading profits (after capital allowances) as follows:

1/12/2006 – 31/3/2007 (4 months)	£20,000
1/4/2007 – 31/3/2008	£50,000
1/4/2008 – 31/3/2009	£60,000

Karen Cabot started trading on 1 October 2006. She produced accounts with adjusted trading profits (after capital allowances) as follows:

1/10/2006 – 30/6/2007 (9 months)	£27,000
1/7/2007 – 30/6/2008	£42,000
1/7/2008 – 30/6/2009	£47,000

David Daley started trading on 1 November 2006. He produced accounts with adjusted trading profits (after capital allowances) as follows:

1/11/2006 – 31/12/2007 (14 months)	£28,000
1/1/2008 – 31/12/2008	£26,000
1/1/2009 – 31/12/2009	£29,000

Edgar Evans started trading on 1 January 2007. He produced accounts with adjusted trading profits (after capital allowances) as follows:

1/1/2007 – 31/7/2008 (19 months)	£47,500
1/8/2008 – 31/7/2009	£36,000
1/8/2009 – 31/7/2010	£41,000

Required

For each of the clients, calculate the assessable profits for each of their first three tax years, and show the amount of any overlap profits, and how it has arisen.

Solution

John Able

Tax Year	Basis Period	trading income assessment	
2006/07	1/7/2006 – 5/4/2007	£18,000 x 9/12	= £13,500
2007/08	1/7/2006 – 30/6/2007		= £18,000
2008/09	1/7/2007 – 30/6/2008		= £30,000

The overlap profits are £13,500, and relate to the period 1/7/2006 – 5/4/2007, which is assessed in both 2006/07 and 2007/08. The following diagram shows the periods.

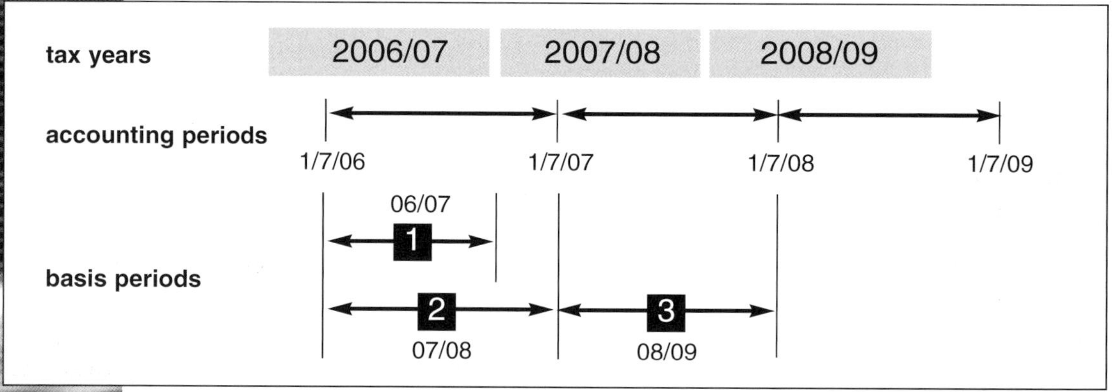

Joe and Jo Barclay

Tax Year	Basis Period	trading income assessment
2006/07	1/12/2006 – 5/4/2007	= £20,000
2007/08	1/4/2007 – 31/3/2008	= £50,000
2008/09	1/4/2008 – 31/3/2009	= £60,000

There are no overlap profits for this business, since the accounting date of 31 March has been chosen. The diagram on the next page shows the periods.

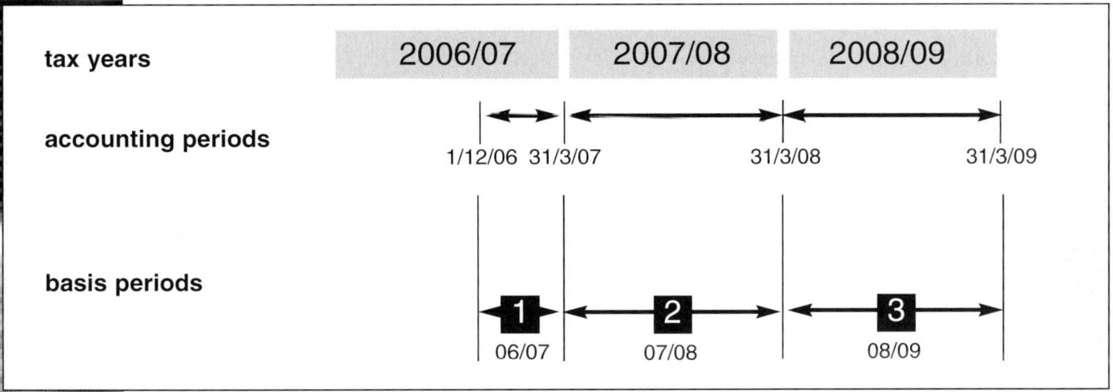

Karen Cabot

Tax Year	Basis Period	trading income assessment	
2006/07	1/10/2006 – 5/4/2007	£27,000 x 6/9	= £18,000
2007/08	1/10/2006 – 30/9/2007	£27,000 + (£42,000 x 3/12)	= £37,500
2008/09	1/7/2007 – 30/6/2008		= £42,000

This situation is a little more complicated than those seen so far.

- Note that the apportionment for the first tax year is 6/9 since the first accounting period is for only nine months.
- For the second tax year there is no 12-month period ending on the accounting date, because the accounting period is only 9 months. This means that the alternative of the first 12 months of the business must be used.
- The overlap profits total £28,500, and arise from two separate periods:

  1/10/2006 – 5/4/2007 (profits of £18,000), and

  1/7/2007 – 30/9/2007 (profits of £42,000 x 3/12 = £10,500)

The diagram on the next page shows the periods.

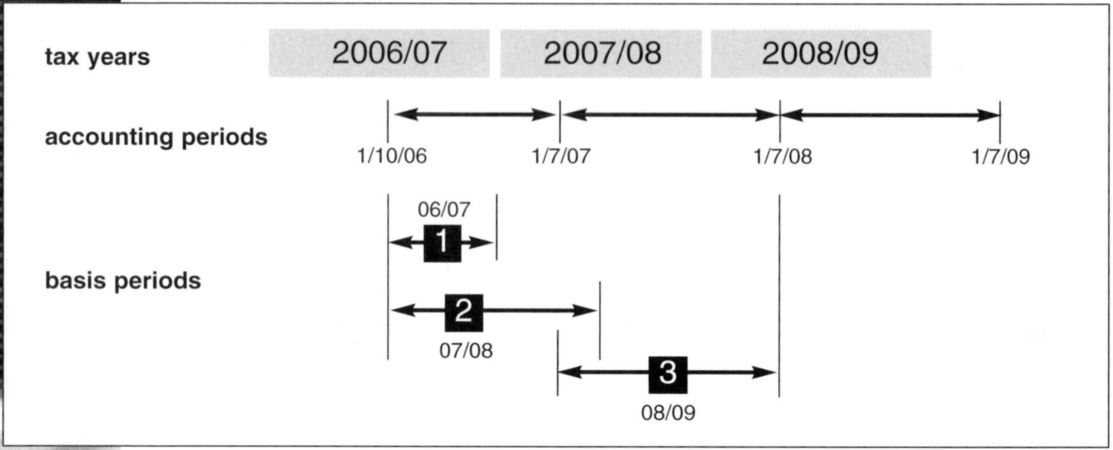

David Daley

Tax Year	Basis Period	trading income assessment	
2006/07	1/11/2006 – 5/4/2007	£28,000 x 5/14	= £10,000
2007/08	1/1/2007 – 31/12/2007	£28,000 x 12/14	= £24,000
2008/09	1/1/2008 – 31/12/2008		= £26,000

The overlap profits are 3/14 x £28,000 = £6,000, and relate to the period 1/1/2007 – 5/4/2007, which is assessed in both 2006/07 and 2007/08.

The fact that 5 + 12 = 17 months of the 14-month period profits have been assessed confirms the 3 months that have been assessed twice. The following diagram shows the periods.

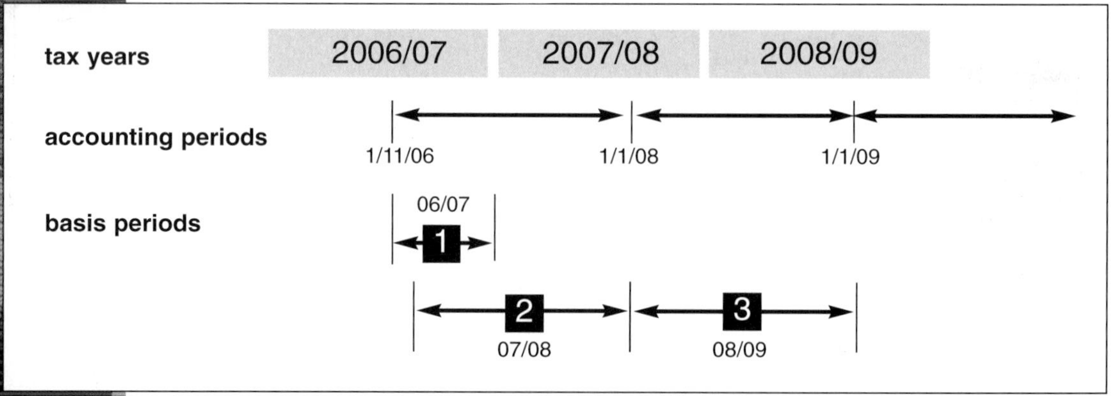

Edgar Evans

Note that we have a situation here where there is no accounting date in the second tax year, and we will therefore follow the special rules noted earlier that apply to the second and third tax years.

Tax Year	**Basis Period**	**trading income assessment**	
2006/07	1/1/2007 – 5/4/2007	£47,500 x 3/19	= £7,500
2007/08	6/4/2007 – 5/4/2008	£47,500 x 12/19	= £30,000
2008/09	1/8/2007 – 31/7/2008	£47,500 x 12/19	= £30,000

The overlap profits are 8/19 x £47,500 = £20,000, and relate to the period 1/8/2007 – 5/4/2008, which is assessed in both 2007/08 and 2008/09. The second and third years are therefore where the overlap occurs in this situation.

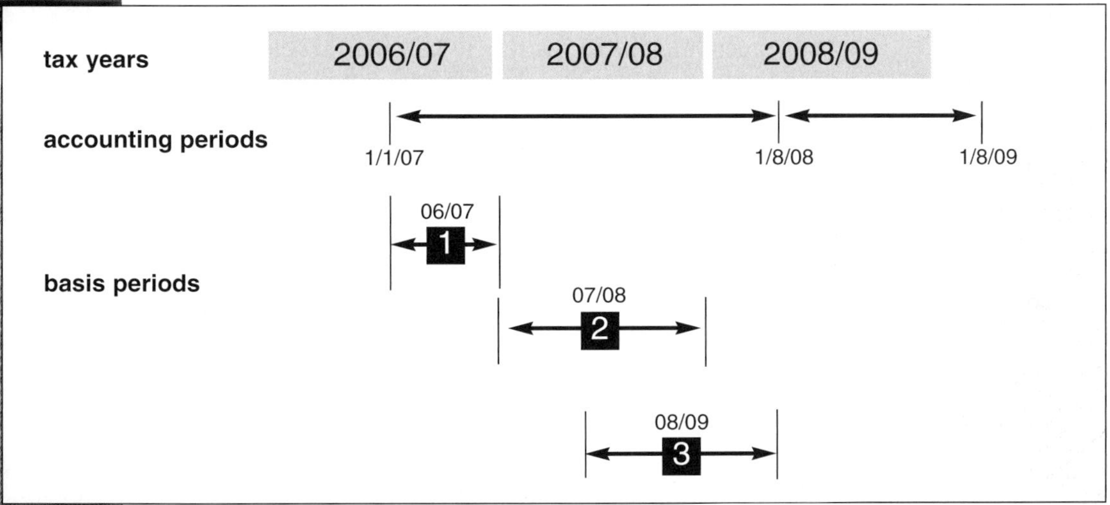

TRADING LOSSES IN OPENING YEARS

Where a loss occurs in the first few years of a new business, the same options that we saw in the last chapter are available. These are:

1 The trading loss can be carried forward to reduce profits from the same trade in the future.

2 The trading loss can be used to reduce (or eliminate) the total taxable income in the tax year of the loss.

3 Whether or not option (2) above is chosen, the loss can be carried back against the total taxable income from all sources in the tax year preceding the tax year of the loss.

In addition to these alternatives, where a loss occurs in the first four tax years of a new business, a further option is available. This allows the loss to be set against the total taxable income of the previous three tax years – earliest year first.

This effectively allows the loss to be carried back against other income two years before it would otherwise be allowed. This may have certain advantages:

- it would probably mean a refund of tax previously paid could be obtained quite quickly
- if the loss occurs early enough in the new life of the new business it may mean that the loss can be set against income from a previous source (for example employment)

calculating the loss

When a loss occurs in the early years of a business it is linked to a tax year, using the same basis periods that we have just examined. Where the accounting period relates to just one tax year, the trading assessment for that tax year is nil, and the taxpayer then chooses how to offset the loss (just as described in the last chapter).

Where a loss occurs in an accounting period that forms part of the basis periods for two tax years, the overlapping part of the loss is only counted in the first of the two tax years. For the other tax year the overlapping period is considered to just have a profit of nil. This mechanism ensures that there is no carry forward of 'overlap losses,' since they do not exist.

Case Study

JUAN LOSS: EARLY YEARS LOSS

Juan Loss left his job (where he earned £20,000 per year), and started a new business on 1 January 2007, and produced accounts to 31 December each year. The adjusted results (after capital allowances) were as follows:

1 January 2007 – 31 December 2007 loss of £24,000

1 January 2008 – 31 December 2008 profit of £30,000

Required

- Calculate the trading income assessments for the first three tax years of Juan's new business.
- Calculate the amounts of any loss, and state the earliest tax years in which the losses could be used against total income.

Solution

Tax Year	Basis Period	Trading Income Assessment	Trading Loss
2006/07	1/1/2007 – 5/4/2007	£Nil	(£24,000) x 3/12 = (£6,000)
2007/08	1/1/2007 – 31/12/2007	£Nil	(£24,000) less allocated (£,6000) = (£18,000)
2008/09	1/1/2008 – 31/12/2008	£30,000	-

The 2006/07 trading loss of £6,000 can be set against Juan's total taxable income of the year 2003/04 (3 years before 2006/07). His employment income will clearly cover this amount.

The 2007/08 trading loss of £18,000 can be set against his total income in 2004/2005 (three years before the year of the loss). Again his employment income will be sufficient to offset the loss.

WHEN BUSINESSES STOP TRADING

basis periods

When a business closes down and stops trading, the last tax year in which the business is taxed is the tax year in which trading ceases. For this tax year only there is a special rule regarding the basis period, so that no period of time is missed out for assessment purposes.

The basis period for the final tax year is from the end of the basis period of the previous tax year to the date that the business ceases i.e. all profits that have not yet been assessed.

The previous year will have been assessed on the normal current year basis, so this means that the final basis period will run from the accounting date in that tax year to the date the business stops. The profits of this final period will be reduced by any overlap profits that are brought forward from the start of the business.

Take, for example, a sole trader who has been in business for several years, making accounts up to 31 December. He ceases trading on 30 June 2008, with the following adjusted profits (after capital allowances) for the final accounting periods:

1/1/2007 – 31/12/2007	£25,000
1/1/2008 – 30/6/2008 (6 months)	£15,000

There are overlap profits of £6,000 brought forward from when he started the business.

The assessable profits for the last two tax years of the business are:

Tax Year	Basis Period	trading income assessment	
2007/08	1/1/2007 – 31/12/2007		£25,000
2008/09	1/1/2008 – 30/6/2008		£15,000
		less overlap profits	(£6,000)
			£9,000

The mechanism for basis periods at the beginning and end of a business, and the way that overlap profits are deducted in the final tax year means that over the whole life of the business all profits are assessed. Therefore,

total adjusted profits over the life of the business

= total assessments over the life of the business

As well as showing that the system has some fairness, this also gives us a useful way to check total assessments if we are presented with data for a business from start to finish. The following Case Study will demonstrate this.

Case Study

HOLE TRADING: ASSESSMENTS THROUGHOUT A BUSINESS

Hole Trading is a shop run by Roger Hole that specialises in caving equipment. The business started on 1/6/2005, and ceased trading on 31/12/2008. The accounts were produced annually up to 31 May, and the adjusted profits (after capital allowances) were as follows:

	£
1/6/2005 – 31/5/2006	18,000
1/6/2006 – 31/5/2007	36,000
1/6/2007 – 31/5/2008	24,000
1/6/2008 – 31/12/2008 (7 months)	21,000
Total	99,000

Required

Calculate the trading income assessments for each tax year in which the business will be assessed.

Solution

2005/06	1/6/2005 – 5/4/2006	£18,000 x 10/12	= £15,000
2006/07	1/6/2005 – 31/5/2006		= £18,000
	(overlap profits 1/6/2005 - 5/4/2006 £15,000)		
2007/08	1/6/2006 – 31/5/2007		= £36,000
2008/09	1/6/2007 – 31/12/2008	£24,000 + £21,000	= £45,000
		less overlap profits	(£15,000)
			£30,000

The trading income assessments for the four years that the business is taxed total (£15,000 + £18,000 + £36,000 + £30,000) = £99,000. This agrees with the total adjusted profits over the life of the business.

capital allowances when a business ceases

Capital allowances are calculated separately for each accounting period of a business, and the result forms part of the adjusted trading profits of each accounting period.

When a business ceases capital allowances will need to be calculated for the final accounting period, but special care must be taken since

- there can be <u>no</u> WDA or FYA in this last period
- all remaining assets will have been disposed of by the business
- balancing allowances and / or balancing charges will occur for all pools (including the main pool) since there can be no written down values to carry forward

Where there is partial private use of assets any allowances or charges will need to reflect only the business proportion of the asset use. However, you may remember that balancing allowances and charges are not time-apportioned if we have long or short accounting periods, so at least that will not create a complication.

Any asset bought from the business by the owner of the business must be included as a disposal at open market value.

Case Study

S. TOPP TRADING: CAPITAL ALLOWANCES AT END OF TRADE

Steve Topp has been running his business for many years, with an accounting date of 31 December.

The written down values carried forward at 31 December 2007 were:

Main Pool	£32,000
Car (80% business use)	£16,000

The business ceased trading on 30/6/2008. The adjusted trading profit for the period 1/1/2008 to 30/6/2008 was £40,000, before deducting capital allowances. There is also £10,000 overlap profit from the start of the business available for set-off.

Steve managed to sell all the remaining business assets (except the car) for £14,000. He bought the car from the business himself to use privately for a market value figure of £17,000.

Required

- Calculate the plant & machinery capital allowances for the accounting period 1/1/2008 to 30/6/2008.
- Calculate the trading income assessment for the final tax year of the business.

Solution

Plant & machinery capital allowances computation

	Main Pool	Single Asset Pool Car (20% Private Use)	Capital Allowances
	£	£	£
WDV bf	32,000	16,000	
Disposals	(14,000)	(17,000)	
	18,000	(1,000)	
Balancing allowances	(18,000)		18,000
Balancing charge		1,000 x 80%	(800)
WDV cf	0	0	
Total Capital Allowances			17,200

Trading Income assessment working:

		£
Accounting period 1/1/2008 – 30/6/2008:		
	Adjusted trading profits (before capital allowances)	40,000
	less capital allowances	(17,200)
		22,800

Tax Year 2008/09	**Basis period 1/1/2008 – 30/6/2008:**	
	Adjusted Profit (as above)	22,800
	Less overlap profits	(10,000)
	Trading Income assessment	12,800

losses when a business ceases

If a business incurs a loss just before it stops trading, the three normal loss options (as explained earlier) still apply in theory. The problem is that one of the options is impossible, since the loss cannot be carried forward against future profits of the same trade, as there can be no future profits.

To provide a further option for offsetting losses in this situation, a **terminal loss** can be offset against trading profits of the three tax years before the final tax year (latest first).

A **terminal loss** is defined as the loss occurring in the **last twelve months of trading**.

DIVIDING TRADING PROFITS BETWEEN PARTNERS

We have seen throughout the last two chapters that a partnership is taxed in the same way as a sole trader. It uses the same adjustment mechanism for trading profits; capital allowances are calculated in exactly the same way, and basis periods throughout the business are also identical.

The way in which partners decide to divide their profits is entirely their choice, and is stated in their partnership agreement. The division agreed will not only apply to the actual profits that the partnership generates, but also to the amount that is assessable on each partner for Income Tax purposes.

simple profit splits

If a partnership is made up of two individuals who agree to share profits and losses equally, then the calculation of each partner's trading income assessment is straightforward. The adjusted trading profits for the partnership (after capital allowances) is simply halved, and each partner is assessed on this figure.

So, for example, suppose the ongoing partnership of Sue and Adam had adjusted profits for the accounting period of 12 months to 31/12/2007 of £40,000 (after capital allowances). If their agreement was to divide profits and losses equally then the trading income assessment for Sue for the tax year 2007/08 would be £20,000, and the assessment for Adam for the same tax year would also be £20,000. Note that the current year basis of assessment is used here, just as it is for sole traders.

The simplest split is to agree a percentage that each partner will be entitled to. This could be a straightforward 50%:50% as just mentioned, or could be any other figures that the partners feel is fair. A partnership of three individuals may, for example agree that a 60%:30%:10% split is fair in their particular circumstances. These divisions could also be expressed as ratios – 50%:50% would be shown as 1:1, while 60%:30%:10% could be expressed as 6:3:1.

more complex profit splits

Some partnerships may, however, agree a more complex division of profits and losses. They may for example agree that out of the profits,

- 'salaries' are to be provided for some or all partners, and/or
- 'interest on capital' should be paid to partners based on their investment in the partnership

Both these types of appropriation would be made out of the total profits that the partnership has made. The larger these payments are, the less profit will remain to be shared by the partners by using the agreed percentages or ratios.

For tax purposes the starting point would always be the adjusted profits of the accounting period (after capital allowances), and this is the amount that the combined trading income assessments of each partner must total. Any salaries or interest on capitals are allocated first, and then the remaining profit (or loss) is shared amongst the partners. Note that partners' salaries and interest on capitals are trading profits, and are taxed as part of trading income. Partner's salaries are not assessed as employment income, which only relates to employees.

If a profit sharing arrangement changes, the agreement that is in existence during the accounting period is the one that applies to dividing the tax-adjusted profits of that accounting period.

The Case Study that follows shows how individual partners' assessments are calculated for an ongoing partnership where the normal 'current year basis' is operating. We will then go on to look at some other situations.

Case Study

PENN, QUILL AND WRIGHT: PARTNERS' ASSESSMENTS

John Penn, Daisy Quill and Sue Wright have been trading in partnership for several years. The partnership produces accounts each year up to the 30 June. Their partnership agreement states that the following salaries, rates of interest on capitals, and shares of remaining profits or losses should apply:

	Salary (pa)	Interest on Capital	Share of Profit/Loss
John Penn	£10,000	5%	30%
Daisy Quill	£15,000	5%	20%
Sue Wright	-	5%	50%

The partnership accounts for the twelve month accounting period to 30/6/2007 shows tax-adjusted profits of £95,000 (after deducting capital allowances):

The capital accounts balances for the partners are:

John Penn	£100,000
Daisy Quill	£50,000
Sue Wright	£250,000

Required

Calculate the trading income assessments for each of the three partners that will be based on the adjusted profits for this period, and state the tax year that the assessments will be for.

Solution

The following calculation shows how the adjusted profits are divided up:

	John Penn	Daisy Quill	Sue Wright	Total Remaining
	£	£	£	£
Adjusted Profits				95,000
Salaries	10,000	15,000	0	(25,000)
Balance Remaining				70,000
Interest on Capitals	5,000	2,500	12,500	(20,000)
Balance Remaining				50,000
Share of Balance	15,000	10,000	25,000	(50,000)
	30,000	27,500	37,500	

The calculation follows the same principles that are used for dividing profits for financial accounting purposes (with which you may be familiar) – the only difference is that here our starting point is the adjusted profits after capital allowances.

Notes

- salaries and interest on capitals are deducted from the original adjusted profit first, leaving a balance of £50,000 to be shared using the profit sharing percentages
- interest on capitals are calculated using the individual partners' balances on their capital accounts
- the overall amounts allocated to each partner of £30,000, £27,500, and £37,500 total the original adjusted profit figure of £95,000

The trading income assessments for each partner for 2007/08 (since the accounting period ends in that tax year) will be:

John Penn	£30,000
Daisy Quill	£27,500
Sue Wright	£37,500

partnership losses

If a partnership incurs a trading loss, each partner's share of the loss can be dealt with independently. This means that each partner has the same choices of how their own share of the trading loss should be relieved as a sole trader. The individual partners could all choose different ways to relieve their own loss, according to their personal circumstances.

when partnerships start or cease trading

When a partnership is first formed and starts trading, the basis periods that apply to each partners' share will be exactly the same as if they were sole traders. Therefore the rules that we saw earlier in the chapter for commencing or ceasing trading apply to both sole traders and partnerships.

CHANGES IN A PARTNERSHIP

when the profit sharing agreement changes

Depending on when the existing partners decide to alter their profit sharing agreement, there are two possible implications:

- If the change is made with effect from a normal accounting date (ie the start/end of an accounting period), then the new arrangement will simply apply to the new accounting period. This will mean that the new share of profits will apply entirely to the basis period of a new tax year.
- If the change is made during an accounting period, the adjusted profits (after capital allowances) will first have to be time-apportioned into the two parts of the period – before and after the change. Each part of the profits will then be divided amongst the partners according to the agreement in force at the time, and the two parts for each partner added together to form their assessment for the tax year.

when a new partner joins a partnership

When a new partner joins an established partnership (or a partnership is formed by an individual joining an established sole trader) the new partner is treated as if they had started a new business on the date that they joined. There will need to be a new profit sharing agreement that incorporates the additional partner, and this will operate from the date the new partner started.

The new partner will be subject to the opening basis of assessment rules, but the established partners (or established sole trader) will carry on applying the normal 'current year' basis to their shares of the adjusted profits. The new partner may therefore have personal overlap profits that will be carried forward until they leave the partnership, or the partnership ceases trading.

If the new partner starts on a normal accounting date for the partnership the situation is not too complicated, as the following example shows.

example: introduction of a new partner at the start of an accounting period

Rose and Daisy have been in partnership for several years, sharing profits and losses equally. They have always made their accounts up to 31 December each year. On 1 January 2007 they are joined by Bud, and the partnership agreement is changed to Rose 40%, Daisy 40%, Bud 20% from that date. They have never used salaries or interest on capitals as part of their profit sharing arrangement.

The first accounting year of the revised partnership (the year ended 31 December 2007) produced adjusted profits (after capital allowances) of £120,000.

For both Rose and Daisy their share of the profits for the y/e 31/12/2007 will be £120,000 x 40% = £48,000 each. The figure will form their trading income assessments for 2007/08 under the normal 'current year basis' rules.

Bud will be treated as if he started a new business on 1 January 2007. His share of the profits for the accounting year ended 31/12/2007 of 20% x £120,000 = £24,000 will be used to calculate the assessments for his first two tax years:

Bud's assessment for the tax year 2006/07 will use the basis period 1/1/2007 – 5/4/2007. His assessment for 2006/07 will therefore be £24,000 x 3/12 = £6,000.

His assessment for the tax year 2007/08 will use the basis period 1/1/2007 – 31/12/2007. His assessment for 2007/08 will therefore be £24,000.

This means that Bud will have overlap profits of £6,000, (relating to the period 1/1/2007 – 5/4/2007) that he will carry forward until either he leaves the partnership or it ceases trading.

a partner joining partway through an accounting period

If the new partner joins partway through an accounting period, the adjusted profits of the period must first be time-apportioned into the parts either side of that date. Each existing partner's assessment will then be generated by adding together their shares from each part of the period, just as if they had simply changed their profit sharing arrangement. The new partner will be treated as if he had started a new business on the date he joined. The following example will illustrate the situation.

example: introduction of a new partner partway into an accounting period

Oak and Ash have been in partnership for several years, sharing profits and losses equally. They have always made their accounts up to 31 December each year. On 1 October 2007 they are joined by Elm, and the partnership agreement is changed to Oak 40%, Ash 40%, Elm 20% from that date. They have never used salaries or interest on capitals as part of their profit sharing arrangement.

The year ended 31 December 2007 produced adjusted profits (after capital allowances) of £120,000. The year ended 31 December 2008 produced adjusted profits (after capital allowances) of £180,000.

The first step is to time-apportion the adjusted profits into the periods before and after Elm joined:

1/1/2007 – 30/9/2007	£120,000 x 9/12 = £90,000
1/10/2007 – 31/12/2007	£120,000 x 3/12 = £30,000

Oak and Ash

For the existing partners, Oak and Ash, they will each have a share of the profits for the whole accounting year madc up of:

1/1/2007 – 30/9/2007 £90,000 x 50%	=	£45,000, plus
1/10/2007 – 31/12/2007 £30,000 x 40%	=	£12,000
		£57,000

For both Oak and Ash this figure will form the assessment for 2007/08 under the normal rules.

For 2008/09 their assessments will each be based on £180,000 x 40% = £72,000.

Elm

The new partner, Elm will be treated as if he started a new business on 1 October 2007.

He has a share of the profits for the period 1/10/2007 - 31/12/2007 of

20% x £30,000 = £6,000.

He has a share of the profits for the period 1/1/2008 - 31/12/2008 of

20% x £180,000 = £36,000.

These amounts will be used to calculate the assessments for his first two tax years:

Elm's assessment for his first tax year - 2007/08 will use the basis period 1/10/2007 – 5/4/2008.

His trading income assessment for 2007/08 will therefore be made up of:

1/10/2007 – 31/12/2007		£6,000, plus
1/1/2008 – 5/4/2008 £36,000 x 3/12	=	£9,000
		£15,000

His assessment for the tax year 2008/09 will use the basis period 1/1/2008 – 31/12/2008. His assessment for 2008/09 will therefore be £36,000.

Elm will have overlap profits of £9,000, (relating to the period 1/1/2008 – 5/4/2008) that he will carry forward until either he leaves the partnership or it ceases trading.

when a partner leaves a partnership

If a partner leaves then the treatment follows the same logic as we have just seen. It is only the leaving partner that has the closing basis period rules applied to his/her share of the profits. The individual's own overlap profits (if any) would be deducted from their final share of profits. The existing partners carry on as normal.

The following example illustrates the situation.

example: partner leaving a partnership

Reddy, Eddy and Go have been in business for several years, sharing profits equally, and making accounts up to 31 December. Go decides to leave the partnership on 30 June 2008.

The partnership had the following adjusted profits (after capital allowances) for their accounting periods.

1/1/2007 – 31/12/2007	£75,000
1/1/2008 – 31/12/2008	£60,000

Go has personal overlap profits of £1,000 brought forward from when he started in partnership.

For **Go**, the assessable profits for his last two tax years of the business are:

Tax Year	Basis Period	trading income assessment	
2007/08	1/1/2007 – 31/12/2007	£75,000 x 1/3	= **£25,000**
2008/09	1/1/2008 – 30/6/2008	£60,000 x 6/12 x 1/3	= £10,000
		less overlap profits	(£1,000)
			£9,000

NATIONAL INSURANCE FOR THE SELF-EMPLOYED

As we saw in Chapter 1, sole traders and partners are liable to Class 2 and Class 4 National Insurance contributions.

- Class 2 contributions are payable at a flat rate of £2.20 per week (unless the 'small earnings exception' is claimed), and in addition,
- Class 4 contributions are payable on the profits above £5,225 per year

The profits for self-employed NIC purposes are the same ones that are used for Income Tax purposes – the assessable trading profits. For partners this refers to their personal share of the assessable profits, not those relating to the whole partnership.

Where an individual's profits are less than £4,635 (2007/08) then the small earnings exception may be claimed and Class 2 contributions need not be paid.

The rates for Class 4 contributions for 2007/08 are:

8% of profits for the year between £5,225 and £34,840, plus

1% of profits above £34,840.

If profits are below £5,225 then there are no Class 4 contributions. You may recognise this lower limit figure as the same as the Income Tax personal allowance.

If a sole trader or a partnership employs other people in the business (not partners) then the business must pay secondary Class 1 National Insurance contributions related to them. This is exactly the same as applies to limited companies, as we saw earlier in the book.

A REVIEW OF INCOME TAX PAYMENT DATES

In Chapter 1 we saw that the final date for payment of Income Tax is 31 January following the end of the tax year (eg 31/1/09 for 2007/08). We also discussed briefly the timing of payments on account that are sometimes due. We will now look a little more closely at these interim payments.

payments on account

The two payments on account are calculated as follows:

Each payment on account is based on **half** the Income Tax amount due for the **previous** year, (after deducting tax paid under PAYE and other Income Tax deducted at source).

Suppose, for example, that a partner only had trading income, and no other income. If his Income Tax for liability for 2006/07 was £7,000, none of this would have been paid by deduction at source.

This means that for 2007/08 he would need to make two payments on account. Each of the two payments on account for 2007/08 would be:

1/2 x £7,000 = £3,500.

These payments on account for 2007/08 would be made on 31/1/08 and 31/7/08. If the Income Tax amount for each year is quite similar, there would not be much left to pay (or have refunded) on the final date of 31/1/09.

Payments on account are not, however, always required. They do not have to be made if, for example, the taxpayer makes a claim that his tax will be much less than the previous year and that therefore a payment on account is not needed.

INTEREST AND PENALTIES

Interest on tax is payable on late payments, and also on any underpayment of the amount due on account. The rate is 7.5% at the time of going to press.

Penalties are also payable for:

Late submission of tax return:

- automatic £100 for missing submission deadline
- possible £60 per day (if tax owed is believed to be substantial)
- further £100 if return still outstanding 6 months after deadline
- further penalty of up to 100% of the tax unpaid if over 12 months late

The tax return submission deadlines are:

- 31 October following end of tax year for paper-based returns
- 31 January following end of tax year for online submission

Late payment of the balancing payment by more than 28 days:

- 5% of the tax due plus
- further 5% of the tax due if still unpaid by 31 July

Note that the penalties are in addition to the interest charges.

The fixed penalties for late submission of the tax return cannot however exceed the tax unpaid on the date that the return is due. If no tax is due there cannot therefore be a penalty.

incorrect returns

If after submitting a tax return, the taxpayer discovers that he has made an error or omission, he should notify HM Revenue & Customs as soon as possible. If the alteration results in less tax being payable than was originally thought, the taxpayer will receive a refund. Where additional tax is due this will of course need to be paid, plus interest that will run from the normal payment date.

COMPLETING THE TAX RETURN PAGES

The tax return for individuals has to be completed and submitted at the latest by 31 January that follows the end of the tax year – for example 31 January 2008 for the tax year 2006/07. The completed tax return contains information about the individual's income from all sources, and supplementary pages are used for those with specific types of income. In studying Unit 18, we are concerned with the supplementary pages that relate to sole traders and partners, and you may be asked to complete these in your examination.

self-employment pages

The self-employment pages (SE1 – SE4) are for completion by sole traders. The pages are divided into several sections, with sub headings that describe each section's content. The pages are reproduced in this chapter (pages 7.26 to 7.29) with the following commentary to help explain the main issues.

Page SE1

This commences with a section for business details. As well as the name, address and description of the business, the relevant accounting period dates are also required. For those starting or ceasing trading in the tax year the appropriate date is also required.

The second section deals with capital allowances. This is quite similar to the equivalent section for limited companies that we examined earlier.

If the sole trader's turnover (sales) is below £15,000, then the following income and expenses summary is completed. This section relates to the accounting period that was outlined in the earlier section. If the basis period is not the same period, then any apportionment will be carried out later on in the form. This is a very simple 'three-line' profit summary that replaces the longer summary that is required for those businesses with a larger turnover.
Box 3.24 is for the sales figure (plus any balancing charges),
Box 3.25 is used for all allowable expenses, including capital allowances
Box 3.26 is for the adjusted net profit.

Page SE2

For those sole traders who have a turnover of £15,000 or more, the two sections on page SE2 need to be completed for the accounting period, instead of the last short section. This provides boxes for a more comprehensive analysis of the profit & loss account. It provides two columns for expenses, the one on the right (boxes 3.46 – 3.63) for total expenses, and the left hand one (boxes 3.30 – 3.45) for any disallowable items that are included in the boxes on the right. Further adjustments (including capital allowances) are then made in the lower section on that page in boxes 3.66 – 3.72, to arrive at the adjusted trading profit for the accounting period.

Page SE3

The first section on page SE3 is where any apportionment of profits from the accounting period is carried out, and also any overlap profits or losses are taken into account. Box 3.92 shows the final trading income assessment figure. There then follows a short section relating to National Insurance contributions.

Page SE4

The final page SE4 is for a balance sheet summary where this is available. You would not be required to complete this page in an examination.

HM Revenue & Customs

Income for the year ended 5 April 2007

SELF-EMPLOYMENT

Fill in these boxes first

Name

Tax reference

If you want help, look up the box numbers in the Notes

Business details

Name of business **3.1**

Description of business **3.2**

Address of business **3.3**

Postcode

Accounting period - read the Notes, page SEN3 before filling in these boxes

Start **3.4** / /

End **3.5** / /

- Tick box 3.6 if details in boxes 3.1 or 3.3 have changed since your last Tax Return **3.6**
- Date of commencement if after 5 April 2004 **3.7** / /
- Date of cessation if before 6 April 2007 **3.8** / /
- Tick box 3.9 if the special arrangements for particular trades apply - read the Notes, page SEN11 **3.9**
- Tick box 3.10 if you entered details for all relevant accounting periods on last year's Tax Return and boxes 3.14 to 3.73 and 3.99 to 3.115 will be blank (read Step 3 on page SEN2) **3.10**
- Tick box 3.11 if your accounts do not cover the period from the last accounting date (explain why in the 'Additional information' box, box 3.116) **3.11**
- Tick box 3.12 if your accounting date has changed (only if this is a permanent change and you want it to count for tax) **3.12**
- Tick box 3.13 if this is the second or further change (explain in box 3.116 on Page SE4 why you have not used the same date as last year) **3.13**

Capital allowances - summary

	Capital allowances	Balancing charges
• Cars costing more than £12,000 (excluding cars with low CO_2 emissions) (A separate calculation must be made for each car.)	3.14 £	3.15 £
• Other business plant and machinery (including cars with low CO_2 emissions and cars costing less than £12,000) read the Notes, page SEN4	3.16 £	3.17 £
• Agricultural or Industrial Buildings Allowance (A separate calculation must be made for each block of expenditure.)	3.18 £	3.19 £
• Other capital allowances claimed (separate calculations must be made). Claims to, and balancing charges arising on, Business Premises Renovation Allowance must also be included in boxes 23.7 and 23.8 respectively	3.20 £	3.21 £
Total capital allowances/balancing charges	total of column above 3.22 £	total of column above 3.23 £

- Tick box 3.22A if box 3.22 includes enhanced capital allowances for designated environmentally beneficial plant and machinery **3.22A**

Income and expenses - annual turnover below £15,000

If your annual turnover was £15,000 or more , or would be if you traded for a whole year, **ignore** boxes 3.24 to 3.26. Instead fill in Page SE2

If your annual turnover was below £15,000 , or would be if you traded for a whole year, **fill in boxes 3.24 to 3.26 instead of Page SE2**. Read the Notes, page SEN4.

• Turnover including other business receipts and goods etc. taken for personal use (and balancing charges from box 3.23)	3.24 £
• Expenses allowable for tax (including capital allowances from box 3.22)	3.25 £
Net profit (put figure in brackets if a loss)	box 3.24 minus box 3.25 3.26 £

You must now fill in Page SE3

SA103

Income and expenses - annual turnover £15,000 or more

You must fill in this Page if your annual turnover was £15,000 or more - r ead the Notes, pages SEN2, SEN4 to SEN7

If you were registered for VAT, will the figures in boxes 3.29 to 3.64, include VAT? 3.27 [ ] or exclude VAT? 3.28 [ ]

Sales/business income (turnover) 3.29 £

	Disallowable expenses included in boxes 3.46 to 3.63	Total expenses	
• Cost of sales	3.30 £	3.46 £	
• Construction industry subcontractor costs	3.31 £	3.47 £	
• Other direct costs	3.32 £	3.48 £	box 3.29 minus (boxes 3.46 + 3.47 + 3.48)
		Gross profit/ (loss)	3.49 £
		Other income/ profits	3.50 £
• Employee costs	3.33 £	3.51 £	
• Premises costs	3.34 £	3.52 £	
• Repairs	3.35 £	3.53 £	
• General administrative expenses	3.36 £	3.54 £	
• Motor expenses	3.37 £	3.55 £	
• Travel and subsistence	3.38 £	3.56 £	
• Advertising, promotion and entertainment	3.39 £	3.57 £	
• Legal and professional costs	3.40 £	3.58 £	
• Bad debts	3.41 £	3.59 £	
• Interest and alternative finance payments	3.42 £	3.60 £	
• Other finance charges	3.43 £	3.61 £	
• Depreciation and loss/(profit) on sale	3.44 £	3.62 £	
• Other expenses	3.45 £	3.63 £	total of boxes 3.51 to 3.63
	Put the total of boxes 3.30 to 3.45 in box 3.66 below	Total expenses	3.64 £
			boxes 3.49 + 3.50 minus 3.64
		Net profit/(loss)	3.65 £

Tax adjustments to net profit or loss

• Disallowable expenses	boxes 3.30 to 3.45 3.66 £	
• Adjustments (apart from disallowable expenses) that increase profits. For instance; goods taken for personal use and amounts brought forward from an earlier year because of a claim under ESC B11 about compulsory slaughter of farm animals	3.67 £	
• Balancing charges (from box 3.23)	3.68 £	
Total additions to net profit (deduct from net loss)		boxes 3.66 + 3.67 + 3.68 3.69 £
• Capital allowances (from box 3.22)	3.70 £	
• Deductions from net profit (add to net loss)	3.71 £	boxes 3.70 + 3.71 3.72 £
Net business profit for tax purposes (put figure in brackets if a loss)		boxes 3.65 + 3.69 minus 3.72 3.73 £

You **must** fill in boxes 3.74 and 3.75 and **all other boxes** that apply to you, on this Page

Adjustments to arrive at taxable profit or loss

Basis period begins 3.74 / / and ends 3.75 / /

Profit or loss of this account for tax purposes (box 3.26 or 3.73) 3.76 £

Adjustment to arrive at profit or loss for this basis period 3.77 £

- Overlap profit brought forward 3.78 £
- Deduct overlap relief used this year 3.79 £
- Overlap profit carried forward 3.80 £
- Averaging for farmers and creators of literary or artistic works (see Notes, page SEN7, if you made a loss for 2006–07) 3.81 £
- Adjustment on change of basis 3.82 £

Net profit for 2006–07 (if you made a loss, enter '0') 3.83 £

Allowable loss for 2006–07 (if you made a profit, enter '0') 3.84 £

- Loss offset against other income for 2006–07 3.85 £
- Loss - relief to be calculated by reference to earlier years 3.86 £
- Loss to carry forward (that is allowable loss not claimed in any other way) 3.87 £
- Losses brought forward from earlier years 3.88 £
- Losses brought forward from earlier years used this year 3.89 £

Taxable profit after losses brought forward (box 3.83 minus box 3.89) 3.90 £

- Any other business income (for example, Business Start-up Allowance received in 2006–07) 3.91 £

Total taxable profits from this business (box 3.90 + box 3.91) 3.92 £

- Tick box 3.93 if the figure in box 3.92 is provisional 3.93

Class 4 National Insurance contributions - see Notes, pages SEN9 and SEN10

- Tick box 3.94 if exception applies 3.94
- Tick box 3.95 if you hold a deferment certificate for 2006–07 3.95
- Adjustments to profit chargeable to Class 4 National Insurance contributions (If you are calculating your tax enter the amount of Class 4 NICs due in box 18.2B on Page 7 of your Tax Return in box 3.96) 3.96 £

Subcontractors in the construction industry

- Deductions made by contractors on account of tax (please send your CIS25s to us) 3.97 £

Tax taken off trading income

- Any tax taken off trading income (excluding deductions made by contractors on account of tax) 3.98 £

Summary of balance sheet

Leave these boxes blank if you do not have a balance sheet

Assets	Plant, machinery and motor vehicles	3.99	£	
	Other fixed assets (premises, goodwill, investments etc.)	3.100	£	
	Stock and work-in-progress	3.101	£	
	Debtors/prepayments/other current assets	3.102	£	
	Bank/building society balances	3.103	£	total of boxes 3.99 to 3.104
	Cash in hand	3.104	£	3.105 £
Liabilities	Trade creditors/accruals	3.106	£	
	Loans and overdrawn bank accounts	3.107	£	total of boxes 3.106 to 3.108
	Other liabilities	3.108	£	3.109 £
Net business assets (put the figure in brackets if you had net business liabilities)				box 3.105 minus 3.109 3.110 £
Represented by	Capital Account			
	Balance at start of period*	3.111	£	
	Net profit/(loss)*	3.112	£	
	Capital introduced	3.113	£	
	Drawings	3.114	£	total of boxes 3.111 to 3.113 minus box 3.114
	Balance at end of period*			3.115 £

*If the Capital Account is overdrawn, or the business made a net loss, enter the figure in brackets

3.116 *Additional information*

Now fill in any other supplementar y Pages that apply to you.
Otherwise, go back to Page 2 of your Tax Return and finish filling it in.

The following Case Study will revise some of the main issues relating to a sole trader that we have examined, and show how in practice the relevant supplementary pages are completed.

Case Study

MARK UPP: A COMPREHENSIVE PROBLEM

Mark Upp commenced in business as a market trader on 1 January 2008. He produced a set of accounts for the period 1/1/2008 – 31/12/2008 as follows:

	£	£
Sales		90,000
less cost of sales:		45,000
Gross profit		45,000
less expenses:		
Insurance	2,500	
Part Time Employees' Wages & NIC	6,500	
Depreciation	3,250	
Motor Expenses	1,000	
General Expenses	3,000	
Bank Interest	1,000	
		17,250
Net Profit		27,750

Notes

1 Mark has agreed that his car is used 75% for business purposes and 25% privately. The motor expenses figure in the accounts relates to both business and private mileage. The car was bought for £13,000 on 1/1/2008.

2 Mark took goods from his market stall shop throughout the year to use privately. The cost of sales figure in the accounts of £45,000 is after deducting the £2,000 cost price of these goods. Mark's normal mark-up is 100% on cost.

3 Mark bought his portable stall for £6,400 when he commenced business. It qualifies as plant & machinery.

Required

- Calculate the capital allowances claimable by Mark for the accounting year ended 31/12/2008.
- Calculate the adjusted profits for the same period, after taking into account the capital allowances.
- Calculate the trading income assessment for Mark for 2007/08.
- Calculate the Class 4 National Insurance contributions payable by Mark for 2007/08.
- Complete supplementary pages SE1 – SE3 of the 2007/08 tax return for Mark.

Solution

Capital Allowances

		Main Pool	Single Asset Pool Expensive Car (25% private)	Capital Allowances
	£	£	£	£
WDV bf		-	-	
Additions				
without FYAs:				
Car			13,000	
WDA 25%			(3,000) x 75%	2,250
Additions				
with FYAs:				
Stall	6,400			
FYA (50%)	(3,200)			3,200
		3,200		
WDV cf		3,200	10,000	
Total Capital Allowances				5,450

Adjustment of Profits

	£	£
Net Profit per accounts		27,750
Add Back:		
Expenditure that is shown in the accounts but is not allowable		
Depreciation		3,250
Private motor expenses (£1,000 x 25%)		250
Adjustment to reflect profit in goods taken for own use		2,000
		33,250
Deduct:		
Allowable expenditure not shown in accounts		
Capital Allowances	5,450	
		(5,450)
Adjusted Profits for y/e 31/12/2008		27,800

Trading Income assessment for 2007/08

This is Mark's first tax year for the business. The basis period is:
1/1/2008 – 5/4/2008

This is apportioned from the adjusted profits as:
£27,800 x 3/12 = £6,950

Class 4 National Insurance

This is calculated based on the trading income:

8% of (£6,950 – £5,225) = £138.

Supplementary tax return pages

These are shown on the next three pages.

Make sure that you can understand where the data has been obtained for each box that has been completed.

HM Revenue & Customs

Income for the year ended 5 April 2007

SELF-EMPLOYMENT

Fill in these boxes first

Name: MARK UPP

Tax reference:

If you want help, look up the box numbers in the Notes

Business details

Name of business

3.1 MARK UPP

Description of business

3.2 MARKET TRADER

Address of business

3.3

Postcode

Accounting period - read the Notes, page SEN3 before filling in these boxes

Start 3.4 1 / 1 / 08

End 3.5 31 / 12 / 08

- Tick box 3.6 if details in boxes 3.1 or 3.3 have changed since your last Tax Return — 3.6
- Date of commencement if after 5 April 2004 — 3.7 1 / 1 / 08
- Date of cessation if before 6 April 2007 — 3.8 / /
- Tick box 3.9 if the special arrangements for particular trades apply - read the Notes, page SEN11 — 3.9
- Tick box 3.10 if you entered details for all relevant accounting periods on last year's Tax Return and boxes 3.14 to 3.73 and 3.99 to 3.115 will be blank (read Step 3 on page SEN2) — 3.10
- Tick box 3.11 if your accounts do not cover the period from the last accounting date (explain why in the 'Additional information' box, box 3.116) — 3.11
- Tick box 3.12 if your accounting date has changed (only if this is a permanent change and you want it to count for tax) — 3.12
- Tick box 3.13 if this is the second or further change (explain in box 3.116 on Page SE4 why you have not used the same date as last year) — 3.13

Capital allowances - summary

	Capital allowances	Balancing charges
• Cars costing more than £12,000 (excluding cars with low CO_2 emissions) (A separate calculation must be made for each car.)	3.14 £ 2,250	3.15 £
• Other business plant and machinery (including cars with low CO_2 emissions and cars costing less than £12,000) read the Notes, page SEN4	3.16 £ 3,200	3.17 £
• Agricultural or Industrial Buildings Allowance (A separate calculation must be made for each block of expenditure.)	3.18 £	3.19 £
• Other capital allowances claimed (separate calculations must be made). Claims to, and balancing charges arising on, Business Premises Renovation Allowance must also be included in boxes 23.7 and 23.8 respectively	3.20 £	3.21 £
Total capital allowances/balancing charges	total of column above 3.22 £ 5,450	total of column above 3.23 £ 0

- Tick box 3.22A if box 3.22 includes enhanced capital allowances for designated environmentally beneficial plant and machinery — 3.22A

Income and expenses - annual turnover below £15,000

If your annual turnover was £15,000 or more, or would be if you traded for a whole year, **ignore** boxes 3.24 to 3.26. Instead fill in Page SE2

If your annual turnover was below £15,000, or would be if you traded for a whole year, **fill in boxes 3.24 to 3.26 instead of Page SE2**. Read the Notes, page SEN4.

- Turnover including other business receipts and goods etc. taken for personal use (and balancing charges from box 3.23) — 3.24 £
- Expenses allowable for tax (including capital allowances from box 3.22) — 3.25 £

Net profit (put figure in brackets if a loss) — box 3.24 minus box 3.25 — 3.26 £

You must now fill in Page SE3

SA103

Income and expenses - annual turnover £15,000 or more

You must fill in this Page if your annual turnover was £15,000 or more - read the Notes, pages SEN2, SEN4 to SEN7

If you were registered for VAT, will the figures in boxes 3.29 to 3.64, include VAT? 3.27 [ ] or exclude VAT? 3.28 ✔

	Disallowable expenses included in boxes 3.46 to 3.63	Total expenses	Sales/business income (turnover)
			3.29 £ 90,000
• Cost of sales	3.30 £	3.46 £ 45,000	
• Construction industry subcontractor costs	3.31 £	3.47 £	
• Other direct costs	3.32 £	3.48 £	box 3.29 minus (boxes 3.46 + 3.47 + 3.48)
		Gross profit/ (loss)	3.49 £ 45,000
		Other income/ profits	3.50 £
• Employee costs	3.33 £	3.51 £ 6,500	
• Premises costs	3.34 £	3.52 £	
• Repairs	3.35 £	3.53 £	
• General administrative expenses	3.36 £	3.54 £ 3,000	
• Motor expenses	3.37 £ 250	3.55 £ 1,000	
• Travel and subsistence	3.38 £	3.56 £	
• Advertising, promotion and entertainment	3.39 £	3.57 £	
• Legal and professional costs	3.40 £	3.58 £	
• Bad debts	3.41 £	3.59 £	
• Interest and alternative finance payments	3.42 £	3.60 £ 1,000	
• Other finance charges	3.43 £	3.61 £	
• Depreciation and loss/(profit) on sale	3.44 £ 3,250	3.62 £ 3,250	
• Other expenses	3.45 £	3.63 £ 2,500	total of boxes 3.51 to 3.63
	Put the total of boxes 3.30 to 3.45 in box 3.66 below	Total expenses	3.64 £ 17,250
			boxes 3.49 + 3.50 minus 3.64
		Net profit/(loss)	3.65 £ 27,750

Tax adjustments to net profit or loss

	boxes 3.30 to 3.45	
• Disallowable expenses	3.66 £ 3,500	
• Adjustments (apart from disallowable expenses) that increase profits. For instance; goods taken for personal use and amounts brought forward from an earlier year because of a claim under ESC B11 about compulsory slaughter of farm animals	3.67 £ 2,000	
• Balancing charges (from box 3.23)	3.68 £	boxes 3.66 + 3.67 + 3.68
Total additions to net profit (deduct from net loss)		3.69 £ 5,500
• Capital allowances (from box 3.22)	3.70 £ 5,450	boxes 3.70 + 3.71
• Deductions from net profit (add to net loss)	3.71 £	3.72 £ 5,450
		boxes 3.65 + 3.69 minus 3.72
Net business profit for tax purposes (put figure in brackets if a loss)		3.73 £ 27,800

Adjustments to arrive at taxable profit or loss

Basis period begins 3.74 1 / 1 / 08 and ends 3.75 5 / 4 / 08

Profit or loss of this account for tax purposes (box 3.26 or 3.73)	3.76	£ 27,800
Adjustment to arrive at profit or loss for this basis period	3.77	£ (20,850)

- Overlap profit brought forward 3.78 £
- Deduct overlap relief used this year 3.79 £
- Overlap profit carried forward 3.80 £
- Averaging for farmers and creators of literary or artistic works (see Notes, page SEN7, if you made a loss for 2006–07) 3.81 £
- Adjustment on change of basis 3.82 £

Net profit for 2006–07 (if you made a loss, enter '0')	3.83	£ 6,950
Allowable loss for 2006–07 (if you made a profit, enter '0')	3.84	£
• Loss offset against other income for 2006–07	3.85	£
• Loss - relief to be calculated by reference to earlier years	3.86	£
• Loss to carry forward (that is allowable loss not claimed in any other way)	3.87	£
• Losses brought forward from earlier years	3.88	£
• Losses brought forward from earlier years used this year	3.89	£
Taxable profit after losses brought forward (box 3.83 minus box 3.89)	3.90	£ 6,950
• Any other business income (for example, Business Start-up Allowance received in 2006–07)	3.91	£
Total taxable profits from this business (box 3.90 + box 3.91)	3.92	£ 6,950
• Tick box 3.93 if the figure in box 3.92 is provisional	3.93	

Class 4 National Insurance contributions - see Notes, pages SEN9 and SEN10

- Tick box 3.94 if exception applies 3.94
- Tick box 3.95 if you hold a deferment certificate for 2006–07 3.95
- Adjustments to profit chargeable to Class 4 National Insurance contributions (If you are calculating your tax enter the amount of Class 4 NICs due in box 18.2B on Page 7 of your Tax Return in box 3.96) 3.96 £ –

Subcontractors in the construction industry

- Deductions made by contractors on account of tax (please send your CIS25s to us) 3.97 £

Tax taken off trading income

- Any tax taken off trading income (excluding deductions made by contractors on account of tax) 3.98 £

partnership supplementary pages

The partnership (short) pages are reproduced on the next two pages. These pages would need to be completed for each partner. There is a further partnership return that shows the position of the entire partnership, but completion of that document is not required for Unit 18.

The supplementary pages consist of page P1, which is very similar to page SE3 for a sole trader, and page P2 that summarises partnership income. We are only concerned with trading and professional profits. These are compiled in the main section on page P1, and re-stated in box 4.73 on page P2.

HM Revenue & Customs

Income for the year ended 5 April 2007

PARTNERSHIP (SHORT)

Fill in these boxes first

Name

Tax reference

If you want help, look up the box numbers in the Notes

Partnership details

Partnership reference number 4.1

Description of partnership trade or profession 4.2

- If you started being a partner during 2006–07, enter the date 4.3 / /
- If you stopped being a partner during 2006–07, enter the date 4.4 / /

Your share of the partnership's trading or professional income

Basis period begins 4.5 / / and ends 4.6 / /

- Your share of the profit or loss of this year's account for tax purposes (enter a loss in brackets) 4.7 £
- Adjustment to arrive at profit or loss for this basis period 4.8 £
- Overlap profit brought forward 4.9 £ Deduct overlap relief used this year 4.10 £
- Overlap profit carried forward 4.11 £
- Averaging for farmers and creators of literary or artistic works (see Notes, page PN3 if the partnership made a loss in 2006–07) or foreign tax deducted, if tax credit relief not claimed 4.12 £
- Adjustment on change of basis 4.12A £

Net profit for 2006–07 (if loss, enter '0' in box 4.13 and enter the loss in box 4.14) 4.13 £

Allowable loss for 2006–07 4.14 £

- Loss offset against other income for 2006–07 4.15 £
- Loss - relief to be calculated by reference to earlier years 4.16 £
- Loss to carry forward (that is, allowable loss not claimed in any other way) 4.17 £
- Losses brought forward from earlier years 4.18 £
- Losses brought forward from earlier years used this year 4.19 £

Taxable profit after losses brought forward — box 4.13 minus box 4.19 — 4.20 £

- Add amounts not included in the partnership accounts that are needed to calculate your taxable profit (for example, Enterprise Allowance (Business Start-up Allowance) received in 2006–07) 4.21 £

Total taxable profits from this business — box 4.20 + box 4.21 — 4.22 £

Class 4 National Insurance contributions - see notes, page PN4

- Tick box 4.23 if exception applies 4.23
- Tick box 4.24 if you hold a deferment certificate for 2006–07 4.24
- Adjustments to profit chargeable to Class 4 National Insurance contributions 4.25 £
  (If you are calculating your tax enter the amount of Class 4 NICs due in box 18.2B on your Tax Return - it does not go in this section)

SA104

Your share of the partnership taxed income

- Share of taxed income (liable at 20%) — 4.70 £

Your share of the partnership's trading and professional profits

- Share of partnership profits (other than that liable at 20%) — 4.73 £ (from box 4.22)

Your share of the partnership tax paid

- Share of Income Tax taken off partnership income — 4.74 £
- Share of CIS25 deductions — 4.75 £
- Share of tax taken off trading income (not CIS25 deductions) — 4.75A £

4.77 £ (boxes 4.74 + 4.75 + 4.75A)

4.79 *Additional information*

Now fill in any other supplementar y Pages that apply to you.
Otherwise, go back to page 2 in your Tax Return and finish filling it in

KEEPING RECORDS

Sole traders and partnerships need to keep records relating to their trading for five years after the online tax return is due to be submitted. For the tax year 2007/08 the return is due on 31 January 2009, and so the records must be kept until 31 January 2014. This date would be extended if HM Revenue & Customs were holding an enquiry into the taxpayer.

The records kept would be very similar to those retained by a limited company, as explained earlier. The records should be able to back up the information on the tax return, and would include:

- profit & loss accounts and balance sheets
- cash books and bank statements
- account ledgers or working papers
- invoices relating to allowable expenses and the acquisition of fixed assets
- fixed asset schedules
- taxation working papers, including capital allowance computations
- copies of tax returns

Chapter Summary

- When sole traders or partnerships commence trading they are subject to special basis period rules. The first tax year in which they are assessed is the year into which the start date falls. The basis period for this tax year is from the date of commencement until the following 5 April. The following tax year will usually have as its basis period as either the 12 months ending on the accounting date in that tax year, or if that is impossible, the first 12 months of the business. Overlap profits may arise that have been assessed twice, and these can be relieved on cessation.

- When sole traders or partnerships cease trading the final tax year will be the one in which the final date of trading falls. The basis period for this tax year will be from the last day of the basis period of the previous tax year to the date of cessation.

- Trading profits and losses for a partnership are divided amongst the partners according to the profit sharing agreement that is in force during the accounting period. This could include the allocation of salaries and/or interest on capitals, as well as a share of remaining profits or losses. These amounts all form part of the individual partners' trading income assessment.

- When an individual partner joins or leaves a partnership they are subject to the opening or closing basis of assessment rules, just like a sole trader. The basis periods for the other partners are not affected.
- Both sole traders and partners are subject to Class 2 and Class 4 National Insurance contributions. Class 2 is a flat rate, whereas Class 4 is based on profits.
- Income tax is payable by the 31 January following the end of the tax year. Payments on account are often also required. These are payable on the previous 31 January, and 31 July, and are based on the last year's Income Tax.
- There are separate supplementary pages in the Income Tax return for sole traders and partners. These must be completed for each tax year and submitted with the rest of the tax return by the 31 October or 31 January following the end of the tax year, the later date relating to online returns.

Key Terms

Accounting Date — The date to which the accounts are made up. Sole traders and partnerships can choose their regular accounting dates without restriction.

Accounting Period — The period for which the business produces its accounts.

Basis Period — The link between accounting periods and tax years. For a continuing business, the basis period for a particular tax year is the twelve month accounting period that ends in that tax year. There are special basis period rules when businesses start and cease trading, which may require time-apportionment of adjusted trading profits after capital allowances.

Adjusted Trading Profits — The trading profits that have been adjusted for tax purposes by excluding income not taxable as trading income, and non-allowable expenditure.

Trading Income Assessment — The taxable trading profit for the tax year. It is made up – after deducting any capital allowances – of adjusted trading profits for the basis period.

Student Activities

Answers to the asterisked (*) questions are to be found at the back of this book.

7.1* Rashid started in business as a sole trader on 1 December 2006. He made his accounts up to 30 November each year from then on. His adjusted profits (after capital allowances) for his first two years trading were as follows:

1/12/2006 – 30/11/2007	£48,000
1/12/2007 – 30/11/2008	£30,000

Required

State what the first three tax years will be for the business, and calculate the trading income assessments for each of these tax years.

State the amount of any overlap profits, and the period in which they arose.

7.2* Zorah started in business as a sole trader on 1 February 2007. She made her accounts up to 31 December each year, with the first set of accounts relating to 11 months. Her adjusted profits (after capital allowances) for the first two accounting periods were as follows:

1/2/2007 – 31/12/2007	£33,000
1/1/2008 – 31/12/2008	£48,000

Required

State what the first three tax years will be for the business, and calculate the trading income assessments for each of these tax years.

State the amount of any overlap profits, and the period in which they arose.

7.3* Adam has been in business as a sole trader for many years, with an accounting date of 30 June. On 31 May 2008 he ceased trading. He had overlap profits brought forward from the start of his business of £5,000. His adjusted profits (after deducting capital allowances) for the last three accounting periods of the business were as follows:

1/7/2005 – 30/6/2006	£40,000
1/7/2006 – 30/6/2007	£36,000
1/7/2007 – 31/5/2008	£20,000

Required

Calculate the trading income assessment for each of the tax years 2007/08 and 2008/09.

7.4 Alice and Bob have been in partnership for several years, sharing profits and losses equally. They have always made their accounts up to 31 December each year. On 1 October 2007 Colin joined the partnership, and the partnership agreement was changed to Alice 45%, Bob 40%, Colin 15% from that date.

The year ended 31 December 2007 produced adjusted profits (after capital allowances) of £96,000. The year ended 31 December 2008 produced adjusted profits (after capital allowances) of £108,000.

Required

Calculate separately the trading income assessments for the tax years 2007/08 and 2008/09 for each of the partners, and note any overlap profits for Colin.

7.5 Mark, Norma and Olga had been trading in partnership for many years, sharing profits and losses equally. They had always used 31 December as their accounting date. On 31 December 2007 Olga left the partnership. She had overlap profits brought forward from when she joined the partnership of £4,000.

The partnership accounts for the year ended 31/12/2007 were as follows:

	£	£
Sales		180,000
less cost of sales:		55,000
Gross profit		125,000
less expenses:		
Rent	12,500	
Employees' Wages & NIC	16,500	
Depreciation	12,250	
Motor Expenses	8,000	
General Expenses	3,000	
Bank Interest	1,750	
		54,000
Net Profit		71,000

Notes

1 There were the following written down values for plant & machinery capital allowances purposes as at 31/12/2006:

General Pool	£35,000
Car (30% private use by Olga)	£16,000

Olga bought the car from the partnership on 31/12/2007 for the market value of £10,000. There were no other transactions in fixed assets during 2007.

2 The motor expenses shown in the accounts include £500 relating to private mileage by Olga.

3 General Expenses includes:

Increase in General Provision for Bad Debts	£200
Gift Vouchers as presents for customers	£400

4 The partnership owns a factory that was brought into use when new on 1 January 2002. The eligible cost for Industrial Building Allowance purposes at that time was £300,000.

Required

- Calculate the capital allowances claimable by the partnership for the accounting year ended 31/12/2007 (Plant & Machinery and Industrial Buildings Allowance).
- Calculate the adjusted profits for the same period, after taking into account the capital allowances.
- Calculate the trading income assessment for Olga for 2007/08.
- Calculate the Class 4 National Insurance contributions payable by Olga for 2007/08.
- Complete the partnership (short) supplementary page P1 of the 2007/08 tax return for Olga.

  (A blank page P1 is reproduced in the Appendix of this book or may be downloaded from the Student Resource pages of www.osbornebooks.co.uk or from www.hmrc.gov.uk)

8 Capital gains tax for sole traders

this chapter covers . . .

In this chapter we examine:

- *the way in which capital gains tax applies to sole traders*
- *indexation allowance, taper relief and annual exemptions for individuals*
- *Capital Gains Tax issues common to individuals and limited companies*
- *dealing with the disposal of a business*
- *gift relief for business assets*
- *when to pay Capital Gains Tax*
- *keeping records*

PERFORMANCE CRITERIA COVERED

unit 18: PREPARING BUSINESS TAXATION COMPUTATIONS

element 18.3

prepare capital gains computations

A *identify and value correctly any chargeable assets that have been disposed of*

C *calculate chargeable gains and allowable losses*

D *apply reliefs, deferrals and exemptions correctly*

E *ensure that computations and submissions are made in accordance with current tax law and take account of current Inland Revenue practice*

G *give timely and constructive advice to clients on the maintenance of accounts and the recording of information relevant to tax returns*

CAPITAL GAINS TAX – A PERSONAL AND BUSINESS TAX

We saw in Chapter 4 that any chargeable gains that a limited company generates arc assessable to Corporation Tax.

Any chargeable gains that an individual makes are instead taxable under Capital Gains Tax (CGT). This tax can apply to the disposal of both **personal** and **business** assets. The disposal of personal assets under CGT is dealt with in Unit 19 'Preparing Personal Taxation Computations' (covered in Osborne Books' *Personal Taxation*). In this book we need to see its impact on business assets. Since disposals by partnerships are excluded from the requirements, we will only be looking in this text at disposals of business assets that are made by sole traders.

Some of the issues that were covered when we examined chargeable gains for limited companies also apply to sole traders. We will begin by examining the differences between disposals under Capital Gains Tax for sole traders and Corporation Tax for limited companies, and note any common ground. It is very important to distinguish clearly between these taxes, and be careful always to apply the correct rules.

basis of assessment

Capital Gains Tax is applied to individuals by using the same tax years as those used for Income Tax. The basis of assessment for Capital Gains Tax is the chargeable gains less capital losses arising from **disposals** that occur during the **tax year** (not in the basis period of the business). Both the definition of a disposal, and the types of asset that are exempt or chargeable are identical to those applicable under Corporation Tax. Most of the situations that we will come across will be based on the sale or gift of an asset. The interaction of capital allowances with chargeable gains is the same as was described for limited companies.

Two situations where disposals do not give rise to Capital Gains Tax are:

- disposals arising because the owner has died
- any disposal between spouses (husband and wife)

HOW IS CAPITAL GAINS TAX CALCULATED?

annual exempt amount

Unlike limited companies, all individuals are entitled to an **annual exempt amount** (or annual exemption) for each tax year. This works in a similar way to a personal allowance under Income Tax. The exempt amount is deducted from the total net gains that have been calculated on the individual assets that have been disposed of during the year. Capital Gains Tax is then worked out on the balance.

The exempt amount is £9,200 in 2007/08 (it was £8,800 in 2006/07). The exempt amount can only be used against capital gains, and is not set against income. It cannot be carried back or forward and used in another tax year.

Once the exempt amount has been deducted, the balance of the gains is subject to Capital Gains Tax. Although this is a separate tax from Income Tax it shares the same tax bands. Gains are treated as if they were added on top of taxable income, and the rates of 10%, 20%, and 40% are applied through the bands. If the individual is already a higher rate taxpayer under Income Tax, he will automatically pay 40% Capital Gains Tax, and this is quite often the case. Because the calculation of Income Tax and the use of the bands are both outside the scope of this unit, you are unlikely to be expected to calculate Capital Gains Tax other than by using the 40% rate.

THE COMPUTATION OF EACH GAIN

The standard format that we saw in Chapter 4 in the treatment of Corporation Tax is largely applicable to disposals by individuals chargeable to Capital Gains Tax. However there are two important issues that distinguish the calculation of the gains under the taxes:

- indexation for CGT purposes cannot extend further forward than April 1998
- a reduction in the gain called 'Taper Relief' applies to many gains on business assets under CGT

The basic computation format is as follows:

		£
	Proceeds on disposal	X
	less	
	Incidental costs of disposal	(x)
=	Net proceeds	X
	less	
	Original cost	(x)
	Incidental costs of acquisition	(x)
=	Unindexed gain	X
	less	
	Indexation allowance	(x)
=	Gain before taper relief	X

indexation allowance

This is a similar calculation to that used for chargeable gains under Corporation Tax. The important difference is that for all disposals after April 1998, the indexation factor is based on the RPI at April 1998 instead of the RPI at the date of disposal.

The factor calculation under CGT therefore becomes:

$$\frac{\textbf{(RPI at April 1998 – RPI at the date of acquisition)}}{\textbf{RPI at the date of acquisition}}$$

The result of this fraction is rounded to three decimal places before being multiplied by the historical cost figure. In the exam you will probably be given the indexation factor.

If the asset was acquired in April 1998 or later there will be no indexation allowance since the whole period of ownership occurs too late.

Just as with a limited company, the indexation allowance cannot either

- turn an unindexed gain into a loss, or
- increase the amount of an unindexed loss

taper relief

Taper relief was introduced to allow for the reduction of some gains that take place after April 1998. It is quite a crude mechanism in comparison to indexation allowance, and works by multiplying the gain before taper relief by a percentage. The percentage depends on how long after 6th April 1998 the asset was owned before it was disposed of. There are different percentage rates for business and non-business assets, but we will only need to use the business figures for this unit.

The percentages that follow are for the disposal of business assets. If the asset is owned for less than one year, 100% of the gain is chargeable.

Number of whole years of ownership after 6/4/98	Percentage of gain chargeable
1	50%
2 or more	25%

As you can imagine, this drastically reduces the amount subject to Capital Gains Tax in many situations. If you have studied personal taxation, you will appreciate that the taper relief for business assets is much more generous than that provided for non-business assets.

dealing with capital losses

Capital losses arise from disposals in the same way as gains. You must remember that when an unindexed loss arises there can be no indexation allowance.

Once losses have been calculated they are dealt with as follows:

- firstly they are set against gains (before taper relief) arising in the same tax year, until these are reduced to zero, then
- any unused loss is carried forward to set against the next gains (before taper relief) that arise in future tax years

The key to offsetting losses is to remember that the order of calculation is:

1 firstly offset losses

2 then deduct taper relief

3 then deduct annual exempt amount

to arrive at the amount subject to Capital Gains Tax.

We will now look in more detail at how this process works.

offsetting against gains arising in the same tax year

Any losses that arise during a tax year are offset against capital gains arising from disposals in the same tax year, before taper relief is applied to the resultant figure. There may be gains in the tax year with different taper relief percentages applying. In these circumstances it makes best use of the loss to set it against the gain(s) with the highest percentage chargeable (ideally 100%). This means that the maximum amount of gain is cancelled out by the loss. Where necessary, the losses are set against gains in descending order of the gains' chargeable percentages.

When dealing with losses arising in the same tax year there can be no safeguarding of the annual exempt amount. If there are sufficient losses the gains will be reduced to zero, wasting the exempt amount, before carrying forward any balance of loss.

offsetting against gains in a later tax year

This will only occur when there are insufficient gains in the same tax year to offset the loss (or no gains at all). The loss must be offset as soon as possible, by using any gains that occur in the next tax year. The system is very similar to the one just described, except that in these circumstances an amount of gain before taper relief equal to the annual exempt amount is not offset, and any loss balance carried on forward again. This provides some protection against wasting the exempt amount.

The Case Study that follows demonstrates the main issues that we have examined so far.

Case Study

JOHN GAIN TRADING: CAPITAL GAINS TAX

John Gain has been in business as a sole trader for several years. During the tax year 2007/08 he disposed of the following business assets:

In June 2007 he sold a piece of land for £20,000. He had bought the land in June 2000 for £30,000 and was originally going to extend his factory onto it. However he was refused planning permission, and decided to sell it.

In August 2007 he sold a shop for £100,000. He had bought it for £72,000 in September 2005.

In December 2007 he sold a factory building for £300,000. He had bought it new in December 1990 for £120,000, and claimed Industrial Buildings Allowance based on that eligible cost each year since then.

John is a higher rate taxpayer in 2007/08.

The indexation factor from December 1990 to April 1998 is 0.252.

Required

Calculate the gain or loss on each disposal, and John's total Capital Gains Tax liability for 2007/08.

Explain (without workings) the impact of the factory sale on Industrial Buildings Allowance.

Solution

Disposal of Land	£
Proceeds	20,000
Less Cost	(30,000)
Loss	(10,000)

There is no indexation allowance as there is an unindexed loss, and it was acquired after April 1998.

Disposal of Shop

	£
Proceeds	100,000
Less Cost	(72,000)
Gain before taper relief	28,000

There is no indexation allowance since all the ownership period occurred after April 1998. The shop has been owned for 1 year so 50% of the gain will be chargeable.

Disposal of Factory

	£
Proceeds	300,000
Less Cost	(120,000)
Less Indexation allowance	
0.252 x 120,000	(30,240)
Gain before taper relief	149,760

The factory has been owned for more than 2 years since April 1998. Therefore 25% of the gain is chargeable.

Summary

	£		£
Gain on Shop	28,000		
Less loss on land	(10,000)		
Gain, 50% chargeable	18,000	x 50%	9,000
Gain on Factory, 25% chargeable	149,760	x 25%	37,440
Total gains			46,440
less annual exempt amount			(9,200)
Amount subject to CGT			37,240
Capital Gains Tax at 40%	£37,240 x 40%		= £14,896

Note that the loss is offset against the gain that is chargeable at the highest percentage. Since neither gain is 100% chargeable, it is offset against the gain that is 50% chargeable. This means that only 50% of the loss reduces the net gains.

The only impact on Industrial Building Allowance is that there is no IBA claimable in the accounting period of disposal.

ISSUES THAT ARE COMMON TO COMPANIES AND INDIVIDUALS

The following techniques and rules that we examined in Chapter 4 in respect of limited companies and Corporation Tax are also applicable to individuals under Capital Gains Tax. We will note them here in outline only – if you need further explanation you should refer back to the earlier chapter.

- **links with capital allowances.**

  The issues outlined for companies are valid here. They are:

  - Where losses occur on items where capital allowances have been claimed, no capital loss arises.
  - Gains on chattels can only arise if the proceeds exceed £6,000, and this is subject to the chattels rules (dealt with below).
  - Gains on industrial buildings can arise where the proceeds exceed the original cost.

- **part disposals**

  These are dealt with in exactly the same way as for limited companies. The original cost of the whole asset is apportioned based on the proceeds of the part disposed of and the market value of the remainder at the time of the part disposal.

- **improvement expenditure**

  This follows the same logic under CGT rules as it does for chargeable gains under Corporation Tax. Each amount of expenditure is indexed separately, based on the time that it was incurred. One point to be careful about is that the indexation allowances cannot go past April 1998. If any expenditure was incurred after that point it will not attract any indexation allowance. Taper relief is based on the time that the whole asset has been owned since 1998, and is not affected by the date of any improvements.

- **chattels**

  The special rules for chattels are identical to those for companies:

  - The gain on chattels sold for over £6,000 cannot exceed 5/3 of (Proceeds minus £6,000).
  - The capital loss on chattels sold for under £6,000 is limited by substituting £6,000 for the actual proceeds in the computation.

- **rollover relief**

  This is applicable to the same classes of business assets owned by individuals as owned by companies and in addition it is available for goodwill acquisitions and disposals by individuals. The rules work in exactly the same way, and defer the gain when the proceeds of one disposal are reinvested in another qualifying asset.

DEALING WITH THE DISPOSAL OF A BUSINESS

We have already seen how trading profits are calculated when a business ceases trading, and how the capital allowances for the last accounting period are calculated.

In addition to these implications, if a sole trader sells his or her business, then Capital Gains Tax will apply **individually** to **each chargeable asset** that is included in the business. The sale of the business can therefore result in a number of separate capital gains computations.

The current assets and current liabilities of a business are not chargeable assets, which leaves **fixed assets** and **goodwill ('non-current assets')** as items on which CGT may be assessable.

fixed assets

As we have already seen, land and buildings are chargeable assets, and could easily form part of a business that is being disposed of. Chattels bought and sold for under £6,000 are exempt, and so are cars. Other plant and machinery could theoretically give rise to a capital gain, but since it is rarely sold for more than it cost is unlikely to do so. Any plant and machinery disposed of for less than original cost would simply be dealt with through the capital allowances computation as we have seen previously.

goodwill

Goodwill is an intangible asset that may exist if the business is sold as a going concern. It arises when the buyer is prepared to pay more for the business as a whole than the market value of the net assets of the business. This could be, for example, because of the businesses' customer base that the new owner wishes to continue selling to. Where a sole trader has built up the business himself the goodwill is unlikely to be shown in the business balance sheet, and will often have an original cost of zero for CGT purposes. If you are faced with a situation where the proceeds relating to the goodwill is not stated, you will need to calculate it as the balance of the proceeds that do not relate to any other assets.

Case Study

DUNN TRADING: DISPOSAL OF A BUSINESS

Jo Dunn had been in business as a sole trader since January 1995. She ceased trading on 31/1/2008, and on that date sold her business as a going concern for a total of £500,000. Jo is a higher rate taxpayer in 2007/08.

The summarised balance sheet of the business on 31/1/2008 was as follows:

	£
Premises	200,000
Plant & Machinery	20,000
Net Current Assets	80,000
Total Net Assets	300,000

The premises were bought in January 1995. No depreciation had been charged on the premises in the accounts. The plant and machinery value is based on amounts after depreciation has been charged. Capital allowances had been claimed on all plant and machinery.

It was agreed with the purchaser of the business that the premises were to be valued at £350,000 in the sale, and that the plant and machinery and the net current assets were valued at their balance sheet amounts.

The indexation factor from January 1995 to April 1998 is 0.114.

Required

Calculate the CGT arising on the sale of the business.

Solution

The first step is to allocate the sale proceeds to the individual assets, including any balance of proceeds to goodwill, and determine which assets are chargeable.

	£	
Premises	350,000	Chargeable
Plant & Machinery	20,000	Proceeds < Cost. Dealt with through capital allowance computation
Net Current Assets	80,000	Exempt
Goodwill	50,000	Chargeable
Total Proceeds	500,000	

The goodwill is calculated as the balancing figure, after accounting for the other assets.

The computations are then carried out individually on the chargeable assets.

	£
Premises	
Proceeds	350,000
Less Cost	(200,000)
Less Indexation allowance	
0.114 x 200,000	(22,800)
Gain before taper relief	127,200
Goodwill	
Proceeds	50,000
Less Cost	0
Gain before taper relief	50,000

Both gains will be chargeable at 25%, since they have been owned for more than 2 years since 1998.

(£127,200 + £50,000) x 25% =	£44,300
less annual exempt amount	(£9,200)
Taxable at 40%	£35,100
Capital Gains Tax @ 40%	= £14,040

GIFT RELIEF

We saw earlier in our studies that the gift of an asset is a disposal for Capital Gains Tax purposes. This means that even though the donor (the person giving the item) has received nothing for the item he/she may still have to pay CGT. The disposal will be treated as if the donor had received the market value for the item, and the recipient will be treated as if he/she had acquired the asset at the same market value.

If an individual gives away a 'business asset', the transaction can qualify for 'gift relief'. This has the effect of delaying the onset of the tax, and transferring the liability to the recipient of the gift.

The relief can only be claimed if both parties agree. It means that the donor has no CGT liability, but that the CGT liability of the recipient in the future could be greater - if the item is disposed of.

Gift relief works by reducing the base cost of the asset for the recipient by the amount of the deferred gain. This means that the base cost would now be the market value less the deferred gain (before taper relief), and any eventual gain would therefore be greater than if gift relief had not been claimed.

Because the deferred gain is calculated before taper relief, it may therefore be a greater amount than the one that the donor would have been taxed on. The recipient can only claim taper relief related to his/her own period of ownership, if he/she later disposes of the asset.

Gift relief applies to business assets, including:

- assets used in the donor's business or in his/her personal trading company
- shares in the donor's personal trading company
- unquoted shares in other trading companies

Case Study

JAN NICE: GIFT RELIEF

Jan Nice bought a shop in October 1998 for £100,000, and used it in her business until June 2006, when she gave it to her niece, Norah. The market value of the shop at that time was £180,000.

Norah ran the shop as a sole trader for a while, but decided to sell the shop in October 2007. She received £220,000 for the shop.

Jan and Norah claimed gift relief on the shop. Norah is a higher rate taxpayer. She had no other disposals in 2007/08.

Required

Calculate the Capital Gains Tax payable by Norah on her disposal of the shop.

Solution

The gain deferred by Jan is (£180,000 - £100,000) = £80,000.

There is no indexation allowance (since it was bought after April 1998), and no taper relief applies to a deferred gain.

The disposal by Norah will have the following gain.

		£	£
Proceeds			220,000
Less	Market value at acquisition	180,000	
	less deferred gain	(80,000)	
			100,000
	Gain before taper relief		120,000

50% will be chargeable, based on the one year that Norah has owned the shop:

£120,000 x 50%		£60,000
less annual exempt amount		(£9,200)
Amount subject to CGT		£50,800
Capital Gains Tax	£50,800 x 40% =	£20,320

SUMMARY OF RULES AND RELIEFS

In this book we have looked at both chargeable gains for companies (taxed through Corporation Tax) and individuals (taxed through Capital Gains Tax). This is an area of study where it is easy to get confused, so the following table is produced to summarise the various rules and reliefs that we have looked at and to whom they apply.

	Individuals (Capital Gains Tax)	**Companies (Corporation Tax)**
Annual Exempt Amount	✔	Not applicable
Taper Relief	✔	Not applicable
Indexation	To April 1998 only	To date of disposal
Links with capital allowances	✔	✔
Part Disposal Rules	✔	✔
Chattel Rules	✔	✔
Improvement Expenditure	✔	✔
Shares: matching rules/bonus/rights issues	Outside scope of unit	✔
Gift Relief	✔	Not Applicable
Rollover Relief	✔	✔

PAYMENT OF CAPITAL GAINS TAX

Capital Gains Tax is payable as one amount on the 31 January following the end of the tax year. This is the same date as the final submission date of the online tax return (the paper-based tax return would be due by 31 October). There is no requirement for payments on account of CGT.

KEEPING RECORDS

Since capital gains can arise when assets that have been held for a considerable time are disposed of, this has implications for record keeping. Taxpayers need to plan ahead, and retain records relating to the acquisition of assets that will be chargeable if disposed of.

Typical records that should be kept include:

- contracts, invoices or other purchase documentation relating to the acquisition of assets
- details of any valuations (eg valuations relating to part disposals)
- documentation relating to the sale of assets

Records for CGT purposes should be retained for the same period of time as those relating to Income Tax. For those in business this is five years after the date that the online return must be submitted (eg for 2007/08, records should be kept until 31/01/14). Where records will also relate to later disposals, for example gift relief claims, rollover relief claims and information relating to part disposals, they will need to be retained until all the relevant assets have been disposed of.

Chapter Summary

- Capital Gains Tax applies to individuals (including sole traders and partners) who dispose of chargeable assets. In this unit we are concerned with the disposal of business assets. Although there is some common ground with the way that chargeable gains for companies are taxed under Corporation Tax, the computations for individuals include restricted indexation allowances, taper relief and annual exempt amounts.
- The treatment of gains for individuals and companies include common areas such as capital allowances, part disposals, improvement expenditure, chattel rules and rollover relief.
- Where a whole business is disposed of, a separate computation is carried out for each chargeable asset that is included in the business. This includes goodwill, which is an intangible asset that may arise when the business is sold as a going concern.
- Gift relief is available on the gift of business assets where both parties agree. It has the effect of deferring the gain, so that the donor is not subject to CGT, but the recipient may pay more tax if the asset is subsequently disposed of.
- CGT is payable on the 31 January following the tax year. Records must be kept for five years after that date, or longer if they relate to assets that are still owned or subject to deferral reliefs.

Key Terms

Capital Gains Tax (CGT) The tax that applies to individuals who dispose of chargeable personal or business assets.

Disposal A disposal for CGT purposes is the sale, gift, loss or destruction of an asset.

Chargeable Asset Assets whose disposal can result in a CGT liability. All assets are chargeable unless they are exempt.

Exempt Asset An asset that is not chargeable to CGT. Exempt assets include the current assets of a business.

Chattel A tangible, movable asset.

Annual Exempt Amount (or Annual Exemption)
The amount that is deductible from an individual's net gains in a tax year before CGT is payable.

Unindexed Gain This is the net proceeds (or market value in some situations) less the original cost of the asset and any other allowable costs incurred. It is the sub total of the gain computation before indexation allowance is deducted.

Indexation Allowance An amount that is deductible in the gain computation that compensates for the effect of inflation on the asset between acquisition and April 1998. It uses the retail price index to calculate a factor that is multiplied by the historical cost of the asset.

Taper Relief This relief is in the form of a percentage of the gain that is chargeable. It depends on the whole years that the asset was owned after April 1998. The amount of taper relief also depends on whether the disposal relates to a business or personal asset.

Capital Loss A capital loss results when the allowable costs of an asset exceed the sale proceeds (or market value). Indexation cannot be used to increase a loss. A loss is used by setting it against a gain in the same year, or if this is not possible, by carrying the loss forward to set against gains in the next available tax year.

Part Disposal This occurs when part of an asset is disposed of, but the remainder is retained.

Improvement Expenditure Capital expenditure that enhances an asset. If the enhancement is still evident at disposal then the improvement expenditure is an allowable cost.

Rollover Relief A deferral relief available to businesses (including sole traders). It has the effect of postponing a chargeable gain when the proceeds of disposal have been reinvested.

Goodwill Goodwill is a chargeable asset. It is the amount of the proceeds on disposal of a business that does not relate to any individual assets, but is instead due to the intangible value of the business as a going concern.

Gift Relief A relief claimable jointly by the donor and the recipient of certain assets, including business assets. It allows the original gain by the donor to be deferred by increasing the possible future gain of the recipient.

Student Activities

Answers to the asterisked (*) questions are to be found at the back of this book.

8.1* Analyse the following list of business assets into those that are chargeable to CGT and those that are exempt.

(a) Moveable plant, sold at a gain for £5,000

(b) Trading stock

(c) Shares in CIC plc

(d) An office block

(e) Goodwill

(f) Land

(g) A car

(h) Government securities

8.2* Vikram is a sole trader, who is a higher rate taxpayer in 2007/08. In January 1995 he bought a small shop for £40,000. In April 1998 he extended the shop at a cost of £20,000. He sold the shop for £140,000 in July 2007. This was his only disposal in the tax year.

The indexation factor from January 1995 to April 1998 is 0.114.

Required

Calculate the amount of Capital Gains Tax payable by Vikram for 2007/08.

8.3* Jane is a sole trader, who is a higher rate taxpayer in 2007/08. In January 1999 she bought 1,000 unquoted shares at £10 each in a similar business to help her increase her market share. The shares are business assets. She sold 600 of the shares in July 2007 for a total of £23,000. This was her only disposal in the tax year.

Required

Calculate the amount of Capital Gains Tax payable by Jane for 2007/08.

8.4 In January 1995 George bought an office building for £60,000 to use in his business. In December 2000 he gave the office building to his son, William, who used it in his business. The building was valued at £100,000 at that time, and they claimed gift relief on the transaction. William sold the building for £200,000 in July 2007. This was his only disposal in 2007/08. William is a higher rate taxpayer in the tax year.

The indexation factor from January 1995 to April 1998 is 0.114.

Required

Calculate the amount of Capital Gains Tax payable by William for 2007/08.

8.5 Josie started a business as a sole trader in January 1990. She ceased trading on 31/1/2008, and on that date sold her business as a going concern for a total of £900,000. Josie is a higher rate taxpayer in 2007/08.

The summarised balance sheet of the business on 31/1/2008 is as follows:

	£
Premises	400,000
Plant & Machinery	30,000
Net Current Assets	50,000
Total Net Assets	480,000

The premises were bought in January 1999. A gain of £60,000 on the previous premises was rolled over into these premises when the whole proceeds of the first premises were reinvested. The amount shown in the balance sheet represents the actual cost in 1999 of the current premises.

The plant and machinery is shown in the balance sheet at cost minus depreciation to date. Capital allowances had been claimed on all plant and machinery.

It was agreed with the purchaser of the business that the premises were to be valued at £700,000 in the sale. The plant and machinery is valued at £20,000 in the sale, and the net current assets are valued at their balance sheet amount.

Required

Calculate the Capital Gains Tax liability arising on the sale of the business.

Answers to student activities

The answers in this section relate to the asterisked Student Activities at the end of each chapter.

The answers to the remaining Student Activities (and also to the Practice Examinations) are contained in the *Business Taxation Tutor Pack*. Please call Osborne Books Customer Services on 01905 748071 or visit our website on www.osbornebooks.co.uk for details and conditions of issue of this publication.

CHAPTER 1: INTRODUCTION TO BUSINESS TAXATION

1.1 The following statements are true: (a), (d), (f).

The other statements are false as follows: (b) the Finance Act is not the only relevant law. (c) the return is completed for each CAP, not each financial year. (e) Companies (and other employers) are liable for employers' NIC. (g) It is unethical to bend rules or omit items. (h) The self-employed do not pay income tax under PAYE.

1.2 (a) Corporation Tax Computation for DonCom plc for year ended 31/12/2007

	£
Trading Profits	1,300,000
Income from Property	100,000
Chargeable Gains	500,000
Profits Chargeable to Corporation Tax (PCTCT)	1,900,000
Corporation Tax on PCTCT (£1,900,000 x 30%)	570,000

(b)

Filing date for CT600 return	31/12/2008
Final Payment date for Corporation Tax	1/10/2008

1.3 (a) Income Tax Computation for 2007/2008

	£
Trading Income (Share of Partnership Profits)	4,300
Other Taxable Income	2,000
	6,300
Less personal allowance	5,225
Taxable Income	1,075
Tax payable at 10%	107

(b) A paper-based return must be submitted by 31/10/2008 whether or not HM Revenue & Customs are to calculate the tax.

Final payment date is 31/1/2009.

1.4 (a) **John**

		£
Class 2	£2.20 x 52 weeks	114.40
Class 4	(£25,000 - £5,225) x 8%	1,582.00
		1,696.40

Class 2 is paid by monthly direct debit or quarterly invoice.

Class 4 is paid with the Income Tax liability.

(b) **Walvern Financial Systems Limited**

Class 1 (secondary) NIC calculation

Julian's earnings:	£25,428 / 52	= £489 per week
NIC	(£489 - £100) x 12.8%	= £49.79 per week
		= £2,589.08 per year

Payment would be made monthly in arrears (with the PAYE tax and primary NIC deducted from employees).

1.5 The Walvern Water Company Limited will require a company tax return (form CT600). This will relate to the chargeable accounting period (CAP) 1/8/2006 to 31/7/2007. The form must be submitted by 12 months after the end of the accounting period, ie 31/7/2008. The final Corporation Tax payment must be made by 1/5/2008 (nine months and one day after the end of the CAP).

Wally Weaver will need a tax return for the tax year 2007/2008. The accounting period of 1/8/2006 to 31/7/2007 will form the basis period for this tax year. The main part of the form will need to be completed, along with the supplementary pages relating to self-employment. The online tax return must be submitted by 31/1/2009. The final income tax payment relating to 2007/2008 will also need to be made by 31/1/2009.

CHAPTER 2: CORPORATION TAX – TRADING PROFITS

2.1

1 no action (allowable)

2 add back (disallowable expense)

3 deduct (not trading income)

4 deduct (not taxable income)

5 no action (allowable)

6 deduct (not trading income – possible chargeable gain)

7 no action (taxable trading income)

8 add back (disallowable expense since tobacco)

9 add back (disallowable expense – not specific)

10 add back (disallowable expense – not trading)

11 no action (allowable)

12 add back (charge against whole PCTCT)

2.2

	£	£
Net Profit per accounts		130,300
Add Back:		
Expenditure that is shown in the accounts but is not allowable		
Depreciation		42,000
Loss on Sale of Fixed Assets		5,000
Gifts of Chocolates		4,900
Entertaining Customers		6,000
		188,200
Deduct:		
Income that is not taxable as Trading Income		
Interest Received	20,000	
Dividends Received	70,000	
Decrease in General Bad Debt Provision	5,000	
Capital Allowances	23,000	
		(118,000)
Trading Income Assessment		70,200

2.3

	£	£
Net Profit per accounts		276,600
Add Back:		
Expenditure that is shown in the accounts but is not allowable		
Depreciation		51,000
Directors' Speeding Fines		2,000
Gift Vouchers		5,000
Entertaining Customers		4,000
		338,600
Deduct:		
Income that is not taxable as Trading Income		
Interest Received	40,000	
Gains on Disposal of Fixed Assets	50,000	
Rental Income Received	60,000	
Capital Allowances	31,500	
		(181,500)
Trading Income Assessment		157,100

CHAPTER 3: CORPORATION TAX – CAPITAL ALLOWANCES

3.1

	eligible for FYA? what rate?	**which pool does balance of expenditure enter?**	**WDA claimable in future periods?**	**Balancing Allowances possible?**
Van costing £9,000	50%	Main pool	25% as part of main pool	No
Lorry costing £25,000	50%	Main pool	25% as part of main pool	No
Car costing £10,000	No	Main pool	25% as part of main pool	No
Computer costing £12,000	50%	Main pool or short life asset	25%	No if in main pool Yes if SLA
Machinery costing £20,000	50%	Main pool	25% as part of main pool	No
Car costing £25,000	No	Single asset pool	25%, but limited to £3,000 pa	Yes
Equipment with short life costing £1,000	50%	Single asset pool (short life asset)	25%	Yes
'Low emission' car costing £18,000	100%	Main pool, but no balance of expenditure after FYA	N/A	No

3.2 Plant & Machinery Capital Allowances Computation:

		Main Pool	Single Asset Pools Exp Car VW	Exp Car BMW	S/L Asset	Capital Allowances
	£	£	£	£	£	£
WDV bf		60,000	13,000	-	10,000	
Additions without FYAs:						
BMW Car				24,000		
Disposals:						
VW Car			(10,000)			
SL machine					(3,000)	
Machine		(3,000)				
Sub totals		57,000	3,000	24,000	7,000	
WDA 25%		(14,250)		(3,000)		17,250
Balancing Allowance			(3,000)		(7,000)	10,000
Additions with FYAs:						
Computer	5,000					
FYA (50%)	(2,500)	2,500				2,500
Fork Lift	30,000					
FYA (50%)	(15,000)					15,000
		15,000				
WDV cf		60,250	-	21,000	-	
Total Capital Allowances						44,750

Trading Income for CAP year ended 31/3/2008:

	£
Adjusted trading profits	154,000
Plant & Machinery Capital Allowances	(44,750)
Trading Income	109,250

3.3

	Factory One		Factory Two	
	£		£	
Land Preparation	40,000		10,000	
Main Factory Building	250,000		170,000	
Design Office	-		40,000	
Warehouse	150,000		80,000	
Definitely eligible	440,000		300,000	
Offices (< 25%)	110,000	(1)	60,000	(2)
Eligible cost	550,000		360,000	

(1) £110,000 is less than 25% of £550,000, and is therefore eligible.
(2) £60,000 is less than 25% of £360,000, and is therefore eligible.

		£
IBA writing down allowances:		
Factory One	£550,000 x 4%	22,000
Factory Two	£360,000 x 4%	14,400
		36,400

Adjusted profits	280,000
less P & M capital allowances	(38,000)
less IBA capital allowances	(36,400)
Assessable trading income	205,600

CHAPTER 4: CORPORATION TAX – CHARGEABLE GAINS

4.1 Chargeable Assets: (a), (b), (c), (d), (f).

Exempt Assets: (e – chattel sold for a gain for under £6,000), (g), (h), (i).

4.2

	£
Proceeds	1,300,000
less Cost	(600,000)
Unindexed gain	700,000
less Indexation allowance £600,000 x 0.348	(208,800)
Chargeable Gain	491,200
less capital loss brought forward	(15,000)
Chargeable Gain to be brought into PCTCT	476,200

4.3

	£
Proceeds	145,000
less Cost	(50,000)
less Indexation £50,000 x 0.249	(12,450)
Chargeable Gain	82,550
less capital loss brought forward	(25,000)
Chargeable Gain to be brought into PCTCT	57,550

CHAPTER 5: CORPORATION TAX – CALCULATING THE TAX

5.1 Corporation Tax Computation

	£	£
Adjusted Trading Profits	1,120,000	
less capital allowances - P & M	(143,000)	
add balancing charge IBA	80,000	
Trading Income		1,057,000
Property Income		23,000
Interest Receivable		60,000
Chargeable Gains		48,000
less Gift-Aid payment		(45,000)
PCTCT		1,143,000

'Profits' = £1,143,000 + (£90,000 x 100/90) = £1,243,000

The company will therefore pay Corporation Tax at full rate minus marginal relief:

	£
PCTCT at full rate: £1,143,000 x 30%	342,900
less marginal relief:	
1/40 x (£1,500,000 – £1,243,000) x (£1,143,000 / £1,243,000)	(5,908)
Corporation Tax Liability	336,992

5.2 Corporation Tax Computation

	£	£
Adjusted Trading Profits	1,420,000	
less capital allowances - P & M	(193,000)	
less capital allowances - IBA	(12,000)	
Trading Income		1,215,000
Property Income		92,000
Interest Receivable		12,000
Chargeable Gains	88,000	
less capital loss bf	(18,000)	
Net Chargeable Gains		70,000
less Gift-Aid payment		(8,000)
PCTCT		1,381,000

'Profits' = £1,381,000 + (£27,000 x 100/90) = £1,411,000

The company will therefore pay Corporation Tax at full rate minus marginal relief:

	£
PCTCT at full rate: £1,381,000 x 30%	414,300
less marginal relief:	
1/40 x (£1,500,000 – £1,411,000) x (£1,381,000 / £1,411,000)	(2,178)
Corporation Tax Liability	412,122

5.3 Corporation Tax Computation

	£	£
Trading Income		0
Rental Income	35,000	
less rental loss bf	(13,000)	
Property Income		22,000
Interest Receivable		40,000
Chargeable Gains	90,000	
less capital loss bf	(8,000)	
Net Chargeable Gains		82,000
		144,000
less trading loss		(120,000)
less Gift-Aid payment		(10,000)
PCTCT		14,000

'Profits' = £14,000

The company will therefore pay Corporation Tax at the small companies' rate:

Since the CAP falls into two financial years with different small companies' rates the PCTCT must be time-apportioned:

Financial Year 2006 (1/1/2007 – 31/3/2007)
PCTCT is 3/12 x £14,000 = £3,500
Corporation Tax for this part of the CAP is £3,500 x 19% = £665

Financial Year 2007 (1/4/2007 – 31/12/2007)
PCTCT is 9/12 x £14,000 = £10,500
Corporation Tax for this part of the CAP is £10,500 x 20% = £2,100

Total Corporation Tax for the CAP is £665 + £2,100 = £2,765.

An alternative option would be to carry the loss forward against future trading profits.

CHAPTER 6: INCOME TAX – TRADING PROFITS

6.1 **Profit motive**. Michelle seems to deliberately buy and sell at a profit. She buys property in need of renovation, and times the sale to obtain most profit. This indicates trading.

Subject matter. Michelle gets personal use from the properties that she buys, and this could indicate that she is not trading. She could argue that she is simply changing homes like most people.

Length of ownership. After renovating the buildings, Michelle only keeps them for a few months. Such a short time indicates trading.

Frequency of transactions. The buying and selling of property seems to be quite a regular activity, although with each transaction spaced nearly a year apart it could be argued that it is not particularly frequent.

Supplementary work. Renovating the properties counts as supplementary work, and this is clearly carried out with a view to a future sale.

Reason for acquisition and sale. Although the first property was bequeathed to her, she seems to have subsequently bought with the ultimate sale in mind. This indicates trading.

6.2

1 add back (disallowable expense)
2 add back (disallowable expense)
3 deduct (not trading income)
4 deduct (not trading income)
5 add back (disallowable expense)
6 deduct (not taxable income)
7 add back (disallowable expense)
8 add back (disallowable expense since food)
9 no action (taxable trading income)
10 add back (disallowable expense - part of drawings)
11 no action (allowable)
12 add back (disallowable expense)

6.3

	£	£
Net Profit per accounts		144,000
Add Back:		
Expenditure that is shown in the accounts but is not allowable		
Drawings		18,000
Depreciation		22,000
Loss on Sale of Fixed Assets		4,000
Gift Vouchers		3,000
Entertaining Customers		4,500
Owner's Pension Contribution		2,400
		197,900

		£	£
Deduct:			
Income that is not taxable as trading income			
	Interest Received	12,000	
	Rental Income	10,000	
Capital Allowances		23,000	
			(45,000)
Trading Income Assessment			152,900

CHAPTER 7: INCOME TAX – FURTHER ISSUES

7.1 The first three tax years for the business will be 2006/07, 2007/08 and 2008/09.

The assessments for these years are calculated as follows:

Tax Year	**Basis Period**	**trading income assessment**	
2006/07	1/12/2006 – 5/4/2007	£48,000 x 4/12 =	£16,000
2007/08	1/12/2006 – 30/11/2007		£48,000
2008/09	1/12/2007 – 30/11/2008		£30,000

Overlap profits are £16,000, relating to the period 1/12/2006 – 5/4/2007.

7.2 The first three tax years for the business will be 2006/07, 2007/08 and 2008/09.

The assessments for these years are calculated as follows:

Tax Year	**Basis Period**	**trading income assessment**	
2006/07	1/2/2007 – 5/4/2007	£33,000 x 2/11 =	£6,000
2007/08	1/2/2007 – 31/1/2008 (First 12 months)	£33,000 + (£48,000 x 1/12)	£37,000
2008/09	1/1/2008 – 31/12/2008		£48,000

Overlap profits total £10,000, relating to the periods 1/2/2007 – 5/4/2007 (£6,000) and 1/1/2008 – 31/1/2008 (£4,000).

7.3

Tax Year	**Basis Period**		**trading income assessment**
2007/08	1/7/2006 – 30/6/2007		£36,000
2008/09	1/7/2007 – 31/5/2008	£20,000	
	less overlap profits bf	(£5,000)	
			£15,000

CHAPTER 8: CAPITAL GAINS TAX FOR SOLE TRADERS

8.1 (a) Exempt, as a chattel
(b) Exempt
(c) Chargeable
(d) Chargeable
(e) Chargeable
(f) Chargeable
(g) Exempt
(h) Exempt

8.2

	£
Proceeds	140,000
less cost	(40,000)
extension	(20,000)
indexation allowance on cost	
0.114 x £40,000	(4,560)
Gain before taper relief	75,440

There is no indexation on the extension, as it was carried out in April 1998.

The shop has been owned for over 2 years since 1998, and therefore 25% of the gain is chargeable.

Gain £75,440 x 25%	£18,860
less annual exempt amount	(£9,200)
Amount subject to CGT	£9,660
Capital Gains Tax £9,660 x 40% =	£3,864

8.3

	£
Proceeds	23,000
less cost (600 x £10)	(6,000)
Gain before taper relief	17,000

There is no indexation, as the shares were bought after April 1998.

The shares have been owned for over 2 years, and therefore 25% of the gain is chargeable.

Gain £17,000 x 25% = £4,250

This amount is covered by Jane's annual exempt amount of £9,200. There is no CGT liability.

Practice examination tasks

There are two types of practice examination in this section:

Half papers (for Section 1 or Section 2 of the examination)
There are two practice half papers for Section 1 and two practice half papers for Section 2 of the examination. The Section 2 half-papers can be tackled after Chapters 1 to 5 have been studied, while the Section 1 'half' papers require familiarity with the content of Chapters 6 to 8.

Full papers
There are three full practice papers provided here. The third paper is reproduced by kind permission of AAT.

Tax forms and tax years
Tax forms for use in these tasks may be photocopied from the Appendix at the back of this book, or downloaded from the Student or Tutor Resources section at www.osbornebooks.co.uk or from www.hmrc.gov.uk

At the time of going to press, the 2007/2008 tax forms were not available and so we suggest that – as elsewhere in this book – the 2006/2007 forms are used for exam answers and are amended as appropriate.

Answers to practice examinations
The answers to all the Practice Examinations and larger size photocopiable tax forms are contained in the *Business Taxation Tutor Pack*. Please call Osborne Books Customer Services on 01905 748071 or visit our website at www.osbornebooks.co.uk for details of this publication.

LIST OF PRACTICE EXAMINATIONS – TAX YEAR 2007/08

'Half' papers - Section 1

'Half' papers - Section 2

Full papers

Tax rates and other data

Tax rates and other data needed for carrying out tax calculations are detailed in the 'Tax Data' section at the beginning of this book.

'half' paper 1 Exam Section 1, tax year 2007/08

You should spend about 90 minutes on this practice half-paper.

DATA

You are employed in the small clients department of a firm of accountants. You have been passed the following information relating to a new client, Clive Gregory, who commenced in business as a sole trader on 1 January 2008. He produced a set of accounts for the period 1/1/2008 – 31/12/2008 as follows:

	£	£
Sales		60,000
less cost of sales:		24,000
Gross profit		36,000
less expenses:		
Rent & Rates	3,000	
Depreciation	3,750	
Motor Expenses	1,500	
General Expenses	3,000	
Bank Interest	1,250	
		12,500
Net Profit		23,500

Notes:

1 Clive has agreed that his car is used 80% for business purposes and 20% privately. The motor expenses figure in the accounts relates to both business and private mileage. The car was bought for £16,000 on 1/1/2008.

2 Clive spent £2,250 entertaining his customers during the year. This is included under 'general expenses'.

3 Clive bought a computer for £1,000 and shop equipment for £4,800 when he started in business.

Task 1.1

Calculate the capital allowances claimable by Clive for the accounting year ended 31/12/2008.

Task 1.2

Calculate the adjusted profits for the accounting year ended 31/12/2008, after taking into account the capital allowances calculated in Task 1.1.

Task 1.3

Calculate the assessable trading income for Clive for

- 2007/08, and
- 2008/09

Task 1.4

State the amount of overlap profits based on Clive's business, and state how and when this can be set off.

Task 1.5

Calculate the Class 4 National Insurance contributions payable by Clive for 2007/08.

Task 1.6

Complete supplementary pages SE1 – SE3 of the 2007/08 tax return for Clive.

You may copy the appropriate form pages from the Appendix in this book or download them, either from the Student Resources Section of www.osbornebooks.co.uk or from www.hmrc.gov.uk

'half' paper 2 Exam Section 1, tax year 2007/08

You should spend about 90 minutes on this practice half-paper.

DATA

You are employed in the small clients department of a firm of accountants. You have been passed the following information relating to an established client, Maxine Cliff. Maxine has been in business as a sole trader for many years, having started the business entirely on her own. She has always made her accounts up to 30 June each year. She ceased trading on 30 June 2007, and produced her final set of accounts for the period 1/7/2006 – 30/6/2007, shown below. Maxine has £5,500 overlap profits brought forward from when she started in business.

Maxine sold the goodwill of the business on 30/6/2007 for £50,000. She has significant income from other sources that means she is always a higher rate taxpayer.

	£	£
Sales		85,000
less cost of sales:		53,000
Gross profit		32,000
less expenses:		
Rent & Rates	4,500	
Losses on sale of fixed assets	2,650	
Motor Expenses	1,800	
General Expenses	2,000	
Bank Interest	1,050	
		12,000
Net Profit		20,000

Notes:

1 Maxine used a car owned by the business, 50% for business purposes and 50% privately. The motor expenses figure in the accounts relates to both business and private mileage. She bought the car from the business for the market value of £6,000 on 30/6/2007.

2 Maxine had a farewell party for her customers in June 2007. This cost £1,200, and is included under 'general expenses'.

3 Maxine sold all the business plant and machinery for £10,000 on 30/6/2007. All items were sold for less than they originally cost.

The written down values for capital allowance purposes at 1/7/2006 were:

Main Pool	£14,000
Car (50% business use)	£10,000

Task 1.1

Calculate the plant and machinery capital allowances for the accounting year ended 30/6/2007.

Task 1.2

Calculate the adjusted profits for the accounting year ended 30/6/2007, after taking into account the capital allowances calculated in Task 1.1.

Task 1.3

Calculate the assessable trading income for Maxine for 2007/08.

Task 1.4

Calculate any Capital Gains Tax arising from Maxine's sale of the business assets, and state the date by which payment should be made.

Task 1.5

You have received a message from Maxine's brother. He is interested in starting a similar business, and has asked for rough figures on the sort of profit Maxine was generating, and how much tax she typically paid. He says he needs this information so that he can see if his plans are viable.

Draft some notes that will form the basis of your reply to him.

Task 1.6

Complete supplementary pages SE1– SE3 of the 2007/08 tax return for Maxine (up to box 3.92).

You may copy the appropriate form pages from the Appendix in this book or download them, either from the Student Resources Section of www.osbornebooks.co.uk or from www.hmrc.gov.uk

'half' paper 3 Exam Section 2, tax year 2007/08

You should spend about 90 minutes on this practice half-paper.

DATA

You work for an accounting practice, Magnum and Company, in the corporate clients department. The following information has been passed to you in respect of Johnjo Limited, an established client, with no associated companies. Because the company has decided to change its accounting date, it has produced the following accounts for the 9-month period 1/2/2007 to 31/10/2007.

	£	£
Sales		1,560,000
less cost of sales		980,000
Gross Profit		580,000
add:		
Profit on sale of fixed assets (note 1)	2,000	
Profit on sale of shares (note 2)	64,000	
		66,000
		646,000
less:		
Depreciation	60,000	
Administrative expenses (note 3)	24,500	
Bad debts (note 4)	19,800	
Selling & distribution expenses	15,700	
		120,000
Net Profit		526,000

Notes

1 The profit on sale of fixed assets relates to the disposal of a Toyota car. The proceeds were £3,000. The car originally cost £11,000.

2 The profit on the sale of shares relates to 10,000 shares in Delta plc that were sold for £10 each in March 2007. The shares had been acquired as follows:

4,000 shares bought for £3 each in December 1990

6,000 shares bought for £4 each in December 1994

3 Administrative expenses include:

Gift-aid payment to charity	£5,000
Entertaining suppliers	£6,000
Staff travelling expenses	£3,200

4 Bad debts are made up of:

Increase in specific provisions	£ 9,800
Increase in general provisions	£14,000
Bad debts recovered	(£4,000)

5 The plant & machinery capital allowance brought forward figures at 1/2/2007 are as follows:

Main pool	£ 45,000
Expensive car (1)	£ 15,000
Expensive car (2)	£ 19,000

6 The following acquisitions of fixed assets occurred during the accounting period:

1/5/2007	Van bought for £15,000
1/6/2007	Computer system bought for £10,000

The company is classed as 'small' for capital allowances purposes.

7 The following indexation factors are available:

December 1990 – December 1994	0.124
December 1994 – March 2007	0.400

Task 2.1

Calculate the plant & machinery capital allowances for the nine month CAP to 31/10/2007.

Task 2.2

Calculate the assessable trading income for the nine month CAP to 31/10/2007, incorporating the result of task 2.1.

Task 2.3

Calculate the chargeable gains on the sale of the shares in Delta plc.

Task 2.4

Calculate the profits chargeable to corporation tax (PCTCT) for the nine month CAP to 31/10/2007.

Task 2.5

Calculate the Corporation Tax payable for the nine month CAP to 31/10/2007, and state the date(s) by which payment should be made.

Task 2.6

Complete the short tax return form extract (page 2) for Johnjo Limited for the nine month CAP to 31/10/2007.

You may copy the appropriate form pages from the Appendix in this book or download them, either from the Student Resources Section of www.osbornebooks.co.uk or from www.hmrc.gov.uk

'half' paper 4 Exam Section 2, tax year 2007/08

You should spend about 90 minutes on this practice half-paper.

DATA

You work for an accounting practice, Bridget and Company. The following information has been passed to you in respect of an established client, Claydermann Limited. This client is part of a group of four companies that the practice serves, ie Claydermann Limited has three associated companies for tax purposes.

Claydermann Limited has produced the following accounts for the twelve month period 1/1/2007 to 31/12/2007.

	£	£
Sales		1,480,000
less cost of sales		990,000
Gross Profit		490,000
add:		
Profit on sale of factory premises (note 1)	95,000	
Profit on sale of shares (note 2)	80,000	
Dividends received (note 3)	54,000	
		229,000
		719,000
less:		
Depreciation	90,000	
Administrative expenses (note 4)	44,000	
Bad debts (note 5)	12,500	
Selling & distribution expenses (note 6)	39,500	
		186,000
Net Profit		533,000

Notes

1 The profit on sale of factory premises relates to the sale of an industrial building to a company outside the group for £300,000 in March 2007. Industrial Buildings Allowance had been claimed by Claydermann Limited for each of the years that it had been owned by them since it was bought new in April 2001 for £205,000. The factory was not depreciated in the accounts.

2 The profit on the sale of shares relates to 20,000 shares in Gamma plc, that were sold for £12 each in March 2007. The shares were part of the shares that had been acquired as follows:

15,000 shares bought for £7.00 each in December 1994

25,000 shares bought for £8.60 each in December 1998

3 Dividends relates to the amount received from Taylor Plc, a company that is not associated with Claydermann Limited for tax purposes.

4 Administrative expenses include:

Gift-aid payment to charity	£4,000

5 Bad debts are made up of:

Increase in specific provisions	£3,800
Increase in general provisions	£3,700
Bad debts written off	£5,000

6 Selling and Distribution Expenses include:

Gifts of Diaries (with adverts) to 500 customers	£3,500
Gifts of Food Hampers to 100 customers	£2,000

7 The plant & machinery capital allowance brought forward figures at 1/1/2007 are as follows:

Main pool	£ 41,000
Expensive car (1)	£ 19,000
Expensive car (2)	£ 11,000

8 The following acquisitions of fixed assets occurred during the accounting period:

1/5/2007	Lorry bought for £25,000
1/6/2007	New electric powered low emission car bought for £30,000.

There were no disposals of plant & machinery.

9 The following indexation factors are available:

December 1994 – December 1998	0.126
December 1998 – March 2007	0.243
April 2001 – March 2007	0.181

10 Claydermann Limited is classed as a small company for capital allowances purposes.

Task 2.1

Calculate the plant & machinery capital allowances for the twelve month CAP to 31/12/2007.

Task 2.2

Comment briefly on any Industrial Buildings Allowance implications arising from the sale of the factory.

Task 2.3

Calculate the assessable trading income for the twelve month CAP to 31/12/2007, incorporating the results of Task 2.1.

Task 2.4

Calculate any chargeable gains arising on the sale of

- the shares in Gamma plc
- the sale of the factory

Task 2.5

Calculate the profits chargeable to corporation tax (PCTCT) for the twelve month CAP to 31/12/2007.

Task 2.6

Calculate the Corporation Tax payable for the twelve month CAP to 31/12/2007, and state whether the company must make payments by instalment.

Task 2.7

Complete page 2 of the short tax return form CT600 for Claydermann Limited for the twelve month CAP to 31/12/2007.

You may copy the appropriate form pages from the Appendix in this book or download them, either from the Student Resources Section of www.osbornebooks.co.uk or from www.hmrc.gov.uk

'full' paper 1 Practice exam, tax year 2007/08

This examination paper is in TWO SECTIONS.

You have to show competence in BOTH sections.

You should therefore attempt and aim to complete EVERY task in EACH section.

You should spend about 90 minutes on Section 1 and 90 minutes on Section 2.

15 minutes reading time will be allowed.

SECTION 1

DATA

You are employed in the small clients department of a firm of accountants. You have been passed the following information relating to an established partnership client, George and Gemma Gale. They have been in business for many years, sharing profits and losses equally. They have always made their accounts up to 30 September each year.

On 1 January 2008 they are joined in the partnership by Julian Jones, and the profit sharing arrangement is changed with effect from that date to George 40%; Gemma 40%; Julian 20%.

The partnership accounts for the accounting period 1/10/2007 – 30/9/2008 include the following:

		£	£
Sales			285,000
less cost of sales:			140,545
Gross profit			144,455
less expenses:			
Rent & Rates		14,500	
Depreciation		12,000	
Motor Expenses	George	11,800	
	Gemma	6,000	
	Julian	4,000	
General Expenses		8,000	
Bank Interest		1,600	
Bad Debts		13,000	
			70,900
Net Profit			73,555

Notes

1 George and Gemma both use cars owned by the partnership 60% for business purposes and 40% privately. The motor expenses figure in the accounts relates to both business and private mileage. Julian's car is used entirely for business.

2 General Expenses include £3,500 for entertaining customers, and £1,000 relating to hotel costs for the partners whilst on business trips.

3 Bad Debts is made up of:

Bad Debts written off	£12,300
Increase in specific bad debt provision	£700

4 The written down values for capital allowance purposes at 1/10/2007 were:

Main Pool	£14,000
Car 1 (60% business use)	£10,000
Car 2 (60% business use)	£18,000

5 During the period, the following acquisitions and disposals were made:

1/1/2008	Purchase of a car for Julian's business use for £10,000
1/3/2008	Purchase of a computer system for £5,000
1/7/2008	Disposal of some equipment for £500 (original cost £3,000)

Task 1.1

Calculate the plant and machinery capital allowances for the accounting year ended 30/9/2008.

Task 1.2

Calculate the adjusted profits for the partnership for the accounting year ended 30/9/2008, after taking into account the capital allowances calculated in task 1.1.

Task 1.3

Calculate Julian's share of the adjusted trading profits of the partnership for the accounting period ending 30/9/2008.

Task 1.4

Calculate the assessable trading income for Julian for 2007/08.

Task 1.5

Write a note for Julian that explains what type of National Insurance contributions he is liable to make since he joined the partnership, and calculate his Class 4 contribution for 2007/08.

Task 1.6

Complete supplementary page P1 of the 2007/08 tax return for Julian.

You may copy the appropriate form pages from the Appendix in this book or download them, either from the Student Resources Section of www.osbornebooks.co.uk or from www.hmrc.gov.uk

SECTION 2

DATA

You have been asked to help out in your firm's corporate clients department. The following information has been passed to you in respect of Grubb Limited, an established client with no associated companies. The company has produced the following accounts for the twelve month period 1/4/2007 to 31/3/2008.

	£	£
Sales		1,455,000
less cost of sales		995,000
Gross Profit		460,000
add:		
Non-trade interest received (note 1)	4,000	
Dividends received (note 2)	18,000	
Profit on sale of shares (note 3)	65,500	
Profit on sale of factory (note 4)	50,000	
		137,500
		597,500
less:		
Factory rent	10,000	
Depreciation	45,000	
Directors' salaries	85,000	
Staff salaries	95,000	
Administrative expenses (note 5)	39,600	
Bad debts written off	9,700	
Selling & distribution expenses	15,700	
		300,000
Net Profit		297,500

Notes

1 The amount received for interest is also the taxable amount under the appropriate category.

2 The dividends were received in April 2007 from Beta Limited.

3 5,000 shares in Beta Limited (Grubb Limited's entire shareholding) were sold in April 2007 for £265,500. They had been acquired as follows:

2,000 bought in May 1993 for £40 each

2,000 bought in January 2000 for £60 each

A bonus issue of 1 for 4 in January 2001.

4 Grubb Limited's factory was sold in April 2007 for £550,000. It had been bought new for £500,000 in January 2004. Industrial building allowances claimed up to 31/3/2007 totalled £80,000. The company rented its subsequent premises.

5 Administrative expenses include:

Entertaining suppliers	£4,000
Gifts of Calendars (with adverts) to 1,000 customers	£7,000

6 The plant and machinery written down values brought forward at 1/4/2007 were:

Main pool	£120,000
Short life asset (bought April 2004)	£20,000
Expensive car	£11,000

There were no acquisitions or disposals of plant and machinery during the accounting period.

7 The following indexation factors are available:

May 1993 – January 2000	0.181
January 2000 – April 2007	0.230 (est)
January 2004 – April 2007	0.120 (est)

Task 2.1

Calculate the plant & machinery capital allowances for the twelve month CAP to 31/3/2008.

Task 2.2

Calculate the assessable trading income for the twelve month CAP to 31/3/2008, incorporating the results of Task 2.1.

Task 2.3

Calculate the chargeable gain, if any, on the sale of the factory.

Task 2.4

Calculate the chargeable gain on the sale of the shares in Beta Limited.

Task 2.5

Calculate the profits chargeable to corporation tax (PCTCT) for the twelve month CAP.

Task 2.6

Calculate the Corporation Tax payable for the twelve month CAP.

Task 2.7

Complete page 2 of the short tax return form CT600 for the company for the twelve month CAP to 31/3/2008.

You may copy the appropriate form pages from the Appendix in this book or download them, either from the Student Resources Section of www.osbornebooks.co.uk or from www.hmrc.gov.uk

'full' paper 2 Practice exam, tax year 2007/08

This examination paper is in TWO SECTIONS.

You have to show competence in BOTH sections.

You should therefore attempt and aim to complete EVERY task in EACH section.

You should spend about 90 minutes on Section 1 and 90 minutes on Section 2.

15 minutes reading time will be allowed.

SECTION 1

DATA

You are employed in the small clients department of a firm of accountants. You have been passed the following information relating to an established client, Minnie Beech. Minnie has been in business as a sole trader for many years, having started the business entirely on her own. She has always made her accounts up to 30 June each year. She ceased trading on 30 June 2007, and produced her final set of accounts for the period 1/7/2006 – 30/6/2007, shown below. Minnie has £10,500 overlap profits brought forward from when she started in business.

Minnie had the goodwill of the business valued on 30/6/2007 at £30,000. This consists of the business trade name 'Beech Goods' and list of established customers. She arranged for her sister to take over the trade, and has given her the goodwill on that date. Minnie has significant income from other sources that means she is always a higher rate taxpayer. She has no chargeable disposals except any arising from her business in 2007/08.

	£	£
Sales		95,000
less cost of sales:		43,000
Gross profit		52,000
less expenses:		
Rent & Rates	6,500	
Losses on sale of fixed assets	2,900	
Motor Expenses	1,000	
General Expenses	2,500	
Bank Interest	1,550	
		14,450
Net Profit		37,550

Notes:

1 Minnie used a van owned by the business, 90% for business purposes and 10% privately. The motor expenses figure in the accounts relates to both business and private mileage. She bought the van from the business for the market value of £9,500 on 30/6/2007.

2 Minnie sold all the business plant and machinery (except the van) for £12,000 on 30/6/2007. All items were sold for less than they originally cost.

3 The written down values for capital allowance purposes at 1/7/2006 were:

Main Pool	£9,000
Van (90% business use)	£10,000

Task 1.1

Calculate the plant and machinery capital allowances for the accounting year ended 30/6/2007.

Task 1.2

Calculate the adjusted profits for the accounting year ended 30/6/2007, after taking into account the capital allowances calculated in task 1.1.

Task 1.3

Calculate the trading income assessable for Minnie for 2007/08.

Task 1.4

Calculate any Capital Gains Tax arising from Minnie's disposal of the business assets, including the goodwill, ignoring any gift relief.

Task 1.5

Minnie has heard that there is a CGT relief called gift relief. Write a note for Minnie that

- explains in outline how gift relief works, and
- recommends, with reasons whether it would be beneficial for Minnie and her sister to claim gift relief in respect of the goodwill

SECTION 2

DATA

You have been asked to help out in your firm's corporate clients department. The following information has been passed to you in respect of Jello Limited, a new client that has started trading on 1/1/2007. It has no associated companies. Because the company is intending to use 31 October as its accounting date, it has produced the following accounts for the 10-month period 1/1/2007 to 31/10/2007.

	£	£
Sales		1,230,000
less cost of sales		790,000
Gross Profit		440,000
add:		
Rental income received (note 1)	12,000	
Non-trade interest received (note 1)	4,000	
		16,000
		456,000
less:		
Depreciation	30,000	
Directors' salaries	60,000	
Staff salaries	80,000	
Administrative expenses (note 2)	31,500	
Bad debts (note 3)	7,800	
Selling & distribution expenses	12,700	
		222,000
Net Profit		234,000

Notes:

1 The amounts received from rent and interest are the taxable amounts under the appropriate categories.

2 Administrative expenses include:

Gift-aid payment to charity	£2,000
Entertaining suppliers	£8,000
Entertaining customers	£7,000
Staff travelling expenses	£3,200

3 Bad debts are made up of:

Increase in specific provisions	£ 1,800
Increase in general provisions	£ 6,000

4 The following acquisitions of fixed assets occurred during the accounting period:

1/1/2007	Plant bought for £32,000
1/5/2007	Van bought for £22,000
1/6/2007	Computer system bought for £10,000.
1/6/2007	Office furniture bought for £15,000

5 In addition, the company purchased a new factory building for £340,000 on 1/1/2007, with the following cost breakdown:

	£
Land	40,000
Land Preparation	20,000
Factory	200,000
Design Office	25,000
Administration Offices	55,000

The company used the factory for a qualifying purpose throughout the accounting period.

6 The company is classed as 'small' for capital allowances purposes.

Task 2.1

Calculate the plant & machinery capital allowances for the ten month CAP to 31/10/2007.

Task 2.2

Calculate the Industrial Buildings Allowance for the company for the ten month CAP to 31/10/2007.

Task 2.3

Calculate the assessable trading income for the ten month CAP to 31/10/2007, incorporating the results of tasks 2.1 and 2.2.

Task 2.4

Calculate the profits chargeable to corporation tax (PCTCT) for the ten month CAP.

Task 2.5

Calculate the Corporation Tax payable for the ten month CAP to 31/10/2007, and state the date(s) by which payment should be made.

Task 2.6

Complete page 2 of the short tax return CT600 for the company for the ten month CAP to 31/10/2007.

You may copy the appropriate form pages from the Appendix in this book or download them, either from the Student Resources Section of www.osbornebooks.co.uk or from www.hmrc.gov.uk

'full' paper 3 Practice exam, tax year 2007/08
(updated sample material, by courtesy of AAT)

This examination paper is in TWO SECTIONS.

You have to show competence in BOTH sections.

You should therefore attempt and aim to complete EVERY task in EACH section.

You should spend about 90 minutes on Section 1 and 90 minutes on Section 2.

15 minutes reading time will be allowed.

SECTION 1

DATA

You work in the tax department of a firm of Chartered Accountants. One of your colleagues, Samantha, who works in the Small Business Accounts department, has contacted you about a new client, Joe Dunn. He commenced trading on 1 January 2006, but has not prepared any accounts. Samantha has completed the accounts for the period ended 30 June 2006, and the two years ended 30 June 2007 and 2008. She asks you to carry out tax work for Joe Dunn for all tax years, up to and including 2008/09.

Samantha supplies you with the following information:

1 Adjusted profits, before deducting capital allowances:

	£
Period ended 30 June 2006	27,055
Year ended 30 June 2007	31,496
Year ended 30 June 2008	30,047

2 Fixed asset additions and disposals:

additions:		£
February 2006	Motor car, no private usage	11,600
February 2006	Motor car, 30% private usage	10,000
May 2006	Plant and machinery	20,000
June 2006	Plant and machinery	14,760
November 2006	Computer	3,200
May 2007	Motor car, no private usage	13,000
disposals:		
December 2006	Plant and machinery	4,600

3 Joe Dunn has paid no National Insurance Contributions since he started trading.

4 Joe Dunn wants to take his brother into partnership to help him run the business, from January 2009.

Task 1.1

Calculate the capital allowances for all three accounting periods.

Task 1.2

Calculate the net taxable profit for each accounting period.

Task 1.3

Calculate the taxable trading income for all tax years, from commencement of trade to 2008/09, clearly showing the dates and amount of overlap profits.

Task 1.4

Calculate the total amount of NIC Class 4 payable by Joe Dunn for 2007/08.

Task 1.5

Explain the implications for Joe Dunn of his failure to:

- notify HM Revenue & Customs of his chargeability to taxation
- complete and submit his tax returns by the due dates, stating what the due dates were, assuming he would make online submissions.

Task 1.6

Outline the key points that you would like to make to Joe Dunn regarding the taxation implications of a business being operated as a partnership.

SECTION 2

DATA

You work for a company, Delta Ltd, preparing its tax information prior to being entered in the CT600 tax form. The company has traded for many years, using a year end of 31 December. However, it has now changed its year end to 31 March.

The Chief Accountant for Delta Ltd has supplied you with the accounts for the fifteen month period ended 31 March 2008.

The profit and loss account shows:

	£	£
Gross profit		1,131,950
Profit on the sale of shares (Note 3)		23,800
General expenses (Note 1)	425,380	
Bad debts (Note 2)	5,850	
Salaries and wages	280,645	
Depreciation	125,630	
		837,505
Net profit		318,245

Note 1: General expenses includes:

	£
Entertaining customers	2,300
Parking fines paid for employees	650
Gifts to customers (100 bottles of wine)	1,000
Staff Christmas party (30 people)	600

Note 2: Bad debts are made up of:

	£
Debts written off – trade	3,800
Employee loan	800
Increase in general provision	1,600
Bad debts recovered – trade	(350)
	5,850

Note 3: Profit on the sale of shares

In January 2008, Delta Ltd sold 30,000 shares in Alpha Ltd for £58,500. These shares had been acquired as follows:

	No of Shares	£
June 1995	20,000	12,000
November 1999	10,000	16,000

In May 1996, Alpha Ltd made a bonus issue of 1 for 10.

Additional information

1 You have already calculated the capital allowances for the plant and machinery at £35,060 for the year ended 31 December 2007, and £10,400 for the period ended 31 March 2008.

2 In September 1996, Delta Ltd had acquired a new industrial building for £250,000. The building had been in industrial use throughout the period of ownership.

3 Delta Ltd has no associated companies.

4 Indexation factors to be used are:

June 1995 – November 1999	0.113
November 1999 – January 2008	0.260 (estimated)

Task 2.1

Calculate the capital gain arising from the disposal of the shares in Alpha Ltd.

Task 2.2

Calculate the adjusted trading profit, before capital allowances, for the fifteen month period ended 31 March 2008.

Task 2.3

Show the PCTCT (profit chargeable to corporation tax) for the year ended 31 December 2007, and the period ended 31 March 2008.

Task 2.4

Calculate the Corporation Tax payable for the twelve month period ended 31 December 2007.

Task 2.5

Calculate the Corporation Tax payable for the three month period ended 31 March 2008.

Task 2.6

DATA

The Chief Accountant tells you that he anticipates that Delta Ltd will make a loss in the year ended 31 March 2009. He has asked if you could advise him about the tax implications of such a loss.

Using the headed paper provided on the next page write a memo to the Chief Accountant, setting out the options available to Delta Ltd for the set-off of the potential loss.

MEMORANDUM

To:	Chief Accountant	Date:	
From:	Accounting Technician	Ref:	Corporation Tax Losses

Appendix
Photocopiable tax forms

This Appendix contains Tax forms for use in student activities and practice examinations. The forms may be photocopied from this book, or alternatively downloaded from the Student or Tutor Resources section on www.osbornebooks.co.uk or from www.hmrc.gov.uk

The tax forms were those available at the time of going to press (July 2007) and therefore cover the 2006-07 tax year rather than the 2007-08 tax year. The forms will still 'work' in the various exercises. If you are using this book in 2008 you will find more up-to-date forms at www.hmrc.gov.uk

The forms included here are:

11.2

HM Revenue & Customs

Company - Short Tax Return form

CT600 (Short) (2006) Version 2

for accounting periods ending on or after 1 July 1999

Your company tax return

If we send the company a *Notice* to deliver a company tax return (form *CT603*) it has to comply by the filing date, or we charge a penalty, even if there is no tax to pay. A return includes a company tax return form, any Supplementary Pages, accounts, computations and any relevant information.

Is this the right form for the company? Read the advice on pages 3 to 6 of the Company tax return guide (the *Guide*) before you start.

The forms in the CT600 series set out the information we need and provide a standard format for calculations. Use the *Guide* which contains general information you may need and box by box advice to help you complete the return form.

Company information

Company name

Company registration number

Tax Reference as shown on the CT603

Type of company

Registered office address

Postcode

About this return

This is the above company's return for the period

from (dd/mm/yyyy) to (dd/mm/yyyy)

Put an 'X' in the appropriate box(es) below

A repayment is due for this return period

A repayment is due for an earlier period

Making more than one return for this company now

This return contains estimated figures

Disclosure of tax avoidance schemes

Notice of disclosable avoidance schemes

Transfer pricing

Compensating adjustment claimed

Company qualifies for SME exemption

Accounts

I attach accounts and computations

for the period to which this return relates

for a different period

If you are not attaching accounts and computations, say why not

Supplementary Pages

If you are enclosing any Supplementary Pages put an 'X' in the appropriate box(es)

Loans to participators by close companies, form *CT600A*

Charities and Community Amateur Sports Clubs (CASCs), form *CT600E*

Disclosure of tax avoidance schemes, form *CT600J*

Company tax calculation

Turnover

1 Total turnover from trade or profession — 1 £

Income

3 Trading and professional profits — 3 £

4 Trading losses brought forward claimed against profits — 4 £

5 Net trading and professional profits — box 3 minus box 4 — 5 £

6 Bank, building society or other interest, and profits and gains from non-trading loan relationships — 6 £

11 Income from UK land and buildings — 11 £

14 Annual profits and gains not falling under any other heading — 14 £

Chargeable gains

16 Gross chargeable gains — 16 £

17 Allowable losses including losses brought forward — 17 £

18 Net chargeable gains — box 16 minus box 17 — 18 £

21 Profits before other deductions and reliefs — sum of boxes 5, 6, 11, 14 & 18 — 21 £

Deductions and Reliefs

24 Management expenses under S75 ICTA 1988 — 24 £

30 Trading losses of this or a later accounting period under S393A ICTA 1988 — 30 £

31 *Put an 'X' in box 31 if amounts carried back from later accounting periods are included in box 30* — 31

32 Non-trade capital allowances — 32 £

35 Charges paid — 35 £

37 Profits chargeable to corporation tax — box 21 minus boxes 24, 30, 32 and 35 — 37 £

Tax calculation

38 Franked investment income — 38 £

39 Number of associated companies in this period — 39

or

40 Associated companies in the first financial year — 40

41 Associated companies in the second financial year — 41

42 *Put an 'X' in box 42 if the company claims to be charged at the starting rate or the small companies' rate on any part of its profits, or is claiming marginal rate relief* — 42

Enter how much profit has to be charged and at what rate of tax

Financial year *(yyyy)*	Amount of profit	Rate of tax	Tax
43	44 £	45	46 £ p
53	54 £	55	56 £ p

63 Corporation tax — total of boxes 46 and 56 — 63 £ p

64 Marginal rate relief — 64 £ p

65 Corporation tax net of marginal rate relief — 65 £ p

66 Underlying rate of corporation tax — 66 • %

67 Profits matched with non-corporate distributions — 67

68 Tax at non-corporate distributions rate — 68 £ p

69 Tax at underlying rate on remaining profits — 69 £ p

70 Corporation tax chargeable — *See note for box 70 in CT600 Guide* — 70 £ p

79 Tax payable under S419 ICTA 1988		79 £ p
80 *Put an 'X' in box 80 if you completed box A11 in the Supplementary Pages CT600A*	80	
84 Income tax deducted from gross income included in profits		84 £ p
85 Income tax repayable to the company		85 £ p
86 **Tax payable - this is your self-assessment of tax payable**		total of boxes 70 and 79 minus box 84 86 £ p

Tax reconciliation

91 Tax already paid (and not already repaid)	91 £ p
92 Tax outstanding	box 86 minus box 91 92 £ p
93 Tax overpaid	box 91 minus box 86 93 £ p

Information about capital allowances and balancing charges

Charges and allowances included in calculation of trading profits or losses

	Capital allowances	Balancing charges
105 - 106 Machinery and plant - long-life assets	105 £	106 £
107 - 108 Machinery and plant - other (general pool)	107 £	108 £
109 - 110 Cars outside general pool	109 £	110 £
111 - 112 Industrial buildings and structures	111 £	112 £
113 - 114 Other charges and allowances	113 £	114 £

Charges and allowances not included in calculation of trading profits or losses

	Capital allowances	Balancing charges
115 - 116 Non-trading charges and allowances	115 £	116 £
117 *Put an 'X' in box 117 if box 115 includes flat conversion allowances*	117	

Expenditure

118 Expenditure on machinery and plant on which first year allowance is claimed		118 £
119 *Put an 'X' in box 119 if claim includes enhanced capital allowances for designated energy-saving investments*	119	
120 Qualifying expenditure on machinery and plant on long-life assets		120 £
121 Qualifying expenditure on machinery and plant on other assets		121 £

Losses, deficits and excess amounts

122 Trading losses Case I	calculated under S393 ICTA 1988 122 £	124 Trading losses Case V	calculated under S393 ICTA 1988 124 £
125 Non-trade deficits on loan relationships and derivative contracts	calculated under S82 FA 1996 125 £	127 Schedule A losses	calculated under S392A ICTA 1988 127 £
129 Overseas property business losses Case V	calculated under S392B ICTA 1988 129 £	130 Losses Case VI	calculated under S396 ICTA 1988 130 £
131 Capital losses	calculated under S16 TCGA 1992 131 £	136 Excess management expenses	calculated under S75 ICTA 1988 136 £

Overpayments and repayments

Small repayments

If you do not want us to make small repayments please either put an 'X' in box 139 or complete box 140 below. 'Repayments' here include tax, interest, and late-filing penalties or any combination of them.

Do not repay £20 or less 139 **Do not repay sums of** 140 £ **or less.** *Enter whole figure only*

Bank details (for person to whom the repayment is to be made)

Repayment is made quickly and safely by direct credit to a bank or building society account. Please complete the following details:

Name of bank or building society 149

Branch sort code 150

Account number 151

Name of account 152

Building society reference 153

Payments to a person other than the company

Complete the authority below if you want the repayment to be made to a person other than the company.

I, as *(enter status - company secretary, treasurer, liquidator or authorised agent, etc.)* 154

of *(enter name of company)* 155

authorise *(enter name)* 156

(enter address) 157

Postcode

Nominee reference 158

to receive payment on the company's behalf.

Signature 159

Name *(in capitals)* 160

Declaration

Warning - Giving false information in the return, or concealing any part of the company's profits or tax payable, can lead to both the company and yourself being prosecuted.

Declaration

The information I have given in this company tax return is correct and complete to the best of my knowledge and belief.

Signature

Name *(in capitals)*

Date *(dd/mm/yyyy)*

Status

HM Revenue & Customs

Income for the year ended 5 April 2007

SELF-EMPLOYMENT

Fill in these boxes first

Name | Tax reference

If you want help, look up the box numbers in the Notes

Business details

Name of business

3.1

Description of business

3.2

Address of business

3.3

Postcode

Accounting period - read the Notes, page SEN3 before filling in these boxes

Start 3.4 / /

End 3.5 / /

- Tick box 3.6 if details in boxes 3.1 or 3.3 have changed since your last Tax Return 3.6
- Date of commencement if after 5 April 2004 3.7 / /
- Date of cessation if before 6 April 2007 3.8 / /
- Tick box 3.9 if the special arrangements for particular trades apply - read the Notes, page SEN11 3.9
- Tick box 3.10 if you entered details for all relevant accounting periods on last year's Tax Return and boxes 3.14 to 3.73 and 3.99 to 3.115 will be blank (read Step 3 on page SEN2) 3.10
- Tick box 3.11 if your accounts do not cover the period from the last accounting date (explain why in the 'Additional information' box, box 3.116) 3.11
- Tick box 3.12 if your accounting date has changed (only if this is a permanent change and you want it to count for tax) 3.12
- Tick box 3.13 if this is the second or further change (explain in box 3.116 on Page SE4 why you have not used the same date as last year) 3.13

Capital allowances - summary

	Capital allowances	Balancing charges
• Cars costing more than £12,000 (excluding cars with low CO_2 emissions) (A separate calculation must be made for each car.)	3.14 £	3.15 £
• Other business plant and machinery (including cars with low CO_2 emissions and cars costing less than £12,000) read the Notes, page SEN4	3.16 £	3.17 £
• Agricultural or Industrial Buildings Allowance (A separate calculation must be made for each block of expenditure.)	3.18 £	3.19 £
• Other capital allowances claimed (separate calculations must be made). Claims to, and balancing charges arising on, Business Premises Renovation Allowance must also be included in boxes 23.7 and 23.8 respectively	3.20 £	3.21 £
	total of column above	total of column above
Total capital allowances/balancing charges	3.22 £	3.23 £

- Tick box 3.22A if box 3.22 includes enhanced capital allowances for designated environmentally beneficial plant and machinery 3.22A

Income and expenses - annual turnover below £15,000

If your annual turnover was £15,000 or more , or would be if you traded for a whole year, **ignore** boxes 3.24 to 3.26. Instead fill in Page SE2

If your annual turnover was below £15,000 , or would be if you traded for a whole year, **fill in boxes 3.24 to 3.26 instead of Page SE2**. Read the Notes, page SEN4.

- Turnover including other business receipts and goods etc. taken for personal use (and balancing charges from box 3.23) 3.24 £
- Expenses allowable for tax (including capital allowances from box 3.22) 3.25 £

Net profit (put figure in brackets if a loss) — box 3.24 minus box 3.25 — 3.26 £

You must now fill in Page SE3

Income and expenses - annual turnover £15,000 or more

You must fill in this Page if your annual turnover was £15,000 or more - r ead the Notes, pages SEN2, SEN4 to SEN7

If you were registered for VAT, will the figures in boxes 3.29 to 3.64, include VAT? 3.27 [ ] or exclude VAT? 3.28 [ ]

Sales/business income (turnover) 3.29 £

	Disallowable expenses included in boxes 3.46 to 3.63	Total expenses	
• Cost of sales	3.30 £	3.46 £	
• Construction industry subcontractor costs	3.31 £	3.47 £	
• Other direct costs	3.32 £	3.48 £	
		Gross profit/ (loss)	box 3.29 minus (boxes 3.46 + 3.47 + 3.48) 3.49 £
		Other income/ profits	3.50 £
• Employee costs	3.33 £	3.51 £	
• Premises costs	3.34 £	3.52 £	
• Repairs	3.35 £	3.53 £	
• General administrative expenses	3.36 £	3.54 £	
• Motor expenses	3.37 £	3.55 £	
• Travel and subsistence	3.38 £	3.56 £	
• Advertising, promotion and entertainment	3.39 £	3.57 £	
• Legal and professional costs	3.40 £	3.58 £	
• Bad debts	3.41 £	3.59 £	
• Interest and alternative finance payments	3.42 £	3.60 £	
• Other finance charges	3.43 £	3.61 £	
• Depreciation and loss/(profit) on sale	3.44 £	3.62 £	
• Other expenses	3.45 £	3.63 £	
	Put the total of boxes 3.30 to 3.45 in box 3.66 below	Total expenses	total of boxes 3.51 to 3.63 3.64 £
		Net profit/(loss)	boxes 3.49 + 3.50 minus 3.64 3.65 £

Tax adjustments to net profit or loss

• Disallowable expenses	boxes 3.30 to 3.45 3.66 £	
• Adjustments (apart from disallowable expenses) that increase profits. For instance; goods taken for personal use and amounts brought forward from an earlier year because of a claim under ESC B11 about compulsory slaughter of farm animals	3.67 £	
• Balancing charges (from box 3.23)	3.68 £	
Total additions to net profit (deduct from net loss)		boxes 3.66 + 3.67 + 3.68 3.69 £
• Capital allowances (from box 3.22)	3.70 £	
• Deductions from net profit (add to net loss)	3.71 £	boxes 3.70 + 3.71 3.72 £
Net business profit for tax purposes (put figure in brackets if a loss)		boxes 3.65 + 3.69 minus 3.72 3.73 £

Now fill in Page SE3

You **must** fill in boxes 3.74 and 3.75 and **all other boxes** that apply to you, on this Page

Adjustments to arrive at taxable profit or loss

Basis period begins **3.74** / / and ends **3.75** / /

Profit or loss of this account for tax purposes (box 3.26 or 3.73) **3.76** £

Adjustment to arrive at profit or loss for this basis period **3.77** £

- Overlap profit brought forward **3.78** £
- Deduct overlap relief used this year **3.79** £
- Overlap profit carried forward **3.80** £
- Averaging for farmers and creators of literary or artistic works (see Notes, page SEN7, if you made a loss for 2006–07) **3.81** £
- Adjustment on change of basis **3.82** £

Net profit for 2006–07 (if you made a loss, enter '0') **3.83** £

Allowable loss for 2006–07 (if you made a profit, enter '0') **3.84** £

- Loss offset against other income for 2006–07 **3.85** £
- Loss - relief to be calculated by reference to earlier years **3.86** £
- Loss to carry forward (that is allowable loss not claimed in any other way) **3.87** £
- Losses brought forward from earlier years **3.88** £
- Losses brought forward from earlier years used this year **3.89** £

Taxable profit after losses brought forward — box 3.83 minus box 3.89 — **3.90** £

- Any other business income (for example, Business Start-up Allowance received in 2006–07) **3.91** £

Total taxable profits from this business — box 3.90 + box 3.91 — **3.92** £

- Tick box 3.93 if the figure in box 3.92 is provisional **3.93**

Class 4 National Insurance contributions - see Notes, pages SEN9 and SEN10

- Tick box 3.94 if exception applies **3.94**
- Tick box 3.95 if you hold a deferment certificate for 2006–07 **3.95**
- Adjustments to profit chargeable to Class 4 National Insurance contributions (If you are calculating your tax enter the amount of Class 4 NICs due in box 18.2B on Page 7 of your Tax Return in box 3.96) **3.96** £

Subcontractors in the construction industry

- Deductions made by contractors on account of tax (please send your CIS25s to us) **3.97** £

Tax taken off trading income

- Any tax taken off trading income (excluding deductions made by contractors on account of tax) **3.98** £

Summary of balance sheet

Leave these boxes blank if you do not have a balance sheet

Assets

• Plant, machinery and motor vehicles	3.99	£
• Other fixed assets (premises, goodwill, investments etc.)	3.100	£
• Stock and work-in-progress	3.101	£
• Debtors/prepayments/other current assets	3.102	£
• Bank/building society balances	3.103	£
• Cash in hand	3.104	£
total of boxes 3.99 to 3.104	3.105	£

Liabilities

• Trade creditors/accruals	3.106	£
• Loans and overdrawn bank accounts	3.107	£
• Other liabilities	3.108	£
total of boxes 3.106 to 3.108	3.109	£

Net business assets (put the figure in brackets if you had net business liabilities)

box 3.105 minus 3.109	3.110	£

Represented by

Capital Account

• Balance at start of period*	3.111	£
• Net profit/(loss)*	3.112	£
• Capital introduced	3.113	£
• Drawings	3.114	£
• Balance at end of period* (total of boxes 3.111 to 3.113 minus box 3.114)	3.115	£

*If the Capital Account is overdrawn, or the business made a net loss, enter the figure in brackets

3.116 *Additional information*

Now fill in any other supplementar y Pages that apply to you.
Otherwise, go back to Page 2 of your Tax Return and finish filling it in.

Printed in the U.K. by Adare Group 5008699 12/06

HM Revenue & Customs

Income for the year ended 5 April 2007

PARTNERSHIP (SHORT)

Fill in these boxes first

Name	Tax reference

If you want help, look up the box numbers in the Notes

Partnership details

Partnership reference number	4.1	Description of partnership trade or profession	4.2
• If you started being a partner during 2006–07, enter the date	4.3 / /	• If you stopped being a partner during 2006–07, enter the date	4.4 / /

Your share of the partnership's trading or professional income

Basis period begins	4.5 / /	and ends	4.6 / /
• Your share of the profit or loss of this year's account for tax purposes (enter a loss in brackets)			4.7 £
• Adjustment to arrive at profit or loss for this basis period			4.8 £
• Overlap profit brought forward	4.9 £	Deduct overlap relief used this year	4.10 £
• Overlap profit carried forward	4.11 £		
• Averaging for farmers and creators of literary or artistic works (see Notes, page PN3 if the partnership made a loss in 2006–07) or foreign tax deducted, if tax credit relief not claimed			4.12 £
• Adjustment on change of basis			4.12A £
Net profit for 2006–07 (if loss, enter '0' in box 4.13 and enter the loss in box 4.14)			4.13 £
Allowable loss for 2006–07		4.14 £	
• Loss offset against other income for 2006–07		4.15 £	
• Loss - relief to be calculated by reference to earlier years		4.16 £	
• Loss to carry forward (that is, allowable loss not claimed in any other way)		4.17 £	
• Losses brought forward from earlier years		4.18 £	
• Losses brought forward from earlier years used this year			4.19 £
Taxable profit after losses brought forward			box 4.13 minus box 4.19 4.20 £
• Add amounts not included in the partnership accounts that are needed to calculate your taxable profit (for example, Enterprise Allowance (Business Start-up Allowance) received in 2006–07)			4.21 £
Total taxable profits from this business			box 4.20 + box 4.21 4.22 £

Class 4 National Insurance contributions - see notes, page PN4

• Tick box 4.23 if exception applies	4.23
• Tick box 4.24 if you hold a deferment certificate for 2006–07	4.24
• Adjustments to profit chargeable to Class 4 National Insurance contributions (If you are calculating your tax enter the amount of Class 4 NICs due in box 18.2B on your Tax Return - it does not go in this section)	4.25 £

SA104

Your share of the partnership taxed income

- Share of taxed income (liable at 20%) — 4.70 £

Your share of the partnership's trading and professional profits

- Share of partnership profits (other than that liable at 20%) — from box 4.22 — 4.73 £

Your share of the partnership tax paid

- Share of Income Tax taken off partnership income — 4.74 £
- Share of CIS25 deductions — 4.75 £
- Share of tax taken off trading income (not CIS25 deductions) — 4.75A £

boxes 4.74 + 4.75 + 4.75A — 4.77 £

4.79 *Additional information*

Now fill in any other supplementar y Pages that apply to you.
Otherwise, go back to page 2 in your Tax Return and finish filling it in

Printed in the U.K. by Adare Group 5008660 12/06

Index

for your notes